ExtraSensory
DECEPTION

ESP, Psychics, Shirley MacLaine, Ghosts, UFOs . . .

By Magician-Columnist
HENRY GORDON

PROMETHEUS BOOKS

Buffalo, New York

To my wife, Zita Shirley—my severest critic, and staunchest supporter.

90 89 88 87   4 3 2 1

Library of Congress Cataloging-in-Publication Data

Gordon, Henry, 1919-
    Extrasensory deception.

        1. Psychical research—Controversial literature.
2. Occult sciences—Controversial literature. I. Title.
BF1042.G64   1987   133   87-16513
ISBN 0-87975-407-9

Contents

PROPHECY

Two Nations Will Go to War, but Only One Will Win   65

SPIRITS

SUPERSTITION

SCIENCE

Foreword

Henry Gordon is one of those people who can fool all of the people all of the time. He's a magician. The kind of magic in which Gordon specializes is categorized as mentalism. But he calls it sleight of mind. On stage he appears to make objects move without touching them, read people's minds, and make plants react emotionally to people. But he admits freely that the things he does are tricks. He is not a psychic, a mind reader, a mystic, or a clairvoyant. He cannot bend forks with the power of his mind, though he can bend them with his fingers and make it look as if he did it with mental power.

What makes Gordon see red is the growing number of people who do the same things he and his fellow mentalists do and claim they are not tricks. In fact, during the past eighteen years Gordon has become a noted crusader. You may have seen him doing his thing on TV or read one of his exposures of psychic frauds in the *Toronto Star*.

It is worth noting that, as befits someone who believes strongly in science, Gordon does not deny that a person *could* have supernatural powers, that he *might* be able to "read minds" or even "see into the future." What he does say is that such a person should be willing to allow scientific investigation of his claims under the kind of conditions any other phenomena would be scrutinized. This is something most psychics refuse to do, which is why Gordon keeps saying: "Every psychic I know or have heard of is an absolute fraud." Mention TV's Kreskin and Gordon will tell you right off that he first met him in a New York magic shop. Mention "mystic" Uri Geller and he'll explain exactly how the keys Geller appears to bend with mind power are actually bent by hand.

In other words, Gordon is a debunker. Some have said he is a better debunker than he is a magician. Some have even said so unkindly. But surely we are now in an age when a little dash of debunking should be part of our regular diet. Surely some expert scrutiny is required when pitchmen can buy time on TV to talk innocent pensioners into sending "$100 or more" to aid some questionable pursuit. Or when cults drag children into mental wastelands and the sick put their faith in quacks instead of doctors. Or when, for that matter, E.T. seems so real to all of us.

As a leading member of the Canadian branch of the Committee for the Scientific Investigation of Claims of the Paranormal and a magician who knows every psychic trick in the book, Henry Gordon is perhaps the best man in Canada to scrutinize the world of the unexplained.

Gerry Hall
Editor, *Toronto Sunday Star*

Acknowledgments

The print and electronic media have always given ample space and time to the controversial subject of the paranormal. Unfortunately, they have usually featured only one side of the coin—the sensationalization of things that go bump in the night—without devoting much coverage to the rational explanations for the various UFO sightings, poltergeist capers, visions of apparitions, Bermuda Triangle disappearances, "successes" of psychic detectives, annual prophecies by puerile prognosticators, and all the other psychic and pseudoscientific recountings.

How often has the reader seen a newspaper story describing a purported UFO sighting or a ghostly cavortation? When some of these events have been investigated and explained, are these explanations published as follow-up stories? Not usually. When year-end lists of prophecies are published, are they analyzed and reported on by the same journal a year later? Rarely.

The reason for this imbalance is very simple. Newspapers are in the business of selling newspapers. An exciting feature on the paranormal will catch and hold the reader's attention. The prosaic explanation is a non-story. This pragmatic approach is quite understandable. Newspapers and broadcasters don't feel that their primary aim is to educate the public, but merely to inform it, although even such a limited guiding credo should grant adequate space for the prosaic explanation.

All of which leads up to the fact that it is quite remarkable that this book is now in your hands. It is a compilation of three years of my columns in Toronto's *Sunday Star,* which ran under the title "Debunking." This book would not exist had they not been published in the first place. That a major metropolitan newspaper *did* feature this type of column is what is remarkable. Even the publication of an occasional skeptical view of the paranormal is rare. To print a regular weekly column of this kind is more than that—it's unheard of in the newspaper business.

The individual mainly responsible for this unlikely occurrence was an editor who supported my view that there was a need for balance in journalism's coverage of the so-called paranormal. Gerry Hall had just taken over as editor of the *Sunday Star* when I approached him with my idea for a column featuring facts and explanations on this very controversial subject. His adoption of the column and his advice and support over the three years of his tenure have contributed, I believe, to a deeper public insight into the murky field of the paranormal—and perhaps to a more critical outlook by some readers. If there were more editors and broadcast producers with this sense of public responsibility, the public would be better served.

My sincere thanks to Paul Kurtz and Doris Doyle for their encouragement, to Reg Gilbert for his help in assembling this book and for his skillful editing, and to the staff of the Committee for the Scientific Investigation of Claims of the Paranormal for their assistance over the years in keeping me informed of the various strange happenings in the wacky world of the paranormal.

ExtraSensory
DECEPTION

Introduction

In the summer of 1977 thousands of handbills were distributed, posters tacked up, and announcements placed in the newspapers heralding Elchonen, an unknown Canadian psychic scheduled to make a one-night personal appearance at the Samuel Grover Auditorium of the Saidye Bronfman Centre in Montreal. He would be giving a lecture and demonstration of psychic phenomena, including telepathy, psychokinesis, precognition, and clairvoyance.

Elchonen, it was announced, had spent years being tested for his paranormal powers in parapsychological laboratories at the universities of Utrecht and Cornell and at the Stanford Research Institute. This was to be his first public appearance.

For days the Bronfman Centre was deluged with phone calls from newspapers and radio and television stations asking for interviews with this new personality. Elchonen's whereabouts were unknown, the callers were told, but they were advised not to miss the presentation—it would be out of the ordinary.

On the evening of the performance the auditorium was packed. Extra chairs were opened wherever space was available. An air of tension hung over the theater as "show time" approached. At exactly eight o'clock a lean, slightly stooped individual shuffled out on the stage and approached the microphone. There was a buzz in the audience as the onlookers noticed he was wearing a vinyl mask, which gave him more than an odd appearance. "I must beg your indulgence for the disguise I am wearing,"

Elchonen explained in a thick accent. "Because of a promise I have made to my colleagues in the scientific community I cannot reveal my true identity."

"I will attempt to demonstrate," he went on, "if I can, the extraordinary powers of psi energy. We know that psi energy exists, but we do not know what it is, exactly."

After explaining the intricacies of the brain's functions, including its production of electromagnetic waves of various frequencies, finally Elchonen got to the meat of the program, the actual demonstration of his psychic powers. At that time, communication with plants was a topical subject among the supporters of the paranormal. To the delight of the audience Elchonen chose that phenomenon for his opening presentation. A galvanometer was connected to a potted plant standing on the stage. Several volunteers were invited up and each was asked whether he or she would like to display animosity or affection toward the hapless plant. Each advanced on it in turn. The needle shot up whenever an adversary approached and remained motionless when a supporter came near. There were no other wires or outside connections, examination confirmed. The audience was enthralled.

Time for another miracle. A spectator far back in the auditorium, chosen at random, was given a sheet of paper and a crayon and asked to draw a simple geometric figure. After due concentration, Elchonen, on stage, also sketched a figure on a large board. The two drawings matched almost exactly. "I can accomplish this at close range," said Elchonen, "but contrary to the claims of many parapsychologists, I do not believe that thoughts can be transmitted over a long distance."

He continued by demonstrating several other unbelievable mental feats. There was no doubt—the audience was his. They were now ready to believe almost anything.

It was time for the climax of the show: a demonstration of psychokinesis, the ability to move physical objects with the power of the mind alone. A large, heavy, antique rocking chair was carried up and placed on stage by two men. The psychic stood about twenty feet away from it. "The ability to cause the movement of an object strictly by the human mind—this is one of the most difficult psychic feats to be attempted," he intoned. "In the Soviet Union, Mikhailova has proven, without a doubt, that this feat is possible. Tonight, for the first time in public, I will try to convince you of this possibility."

Elchonen raised his arms in the direction of the chair. The silence in the auditorium was deafening. As he gestured dramatically, there was no visible phenomenon to observe. Again he slowly moved his hands—and then it happened. The huge chair began to rock, very slowly, almost imperceptibly, then with greater and greater momentum, until it finally was rocking violently back and forth.

While it was still moving, Elchonen called out, "Anyone who would like to can come up and examine the chair, examine the stage, look backstage, examine me—come up right away, quickly." In a moment half a dozen men jumped onto the stage, picked up the chair, examined it rigorously, prowled around and looked everywhere. After a few minutes they retired, shaking their heads in disbelief.

Elchonen then announced a short intermission and retired to his backstage dressing room, leaving an audience that was too astounded to applaud. In his dressing room he slowly removed the mask, washed his perspiring face, changed his sweat-soaked shirt and his suit jacket, and straightened up from the semi-stooped position he had assumed for the past hour.

I looked into the dressing-table mirror with a sigh of relief. At last that ordeal was over. I had pulled a couple of hoaxes of this kind before—one on radio and another at McGill University—but never one of this dimension, with all the advertising and attendant publicity.

Now came the shedding of the masquerade. I would reveal my true identity and tell the audience they'd been had—and why I had pulled this stunt. How would they react? Obviously the majority of the crowd consisted of believers. Otherwise they would not have been so attracted by the content of the publicity. Previous lectures by Henry Gordon on a skeptical theme had attracted much smaller audiences. Elchonen, the psychic, had packed them in. And their reaction to Elchonen's "miracles" left no question as to their beliefs.

As an active skeptic I had never been a favorite of such people. Why would I be? People do not appreciate attempts to shatter their beliefs. Now, bringing them out for an evening of what they expected would be a reinforcement of such beliefs, with all the inconvenience and expense that entailed—well, I suddenly realized the amount of *chutzpah* it had taken on my part. Now came the moment of truth. Would they throw things? Would they tear me apart with their bare hands?

As the house lights dimmed and the stage spot came on I drew a deep breath and strode out. The first thing I heard was a loud shout from out in the semi-darkness—"My God, it's Henry Gordon."

I should explain. I was rather well known in Montreal, my home town. For many years I had been in the public eye as a performing magician and as a psychic debunker on stage, television, and radio. I had made presentations on this very stage during the previous two years. Hence Elchonen's need to disguise his appearance, and his voice.

Which also explains Elchonen's strange absence from the local airwaves. When the radio people had called the Bronfman Centre to set up an interview with the eminent psychic prior to his appearance, I had to beg off. Elchonen couldn't cash in on this extra publicity because Henry Gordon couldn't show up at a studio. I also doubted if I could carry off the foreign accent for a protracted interview.

As soon as I reached the microphone at center stage I began speaking—and quickly, because I feared a riot. I tried to explain the reasons for this public hoax. I was not trying to garner cheap publicity, neither was this an ego trip. I was just trying to make a point. Did these people not see how easy it was to be taken in? Anyone with the knowledge, experience, and skills of a mentalist-magician could masquerade as a psychic and get away with it. Watching Elchonen the psychic, the members of this audience had to admit they had been deceived. Did they not realize this had happened countless times before, that these were the methods of the so-called psychics? Would this experience at least give them food for thought?

It was, for some perhaps, a bitter pill to swallow. One woman jumped up and shouted, "This is a fake. I paid five bucks to get in, had to pay a baby sitter, and wasted my evening. I want my money back." I immediately announced, "Anyone who feels that way, please go to the box office immediately. Your money will be refunded. I will guarantee it." Several people jumped up and filed out. I was relieved—at least they hadn't headed in my direction. I later found out that many of these people took their refund only to return to the auditorium to catch the rest of the show. I proceeded to present my usual arguments and explanations regarding the pseudosciences, followed by a lively question period. But I must admit that the second half of the program was anticlimactic.

The hoax generated a mountain of publicity. The *Montreal Star* carried a picture of Elchonen on the front page, followed by a banner headline over a story on page three. The *Gazette*, which hadn't covered the presentation, called me the next day and ran a good-sized piece under a huge picture of the masked Elchonen. Several radio stations interviewed me, including the Canadian Broadcasting Corporation national network.

I had made my point.

The question I am most often asked is how I got started in this debunking business. There are probably several answers, though some are surely buried in my subconscious. Perhaps the most important reason is my congenital dislike for hypocrisy. I can think of nothing more hypocritical than the claims of the so-called psychics, the astrologers, the crystal ball gazers, the tarot card readers, and all the phony practitioners of paranormal pretense. As a professional mentalist (a conjurer playing the part of a psychic), I have always been in contact with much of the profession across the continent. I observed, many years ago, that many mentalists tried to convince their audiences that they had paranormal powers. Indeed, a few of the more prominent ones later adopted careers as out-and-out psychics—and made a bundle in their new profession. For these people I have nothing but contempt, and it is probably because of them that I became active in the practice of unmasking the con artists in this field.

Mentalism is the practice of sleight of mind, so to speak. The methods of deception used by the mentalist are strictly the methods of the conjurer-magician: some actual sleight of hand, and a great deal of psychology. The mentalist is an entertainer, nothing less and nothing more. His or her audience deserves to be aware of that fact. Mentalists who profess to be something more are deceiving their audiences in more ways than one. They are asking them to believe that they are possessed of some power above and beyond human limitations.

I am always amused when my occultist opponents accuse me of making easy money as a debunker. They confuse earning a fee as an entertainer with profiting from ignorance. Should I choose to grow a beard and speak in a foreign accent, presenting myself to the public as a psychic, I have absolutely no doubt that I would increase my earnings enormously. There is only one thing that prevents me from doing this, however—my conscience.

To write a column titled "Debunking" and to be labeled a "debunker" could convey the idea of a person who is cynical, ready to put down everything in sight. Not so. To be skeptical does not require one to be cynical. And to debunk simply means to unmask, to explain.

Don't misunderstand—I consider debunking an honorable profession. But it's not an easy one. I have to constantly dwell on the subject of public gullibility. People do not like to see themselves as being gullible or credulous. They don't like to be told they are being deceived.

A recent letter from a reader underscored this point. He said he enjoyed my column, and he commended me for writing things he didn't really want to find out. I suppose it takes a particularly objective thinker to make that kind of statement.

Many would rather believe a liar who promises them wonderful things than a debunker who tries to pull them back to reality, and in doing so perhaps make things a little uncomfortable.

In addition to three years of "Debunking" columns in the *Sunday Star* of Toronto, this book also contains several of my feature articles taken from the daily *Star* dating back to 1981 and which were relevant to the theme of this book. Readers will also find discussions of many subjects not strictly related to claims of the paranormal. A varied diet is always more appealing.

THE PARANORMAL
An Infinite Number of Rabbits

The roots of psychic research lie in the distant past—in myth and superstition, in magic, in the mysteries of ancient priestly cults, in the tendency of the human mind to attribute to the supernatural that which it cannot understand.

The history of parapsychology, the study of so-called psychic phenomena, can be traced back over a century. The terminology has changed from "psychic research" to "parapsychology," but little else has varied in the pursuit of bumps in the night. Psychic investigators have not changed very much. In most cases they remain strong believers in the paranormal. They are out to satisfy their need to find truth in the supernatural. They select their evidence, always on the lookout for facts favorable to preconceived beliefs and theories. Sometimes, and I stress sometimes, the psychic investigator is slightly fraudulent.

Much of the public seems to be under the impression that parapsychology has established the case for extrasensory perception. That is definitely not so, but the parapsychologists have not gone out of their way to set the record straight. Some experiments have provided very modest support for the existence of psychic phenomena, but they are a long way from being accepted as conclusive by science. They still require widespread replication under conditions that allow for no alternative explanations.

There are four basic weaknesses in parapsychological research. The first, and the most-often mentioned even by leading parapsychologists, is the failure so far to repeat the results of major experiments. Then there is the lack of theoretical foundation for the alleged phenomena—a fact that plagued J. B. Rhine, the father of modern parapsychology, to the end of his life. There is a lack of professionalism among some researchers, who seem to welcome and support any evidence that is dredged up. A lack of rigorous controls in experimentation has often been the target of skeptics. At long last some parapsychologists are admitting that perhaps knowledgeable conjurers should be allowed to take part in the establishment of these controls.

So-called psychic readers and/or psychic spoon-benders are the modern-day equivalent of the con men of old. The average person doesn't like to be conned but usually takes delight in reading about a scam pulled on someone else. It's almost like stopping at the scene of an accident. Hence the success of films like *The Sting.* However, as long as gullibility remains pervasive, the psychic will hold sway. Expose one and three more will spring up. The media, particularly radio, have given them a platform larger than any they have ever enjoyed.

The methods used by the psychic readers have been developed and polished by generations of carnival performers. The cold reading—the ability to translate one's perception of a client's characteristics into concrete statements and predictions—is an art form that can have quite an impact on an impressionable subject. The various methods of obtaining information from a subject by subtle means are well known to experienced mentalist-magicians. But they use these skills to entertain. The psychic uses them to gain a client's confidence and to parlay that confidence into the dollars of repeat visits.

We are now living in the age of the self-help seminar. Opportunists and entrepreneurs take advantage of every fad that catches the public imagination, from hypnotic regression to past lives to walking on hot coals. Anything with an occult connotation is fair game. Everyone has ESP powers, they claim—all you have to do is develop them. Some offer expensive courses to do just that.

The endorsement of paranormal gobbledygook by prominent personalities only adds to the public confusion and the tendency to believe in inanities. The Shirley MacLaine phenomenon is a good example of how a person in the public eye can exert a strong impression on a gullible public through the media. With the publication of each of her latest books and the presentation of her made-for-television movie, MacLaine was swamped with requests for appearances on almost every major public affairs television show on the continent. When she appeared on these various shows, and when she was interviewed by journalists, MacLaine was treated with almost unbelievable respect and deference. As an entertainer she rated this treatment, but not as the author of books loaded with paranormal nonsense.

Why did the interviewers fail to challenge some of her ridiculous claims and assertions? It was obvious that most of them did not even have enough knowledge of the subject to ask intelligent questions. It is a failing shared by a large percentage of the public.

The psychic cheats

Does extrasensory perception (ESP) exist, and if so, what is it? This question has gone unanswered for years. ESP is a term that covers several phenomena: telepathy, the transference of information from one mind to another without normal sensory contact; clairvoyance, the knowledge of a remote object or a remote happening without use of the normal senses; precognition, the ability to predict future events through some psychic insight; and psychokinesis (PK), otherwise known as mind over matter, the ability to move physical objects with the power of the mind. There is a general feeling among the public that some of these phenomena exist—but the truth is that there has never been any strong evidence to prove it. Some parapsychologists have made claims to the contrary for years. The record does not back them up. It shows parapsychology to be cluttered with loosely controlled experiments, self-delusion, and glaring examples of fraud.

Dr. J. B. Rhine, the grand old man of parapsychological research, coined the phrase *extra-sensory perception.* His experiments at Duke University in the 1930s kicked off the modern ESP craze. Rhine's interest in the paranormal began when he became convinced of the mind-reading feats of Lady Wonder, a performing horse. He didn't dig deep enough to find that the horse was merely responding to his master's cues.

Looking back to the last century, we find famed scientists Sir Oliver Lodge and Sir William Crookes completely duped by spirit mediums. Later, there were the British scientists John Taylor and John Hasted. Taylor wrote a book called *Superminds,* in which he supported the feats of psychic trickster Uri Geller. Hasted wrote *The Metal Benders,* endorsing the ability of some people to alter the shape of metals through mind power.

Taylor subsequently published a paper retracting his conclusions about Geller, but only after Geller's methods were exposed by knowledgeable magicians. When a so-called psychic endorsed by Hasted was carefully tested by an objective scientific committee, he failed the tests. Hasted didn't accept the results. Why not? Because, he claimed, the complicated rules of the experiment inhibited "spontaneous phenomena." This is a standard cop-out by parapsychologists—if the test controls are tightened, psychic powers are inhibited.

Two eminent scientists in California, Russell Targ and Harold Puthoff, conducted a series of tests on Geller in 1972 at the Stanford Research Institute. They put their stamp of approval on Geller—he did indeed have paranormal powers, they said. Subsequent investigations revealed the tests to have been very loosely controlled, with countless opportunities for trickery. Geller actually laid down the conditions for many of the experiments—an unheard-of thing in science.

The parapsychological community was rocked by a story released at a New York press conference in January 1983. An elaborate hoax had been engineered by magician James Randi. Back in 1979, he had enlisted the aid of two teenage magicians, Michael Edwards and Steven Shaw, and rehearsed them in the tricks of the psychic trade—e.g., bending keys, spoons, and other metallic objects "through the power of the mind," aided, of course, by a little sleight of hand. The pair applied, as psychics, to the paranormal research laboratory of Dr. Peter Phillips, in St. Louis. This lab had been established by a $500,000 donation given to St. Louis's Washington University by the McDonnell Foundation, created by the late chairman of the McDonnell Douglas Corp. The two young impostors were accepted by Phillips and tested over a period of more than three years.

Strangely enough, as often happens in parapsychology, when controls were tightened on successful tests, and the subjects failed to score, these new tests were ignored and new experiments were set up. Even more strangely, the researchers were warned by Randi himself that the subjects might be magicians. The warnings had no effect. The researchers at the St. Louis lab finally convinced themselves that the young men had paranormal abilities, and stated as much. As one of them later said in an interview, "They want to believe—why else would they be studying this? We agreed beforehand to answer 'yes' if ever asked if we cheated. They never asked us that."

Debunking psychic myths

Extrasensory perception, the so-called ability to perceive or communicate without using normal senses, would be better named extrasensory *deception.* The history of parapsychology, of psychic phenomena, has been studded with fraud and experimental error.

When Dr. J. B. Rhine conducted ESP experiments at Duke University in the 1930s, C. E. M. Hansel, a psychology professor at the University of Wales, poked holes in them. His book, *ESP and Parapsychology —A Critical Re-evaluation,* showed up the lack of sufficient controls and the possibilities of human error in the Rhine experiments.

In his experiments, Rhine used Zener cards, now known as ESP cards. A deck consists of five sets of five symbols: a cross, a circle, a square, a star, and three wavy lines. One person would try to transmit the symbol he or she was looking at to another person by telepathy. Concentrating on the symbol, the sender would hold the card up with its back to the other person, who would then mark down what he or she thought the symbol was. The list was then checked off. If the score was much higher than chance would suggest, ESP was thought to be operating.

Some subjects did get high scores. Rhine was elated and later wrote his first book on the subject. ESP became the number one topic of cocktail party conversation.

Hansel points out two glaring errors in these tests: some of the symbols were printed so that they touched the edges of the cards and therefore could be deduced when viewing the edges; and the cards were slightly transparent so that when the light was right one could see the symbol right through the backs of the cards. Whenever subjects got high scores and were retested with tighter controls, their scores invariably dropped off. Rhine explained this by saying the subjects were tired.

A test for clairvoyance went like this: The subjects would sit in one room with pencil and paper and a watch. The testers, in another room, would deal the cards face down, at one-minute intervals, without looking at the symbols. The subjects, also at one-minute intervals, would jot down what they believed each card was. At the finish, the testers would turn over the cards and write a list of the order in which they fell. A comparison was then made between the two lists. Again, some subjects got very high scores.

Years later, Hansel visited the labs where these tests were done. After checking the layout of the building, he showed how the subject, who unbelievably was unsupervised, could have easily gone to the door of the room where the tester was sitting, stood on a chair and peered through the transom, and copied the list being written. The point Hansel makes is this: Unless experiments of this kind are conducted under conditions that preclude any possibility of cheating, they cannot be considered valid.

The key to mind over matter

There are literally thousands, perhaps millions, of people who still believe that Israeli psychic Uri Geller is authentic, that he bends keys, spoons, and assorted cutlery through the power of his mind.

Does psychokinesis really exist? Can people bend metal with the power of thought?

Geller has already been exposed as a magician, a psychic fraud. His methods have been revealed on stage and on television. But the myth lives on. The rationalization never changes. "Sure, he's been caught faking it. But how about the times he wasn't caught? How can you prove he doesn't have paranormal powers at these times?" Well, would you trust your bank manager with your portfolio after he was caught embezzling?

Geller always got away with his psychic stunts because he was performing for believers. The skeptics were bad medicine for him. Magicians were poison. He would not perform when he was aware there would be magicians in his audience. It was when he was unaware of their presence that his methods were spotted and he was unmasked.

The first time I saw Geller perform I was amazed that he could get away with the simple methods he employed. He stood with his back to a blackboard, had someone write something on it, and then revealed without looking at it what had been inscribed. A standing ovation! Even his confederate in the audience, who had signaled to him what was on the board, applauded.

When a dozen people crowded around a table at which he then seated himself, tossing keys on the table for him to bend, the tension was heightened. Geller always makes one thing clear: "It may or may not work. It depends on you, the audience. You must believe, you must concentrate, you must help." As a professional magician I dearly wish I could use those lines. What a beautiful cop-out. "Heads I win, tails you lose."

After fiddling with several keys Geller picks one up, covers it with his thumb and forefinger, and asks, "Whose is this? It's yours? Concentrate, please help me." He gently strokes his thumb over the key and gradually reveals its full length. Fantastic—it's got a good thirty degree bend in it. Will miracles never cease?

What the excited audience misses, however, is the method. Here are the facts—so you, too, can bend keys. Remember, you're supposed to be doing it through psychokinesis—mind over matter. So you must conceal the physical method of the scam. First—the easiest part—the actual bending of the key. Grasp the bow, or head, of the key firmly between your thumb and index finger. Place the tip of the key against a firm surface and push down hard. The key will bend. That's all. Now, a tip about the type of key. The easiest to bend is a car key. The metal is usually weaker than a house key. If you can spot one with a notch cut very low, it will bend even more easily.

The second, and more difficult, part of the operation is the proper use of misdirection—diverting your audience's attention. After all, you can't just bend a key against a tabletop in full view of the onlookers— unless they're wearing glasses half an inch thick. You're supposed to be a psychic—the keynote is deception.

The possible methods are numerous. You can be standing behind a table with the key in your right hand. Reach for any other object with your left hand. Your bemused audience will be following the moving hand. At the critical moment press the key against the tabletop. Or you can be seated at the table, again with the key in your hand. As you pull your chair closer to the table, press the key against the solid frame of the chair.

Geller would sometimes say, after stroking the key, "It doesn't seem to be bending. I think we need to be near the energy of water." He would then quickly stride over to a nearby radiator to hold the key near it. Before anyone else could get near him, he had already pressed the key against the rad and put a good bend in it.

Geller also wore a belt with a huge buckle, which came in handy for key-bending purposes. The point is to have a variety of methods available for different circumstances. The methods you use depend only on your ingenuity.

An important point: Never bend the key and then immediately display it. This is supposed to be a miraculous, mystical maneuver. As Geller does, you must struggle with your soul to accomplish the impossible. Make it look difficult.

Always have several keys offered to you. Scatter them on the table. After you have bent one, find some way of semi-concealing it. Pick up a few others. Stroke them by sliding your thumb tip back and forth over their length. After seeming to fail, apologize for the "lack of vibes." Finally, produce the key which is already bent, concealing the bend. Do the same stroking and *voila!*—a miracle of a semi-religious nature.

Another important point: Get the audience into the act. Preface your performance, as Geller does, by telling them that the energy comes from their collective thoughts. You're nothing without them. That way, if you succeed, they feel good—having aided in the experiment. If for some reason you can't get the job done, you can blame the onlookers: "Someone is upsetting the vibes—there must be a non-believer among you."

I know this all sound ridiculous, and it is. But Uri Geller became famous and made a fortune using these very methods. And most people still don't realize what a fraud he is.

Woody examines psychic phenomena

I just read a couple of Ballantine books by my favorite satirist, wacky Woody Allen. *Without Feathers* and *Side Effects* were written a few years ago, but they recently caught my attention when I spotted chapters on the paranormal. Woody Allen writing about the paranormal? Well, here are a few gems from the chapter titled "Examining Psychic Phenomena."

First of all, he claims that there is no question that there is an unseen world. The problem is, how far is it from midtown and how late is it open?

Discussing apparitions, he tells us the strange story of the man who woke up during the night and saw his brother, who had been dead for fourteen years, sitting at the foot of his bed. Disturbed, the man asks the ghost what he's doing there. Not to worry, says his brother, he's only in town for the weekend. He has returned, he says, to give his brother a message. It's a mistake to bury a man in a dark-blue suit and bright argyle socks. As dawn is breaking the ghost arises and leaves, walking through a wall. His brother, trying to follow, breaks his nose.

On the subject of prognostication, Woody describes Aristonidis, the sixteenth-century prophet whose predictions "continue to dazzle and perplex even the most skeptical." A couple of examples: "A leader will emerge in France. He will be very short and will cause great calamity. (This is a reference either to Napoleon or to Marcel Lumet, an eighteenth-century midget who instigated a plot to rub bearnaise sauce on Voltaire.)" "Two nations will go to war, but only one will win. (Experts feel this probably refers to the Russo-Japanese war of 1904-05—an astounding feat of prognostication, considering the fact that it was made in 1540)."

As to astral projection, Woody describes it as the process whereby a person will suddenly dematerialize and rematerialize somewhere else in the world. As he observes, "This is not a bad way to travel, although there is usually a half-hour wait for luggage." Woody recounts the strange case of Sir Arthur Nurney, who vanished with an audible pop while taking a bath and suddenly appeared in the string section of the Vienna Symphony Orchestra. He stayed on as the first violinist for twenty-seven years, although he could only play "Three Blind Mice."

On clairvoyance, Woody refers to the noted Greek psychic, Achille Londos, who realized he had strange powers at the age of ten, when he found that by concentrating he could make his father's false teeth jump out of his mouth. In 1964 he helped the police find the Dusseldorf Strangler. Just by sniffing a handkerchief he led police to the culprit, who confessed he was the strangler and asked if he could please have his handkerchief back.

In a chapter titled, "The UFO Menace," Woody satirizes the whole flying saucer flap. He admits that all UFOs may not prove to be of extraterrestrial origin. "But," he writes, "experts do agree that any glowing cigar-shaped object capable of rising straight up at 12,000 miles per second would require the kind of maintenance and spark plugs available only on Pluto."

You might assume that this has been a light, harmless treatise on the subject of the paranormal, nothing that could possibly stir up controversy. Wrong. I'll be hearing from the purveyors of the paranormal—for poking fun at their beliefs.

The long history of the con game

Get ready to be diddled. According to the dictionary, to *diddle* is to cheat, swindle, victimize. In "Diddling Considered as One of the Exact Sciences," Edgar Allen Poe expresses it more dramatically: "A crow thieves; a fox cheats; a weasel outwits, a man diddles."

What I'm getting at, in a roundabout way, is that once again April Fool's Day is sneaking up on us. Be prepared.

The history of the hoax or con game is a long and colorful one. Phineas T. Barnum made it into a respectable career and parlayed it into a fortune. He learned early on that the public loved to be fooled and that he did not have to guarantee truthfulness. He just had to promote doubt and controversy. Barnum's first promotion, in 1835, was the exhibition of Joice Heth, a slave who was supposed to be 161 years old, and to have been the nurse to George Washington. Then there was the Fejee Mermaid —a monstrosity with the body of a fish and the head and hands of a monkey. Not your everyday idea of a beautiful mermaid. It wasn't even alive, but it pulled in the customers.

Barnum went on to more spectacular things, of course—Tom Thumb, Jumbo the giant elephant, and finally the three-ring circus that made his name immortal.

On a smaller scale, the list of con men and hoaxers is endless. The Howard Hughes rip-off by author Clifford Irving, who wrote the supposed autobiography of Hughes, is a classic. The infamous con man, Victor Lustig, read a newspaper item in 1925 that said the Eiffel Tower would have to be renovated. Acting on that, he was able to pull a scam and "sell" it as scrap metal. He even had the gall to repeat the scam with a second dupe—becoming the only man to sell the Eiffel Tower not once, but twice.

Then there's this little anecdote from Miller's *The Founding Finaglers,* quoting a nineteenth-century entrepreneur: "I rented an empty store and printed 'Bank' on the window. The first day I was open for business a man came in and deposited 100 dollars. The second day another man deposited 250 dollars, and so along about the third day I got confidence enough in the bank to put in a hundred myself."

One of my favorite hoaxing characters was a man I knew personally, and with whom I shared many interesting and educational hours several years ago. Joe Kara was a fellow magician in Montreal, and a very accomplished one. But Joe made his living traveling with a carnival in the Maritimes, running the sideshow attraction. He would work at this during the summer, and spend the winter dreaming up crazy ideas with which to con the paying customers. I have to admit that I sometimes would supply the small germ of a modest idea. All in good clean fun—for entertainment purposes only, of course.

One of Joe's wackiest ideas was his most profitable one—the Human Fountain. Visualize a living, breathing man sitting in a chair with water spouting out of the top of his forehead. You could get as close to him as you wished to examine this phenomenon. How did Joe carry it off? Believe this—it's true. He had a surgeon insert a tiny plastic tube under the man's scalp, from the rear, hidden under his coat. The pump was supplied from a reservoir concealed at the rear of the chair.

"Step right up, folks—only fifty cents, and see the Human Fountain."

Of scams—and bumps

Scam. It's a slang word, now used quite regularly in the public prints. But until about twenty years ago it had to be defined for the everyday reader—it was a term used only by the criminal element and those who were familiar with that stratum of society.

It was supposed to have originated in the carnivals—meaning to "fleece the public." It's now been updated to cover any kind of dishonest scheme, whether perpetrated by criminals or by seemingly reputable members of our society. The word really came into its own when the infamous Abscam scandal was unearthed in Washington.

If there is one place where the word *scam* applies, it is in the field of the paranormal, where so many take advantage of public gullibility. Just look at some of the perpetrators of scams in this area: those who practice hypnotic regression to past lives; the "psychic advisers" who hook the uncritical believers; the fake faith healers who pry countless dollars from the sick and the afflicted; the psychic surgeons in the Philippines, who still practice their fraudulent sleight of hand; the spiritualists who prey on the bereaved—just to name a few.

Some time ago, *Psychology Today* conducted a "Scamarama Contest," offering cash prizes for the best suggested scams. The contest was inspired by the magazine's annoyance with the baseless claims in the supermarket tabloids. You've all seen the lurid headlines when on line at the checkout counter.

The editors felt that their readers "could come up with much more creative pseudosciences if only they were not burdened with so many scruples and the blind devotion to making an honest living."

One reader won a prize when he suggested "Phrenotherapy." Centuries ago, he wrote, certain people claimed to be able to read character by examining bumps on the head—phrenology. Why not go beyond that? "Actually change a client's character by producing bumps at just the right places. Let our experts knock that noggin where it will do the most good."

Another contestant suggested "Palmistherapy"—a new laser-surgery process that would lengthen the lifeline on a person's palm. Still another came up with: "Improve Your Aura. Why be stuck with the same old aura? Our device can be worn in pocket or purse to enhance and magnify your personal aura, to make a better impression on those who can see auras. Upgrade your aura from one to five levels. Runs on batteries." Another suggested "Autozodiac," a scheme to draw up an astrological chart for one's car—so you will know the best and worst days for trips and repairs. You would first have to provide the day and moment of its birth at the factory.

The grand prize winner was a gem: "Wish you were Born Rich? Now you can be! If you are one of the growing millions who are convinced of the reality of reincarnation, here's a once-in-a-lifetime offer. First, leave us $10,000 or more in your will. After you pass away, our professional medium will contact your spirit in the other world. Then you tell us when you're coming back and under what name. Upon your return, we regress you, at age twenty-one, through this lifetime and ask you for your seven-digit account number. Once you give us the number, we give you a check—on the spot—for your original investment plus interest! The longer you're gone the more you will receive. You may come back to find yourself a billionaire! Show your future self how much you care—leave a generous 'welcome-back' present. We'll take care of the rest."

The magazine claimed that several readers suggested what was probably the best scam of all—to offer cash prizes for get-rich-quick schemes, then to get rich quick with someone else's idea.

This is all good clean fun. But perhaps it doesn't tickle the funnybones of those who have been ripped off by practitioners of the paranormal. Just one word of warning—superstition and scam often go hand in hand.

ESP is a problem for science

It isn't often that a psychologist will comment on the subject of extrasensory perception, particularly a psychologist as eminent as Donald Hebb.

Better known as D. O. Hebb, he has for years been one of the world's leading psychologists, a writer of textbooks in his field, a former chairman of the psychology department and chancellor of McGill University.

Now comes Hebb's *Essay on Mind,* published by Lawrence Erlbaum Associates of New Jersey. One section is headed "Extrasensory Perception: A Problem." Why a problem? Because, according to Hebb, "our present knowledge of the physical world and of the physiology of the human body makes telepathy extremely unlikely and clairvoyance impossible, but at the same time there are experiences that may seem to admit of no other explanation."

I should explain that telepathy is the communication of one mind with another without any sensory connection. Mind reading, in other words. Clairvoyance is the awareness of an event or of an artifact outside the range of one's senses. For example, if you could accurately describe an auto accident taking place ten miles away, or if you could give the correct order of the cards in a deck without having seen them, that would be clairvoyance.

Hebb accepts the possibility that telepathy could exist. It isn't likely—there's no evidence for it as yet—but we are talking about two minds communicating. Could there be some electrical or electromagnetic activity taking place? We know that the brain engages in electrical activity that results in brain waves. We can measure them by connecting the scalp to a device called an electroencephalogram. But that's as far as it goes. The brain-wave activity we are aware of does not have the power to transmit for any distance. Furthermore, Hebb points out, this would just be a blanket transmission. In other words, even if these waves were projected over a distance, how would they project individual images or ideas? The whole concept makes no sense in our present state of knowledge. It is conceivable, but extremely unlikely.

If telepathy is a problem, clairvoyance is even more of a problem. At least in telepathy we're dealing with two or more electrically functioning brains. In clairvoyance we have one mind and one inert object. If a pack of cards is not transmitting some sort of energy, how can the mind possibly receive a message from it? If either telepathy or clairvoyance can really be proven to exist, then, as Hebb says, we would have to revise the laws of science.

But one thing more than anything else convinces many that ESP does exist—the strange experiences we sometimes encounter. Whenever I lecture on ESP I get more questions on that aspect of it than anything else. "I had a dream about Aunt Clara in Vancouver. She was very ill. The next day they phoned me from there. It really happened. Can you explain that?" Or "My husband didn't come home at the usual time. I knew he was in a car accident. It turned out to be true." Perhaps you've had a strange experience. You were at a cocktail party. Suddenly, for no apparent reason, you thought of a friend you hadn't seen for twenty years. Nothing too strange there—these things can happen. But ten minutes later, as you navigate your way through the milling crowd, who do you come face to face with? That's right, the long-lost acquaintance. Shakes you up, doesn't it? File it away in your computer under "paranormal phenomena."

Hebb has other theories about experiences of this kind. He reminds us of the premonitions people have had of an accident happening to a loved one—and of how that mishap was later confirmed. As Hebb states: "The answer of the skeptic is that it all is coincidence, but this does not convince the person who has had such an experience. For him the coincidence is altogether too coincidental."

But, as Hebb points out, there is a statistical argument. Consider the millions of people who are worrying at any one time about the welfare of an absent relative. We never hear about the countless cases where nothing happens. But the odd case where something does happen is the one we always hear about. Just take the extremely small percentage of these cases as against the unreported ones. Isn't it more likely to be a coincidence than a case of ESP, which is highly improbable?

To which I might add the shower phenomenon. When you're in the shower and the phone rings, how many times have you said in exasperation, "Every time I'm in the shower the phone rings." Have you ever considered the number of times you've showered when the phone *didn't* ring? There's more than coincidence involved here. There's the matter of memory, which is very often unreliable.

Almost any psychology textbook will mention that distortions of memory are very common. These distortions are caused by many factors: omissions of certain details of an experience, distortions in one's perceptions of an event caused by built-in beliefs, and distortions caused by the passage of time.

The passage of time—this is the type of case that comes up constantly. Almost every psychic experience I hear about is one that happened ten, twenty, thirty years ago. How many distortions have accumulated in these anecdotes over the years, even when recounted by sincere people? We'll never know. But I can tell you this—I seldom hear of a case that has just happened, that can be immediately investigated with some chance of coming up with definite explanations.

To get back to your cocktail party experience—perhaps I can come up with a rational explanation. Have you heard of subliminal perception? That is your reception of a sensory message without conscious awareness. Remember the "Eat Popcorn" messages flashed at high speed on drive-in movie screens? You got the message without realizing it. Well, here you are in this crowded room filled with the babble of voices. You hear this familiar voice from across the room, but it doesn't immediately dawn on your consciousness. It does make you think of the former friend, however, without realizing why.

When you finally see him or her it's a shocker. Another psychic anecdote has been added to that huge storehouse of the unexplained.

Of energy, the mind, and ESP

The study of the human brain can discourage the average person. Highly technical and complicated, it would seem to be something better left to the psychologist and the neurologist.

But it can be extremely interesting and informative to the layman—particularly one who is interested in some of the scientific-sounding claims of the paranormalists. Today, more than ever before, these people latch on to the coattails of science. They use every advance in scientific discovery for their own purposes.

Take ESP, for example, and the claim that thought can be transmitted from one person to another. Science has established that the brain generates electrical activity, that it produces electromagnetic waves.

There's the answer, say the occultists. Those brain waves are a form of energy. *Energy* is the magic word favored by the believers. If the energy exists, why can't it be transmitted from person to person? They overlook two basic factors. First, to transmit electromagnetic waves, whether radio waves or any other frequency, one must have a sufficient power source. The brain does not have enough power to project these waves beyond the skull. Second, parapsychologists claim that thoughts can be transmitted just as easily around the world, or to outer space, as they can to a person three feet away. This completely overlooks attenuation—the scientifically established fact that electromagnetic signals diminish in strength over distance.

Anthony Smith's *The Mind* provides an insight into the functions of the brain that is mind-boggling—if I may use the expression—and still makes for easy reading. In these days of high technology in medicine, many people have a friend or family member who has been admitted to a hospital or laboratory for an EEG—an electroencephalograph. Smith clarifies what this is all about and helps remove the mystery and the fear associated with the procedure. It is simply a recording of the brain waves by the application to the scalp of contacts that conduct signals to a graph-paper machine.

The brain produces four principal rhythms, or waves of different frequencies. The dominant one is the alpha wave, around ten cycles per second. This is produced when the mind is at rest. When the brain is consciously attentive, the beta wave is produced, at something above thirteen cycles. When you are drowsy the theta waves take over at from four to eight cycles per second. The brain never sleeps. The recording of these rhythms on an EEG chart can be very useful for revealing the existence of certain brain tumors, and of epilepsy and other disorders.

It has still another function. There is great controversy over when death occurs. At the moment, the indication by an EEG is still considered the factor for determining death—brain death, as indicated by the total absence of brain waves. Even this definition is still in dispute, according to Smith, because the EEG does not monitor every part of the brain.

As in every aspect of science, the arguments go on and on. One theory replaces another, or is added to it. But science keeps building on established evidence—as compared to the paranormal, which seldom discards outdated theories, and thrives on wild claims and speculation.

A tremendous amount has been learned about the brain in recent years. But it is just a glimpse into the massive mystery that still exists. Understanding some of the natural functions of this wonderful organ will at least help to dismiss the unfounded claims of those who see the supernatural around every corner.

The ambiguous Kreskin

Over the years there are probably two questions I have been asked more often than any other. "What got you started on the debunking of psychics?" and "What do you think of the Amazing Kreskin?"

Answering the first question is difficult, because there are several things that motivated me. The most basic was this: As a performing mentalist, or magical mind reader, I was often criticized by other mentalists for bending the rules of the game. I didn't pretend to have any supernatural powers. I was quite content to entertain my audience with a supposed demonstration of ESP, while acknowledging that I was merely using the art of deception.

That is still my philosophy—I like to call myself an honest fraud. It was another type of deception used by mentalists that propelled me into the debunking phase of my career: the outright conning of the public into believing that the so-called psychic had God-given supernatural powers. This of course was the approach that spawned Uri Geller and others of his ilk.

As to the second question about George Kreskin, my stock answer is that he is a very clever and a very successful mentalist—and nothing more. You might ask how I can be so sure he hasn't got some special powers of supernormal communication. Simple. In all the years I have seen his performances he has not yet done anything I cannot duplicate. As a matter of fact, most of his effects are standard commercial tricks found in the magic market, dressed up to be more entertaining than usual. And there's nothing wrong with that at all. It's good showbiz, and very commercial.

I part company with Kreskin when he implies that he has special powers of ESP. He'll seldom make that claim on television—for obvious reasons. There are certain rules and regulations that could make it embarrassing. But try reading his books. You'll get a different slant.

On a recent Larry King program on TV's Cable News Network, Kreskin made the flat statement, "I'm not a psychic—I've never claimed supernatural powers." Now, scan his autobiography, Random House's *The Amazing World of Kreskin,* and read, "I used both thought projection and suggestibility," and "Perhaps some of what I do fits into the category of 'psychic,' so-called, under certain conditions." Read his latest book, Doubleday's *Kreskin's Fun Way to Mind Expansion.* The man describes how he tells a volunteer member of his audience her social security number, and adds, to his readers, "I would love to tell you how I do it, but I honestly don't know"—thereby implying that something in the great beyond is assisting the act.

Come on, Kress, I know how you do it, and so does every other professional mentalist. It's been a standard stunt for decades. The effect is powerful enough to stand on its own without the psychic nonsense. Kreskin cleverly obfuscates the issue. He says ESP doesn't mean extrasensory perception. It means "extremely sensitive perception." He claims to be extrasensitive, not psychic.

Kreskin then undermines this argument by relating an effect he did with TV's Sonny and Cher, in which Cher wrote down a name that Sonny had thought of. "I did this," he says, "by first perceiving Sonny's thought, then mentally telegraphing it to Cher." I'm confused. Would mere "sensitivity" produce this kind of ability?

I'll say this. Some mentalists and others who make psychic claims are perhaps quite sincere. They may, to some extent, believe in their own powers. They could be victims of their own role-playing.

It's not up to skeptics to refute psychic claims

The magnet that attracted me a few years ago to the annual convention of the American Association for the Advancement of Science was a symposium labeled "The Edges of Science." This meeting was held in one of the larger ballrooms at the Hilton, and the room was jam-packed—one of the most heavily attended of the hundreds of symposiums held during the week.

What does the scientific community mean by the "Edges of Science"? According to the program book, the edges are those areas "where there is disagreement about whether there are phenomena to be investigated, and whether the tools of science can yield anything."

In the allotted three hours only three subjects could be covered—the study of ESP, the UFO controversy, and the search for extraterrestrial intelligence.

Parapsychologist Stanley Krippner, a leader in the ESP field, led off the session. Krippner is faculty chairman of the Humanistic Psychology Institute in San Francisco. He served as director of the Dream Laboratory of Maimonides Medical Center in New York. This was the renowned lab in which experiments were conducted for several years on the possibility of telepathic transmission during a subject's dream cycles. As in most experiments of this kind, claims of success were made, but conclusive evidence was not forthcoming. The controversy still rages.

A reading of Krippner's book, *Human Possibilities,* published by Doubleday, convinces me that here is a man sincere in his beliefs in the paranormal and bending over backward to be fair and open-minded—but incredibly naive. In his book he endorses the feats of several psychics who have already been exposed as frauds.

At the conference Krippner mentioned an experiment in which a "psychic" caused a small plastic bottle to move by the "power of her mind." The parapsychologist conducting the experiment, Charles Honorton, was considerably impressed and labeled this a true psychic feat.

For years I have exposed the method used in this effect in lectures and on television. A fine thread, invisible a few feet away, is tied to an endless loop and draped over the performer's thumbs. The vial is placed on a table, with the performer's hands on either side of it; the thread is now stretched out loosely behind the vial, barely touching it. The slightest rotation of the thumbs will tighten the thread, pushing the vial forward. The effect is startling.

Practice this. You, too, can be a psychic.

Magician and psychic debunker James Randi followed Krippner with a well reasoned and entertaining talk he called "Parapsychology: A Doubtful Premise." One of the points he stressed was that paranormalists continually put forward claims that they ask the skeptics to refute, rather than proving the point themselves. Well, skeptics take a negative viewpoint, and you often cannot prove a negative.

Suppose someone, most likely Santa Claus, claims reindeer can fly. Randi makes a good case when he says: "We may assemble one thousand reindeer atop the New York World Trade Center and push them off, one at a time, to prove whether they can fly. . . . Based upon my good common sense I strongly suspect that we would end up with a large pile of very unhappy reindeer in very poor condition. But what have we proven? We have only shown that these particular subjects either could not fly, chose not to fly, or perhaps could not fly on this occasion. We have not shown that there are *not* eight tiny reindeer at the North Pole who, on one night of the year, can and do fly."

The burden of proof is on the claimant of the miracle. So far it has not been forthcoming.

Not necessarily bunk

This is as appropriate a time as any to reply to some of the mail I have received from my readers. I've had my share of bouquets and brickbats, with the latter in preponderance. This is to be expected by a well-meaning, sometimes controversial skeptic.

I can't say enough about the need for the public, particularly our young people, to take an interest in the methods of science, in rational and critical thinking. I've received a good deal of criticism about science's lack of interest in such subjects as emotions, love, appreciation of art, belief in religion, and so on. I see no reason why scientific and critical thinking should negate any of the above. Scientists in general are not ogres in white lab coats plotting to blow up the world. They are ordinary people, like you and me—and have the same emotions, feelings and hangups as anyone else. This is not to say that they cannot exercise the prerogatives of their discipline—not to accept claims of any kind without strong evidence produced by observation and empirical experiment.

I've received letters accusing me of being cynical when it comes to debunking the purveyors of the paranormal. Not guilty. There's a big difference between cynicism and skepticism. Several readers have been kind enough to say they support my debunking many of the claims of psychic phenomena. Their reason? "Because," they say, "it's a lot of bunk." It's very encouraging to receive approval, but I can't agree with this philosophy. It's not just enough to state that "it's a lot of bunk." One should be able to explain why it's bunk. If a person sees something strange in the night sky and believes it's a spacecraft from another world, he's not necessarily psychotic. There are literally hundreds of reasons why such conclusions could be incorrect.

When a visit to a psychic adviser makes a strong impression on an individual, he or she is not necessarily more gullible than the average. The methods of fraudulent psychics are varied and numerous. They have been exposed by myself and others again and again. To say that bending spoons, keys, and metal bars through the power of the mind is ridiculous doesn't get to the root of the matter. Better to learn how they are actually done, through perfectly natural physical means—with a touch of deception thrown in. To accuse psychic healers of being charlatans is not enough. Better to take the trouble to study their methods. After all, some psychic healing does work. We should at least understand why, and we should also understand how dangerous much of it is.

I've received several letters to which I cannot reply, even in general terms. They are obviously sincere, but some of the arguments are so abstract I simply cannot understand them. There again, I'm often accused of being simplistic in my approach. My reply to this is that I find that paranormalists love to obfuscate. It's so much easier to muddy the waters with jargon and fuzzification. Good arguments are usually clear and simple. So are good letters.

Demonstration of "psychic" powers isn't hard

Some of the most interesting parts of a television program, for me, take place behind the scenes. My TV appearances are usually on public affairs shows in which I have a confrontation with one or more so-called psychics. A recent one was on "People Are Talking," at KYW-TV in Philadelphia.

I usually meet my opponents in the Green Room before we proceed to the studio. The Green Room is the term used for the waiting room for guests on a program. I've yet to find one decorated in green. On this program the other guests were three self-styled psychics from different states, two women and a man. It was interesting to observe how they greeted one another—obviously this was their first meeting. "What's your sun sign, dear? Aries? I knew it, I knew it,"—and on and on. Of course she knew it. She's psychic, isn't she? Then why ask?

I, the skeptic in the lion's den, am usually greeted cordially, but warily, by the psychics. Not surprisingly, I usually find their attitude toward me friendlier before the program than after. I must admit something: psychics are easy to like. They are usually mild mannered, seemingly sincere, and personable. It's all part of the professional manner, but I'm sometimes tempted to admire them—until I think of the lives that have been ruined by some of them. To paraphrase Will Rogers, I never met a psychic I didn't like—until I knew him or her better.

The hosts of the program impressed me with their objectivity. Richard Bey and Dana Hilger handled the controversial subject evenly and professionally. Usually the host of a program on the paranormal seems to lean over backward to accommodate visiting psychics. The producer, Pamela Browne, asked me to revive my Elchonen character, in which I am introduced as a psychic and perform one or two unexplainable miracles. Could I do a character assessment for host Richard Bey? He, of course, knew who I was, and expected the usual generalities.

On camera, he was due for a shock. I began to describe events from his past that I couldn't possibly have known—by normal standards. I told him about his educational background, about his sex life, and really shook him when I recounted a traumatic event at his birth. I couldn't go back much further than that. Remember, we had not met previously. I had just entered the building a half an hour before and didn't even know who the hosts would be.

In Bey's eyes, Gordon the debunker was now Gordon the psychic, and his amazement and confusion were obvious. "All right, Henry, how could you possibly have known these things?" I knew it was time to blow my cover, but I hesitated to do so. I was beginning to feel a sense of power. Once again I got the feeling that psychics get when they score a "hit." The problem is, they often begin to believe in their own powers. But rationality got the better of me. "It wasn't too difficult, Richard. I got the information from some people right here at the station, just prior to going on the air. How do you think the psychics do it?"

The psychics on the program immediately took issue. They didn't believe me. One of them kept insisting throughout the program, and even during the commercial breaks, that I really was a psychic but wouldn't admit it. I've been hearing this bizarre line for twenty years.

How to expose psychic nonsense

Psychologists have always been the strongest critics of parapsychologists. That this situation hasn't changed was underlined at the 1984 convention of the American Psychological Association in Toronto.

At a symposium on "Anomalistic Psychology" a number of leading psychologists stated their views on superstitious and paranormal beliefs, on critical thinking, and on parapsychology in general.

Dr. James Alcock of York University traced the history of parapsychological research, which began even before that multisyllabic word was concocted. More than a hundred years ago a group of scholars at Cambridge University decided that the time had come to set up a learned society to examine "psychic phenomena." The Society for Psychical Research (SPR) was founded in England in 1882, ten years before the founding of the American branch (ASPR). As Alcock pointed out, the SPR leaders "hoped that they would one day be able to put the postmortem existence of the soul on a scientific footing, or at the very least demonstrate that there is a non-material component to the human mind."

The eminent American psychologist, William James, was one of the founders of the American SPR. James himself was not necessarily a strong believer in the paranormal, but he strongly supported scientific research into paranormal phenomena.

Alcock made a good point when he stressed that although most psychology professors are very skeptical of so-called paranormal phenomena, students have a tendency to lean in the other direction. Controlled studies have corroborated this. In several years of lecturing at universities I have observed this fact repeatedly. The reason, of course, is that most psychology professors prefer to ignore the claims of psychic phenomena, perhaps hoping they will go away. What they should do is to incorporate paranormal studies in their courses, instead of looking down their noses at them. There are natural explanations for most "psychic experiences." If those with the explanations would reveal them to the believers, a good deal of the nonsense would be exposed.

My own experience in dealing with students convinces me that they are open-minded, hungry for explanations, and ready to adopt critical thinking. What they need is proper direction—and who better to give it than their psychology professors. An incident that took place at the close of the Toronto symposium was revealing. During the discussion period an audience member stood up to complain bitterly that his observations on his own personal psychic experiences were ignored by the psychology establishment, that he couldn't get his writings published. Why sweep these things under the rug? If intelligent, educated members of society believe even in the tooth fairy, and claim to have evidence for it, their views should be aired—and then challenged and debated. That's what science is all about.

Psychics can trick even the most intelligent

It's one o'clock on a sunny afternoon at the end of March. In a large, bright lecture room at the State University of New York at Buffalo, philosophy students are crowding in for their afternoon class. Attendance is particularly heavy for this session. A guest lecturer has been announced, one a little out of the ordinary. He claims to be a genuine psychic. He will not only speak on the paranormal, he will also attempt to perform some psychic feats—something probably none of the students has ever witnessed. The lecture room is jammed. Extra seats have been set up. There is a definite sense of anticipation in the air.

The philosophy professor walks in, accompanied by another man whom he proceeds to introduce: "This man is a psychic who rarely makes public appearances. Most of his time is spent in parapsychology labs, where he has participated in many experiments in extrasensory perception. I'm pleased he's agreed to come here today. He will now take over."

The guest lecturer begins in a quiet voice. "I know you have mixed feelings about psychic claims, but I would just ask you to cooperate in a few experiments I'll attempt, and then use your own judgment as to their validity. I can't tell you how I do these things—they just seem to happen. But they will only happen if I can count on your cooperation and on your concentration."

The guest lecturer then passes out a sealed envelope, which he asks someone to retain. "This will be an attempt at precognition, the prediction of something that will take place in the future." A notepad is produced, on which four volunteer students each write four digits of their choice, in columns of four. A fifth volunteer is asked to add the figures and announce the total. The person who has the sealed envelope is directed to open it and read the prediction inside. The total of the added figures has been accurately predicted.

There's a quick buzz of conversation around the room. Without delay, the psychic announces: "I'll now try to outdo Uri Geller. As many of you know, he claimed to be using psychokinesis to cause the hands of a watch to change position. Here is a small hand calculator. Will someone take it and enter any four digits on the display? Now, hand the calculator to someone else, anyone. Good. Now, while you are holding it, I will direct my mind to change the four numbers now showing to four completely different numbers"—which he calls off. After suitable concentration, the feat is accomplished—to the accompaniment of puzzled looks and more murmurs from the students. The psychic then proceeds to demonstrate telepathy and psychometry—discerning facts about people merely by handling their personal belongings—in a series of further experiments.

Finally, the psychic lecturer asks his mesmerized audience for a show of hands—"How many of you are now convinced that these things can be done through the hidden powers of the mind? Please be honest about it." There's a decided vote in his favor. "Well, you've been had. I'm not a psychic—I'm a mentalist-magician. I've done these little miracles through perfectly natural means, using the deceptive methods of conjuring. Your professor and I have cooked up this little charade to show you how easily you can be deceived, and how critical you should be of anyone claiming to have paranormal powers."

There's a burst of self-conscious laughter, followed by applause, followed by a hundred questions—which is a good sign.

It occurs to me that I've neglected to mention the identity of the mentalist-magician. It was I.

Variations on the term "intuition"

I finally found one—a psychic who claims he is not psychic. Earl Curley of Ottawa tells strangers intimate facts about themselves, makes predictions of future events, claims to have aided law enforcement agencies in finding criminals and missing persons—all this, but he's not psychic.

How does he do it? Nothing to it—it's "intuition."

Curley and I met head-on at a recent taping of the "Brian Gazzard Show" at the studios of CFCF-TV in Montreal. This syndicated program has been aired weekday mornings on the Global network in the Ontario region for the past couple of years. The host of the show, Brian Gazzard, usually has one or two guests interacting with a studio audience. My first appearance last year was solo, and a breeze. This year, appearing with a member of the opposition, the atmosphere was definitely more charged.

If Curley is not psychic, and operates through intuition, what, I asked, is his definition of *intuition* then? "Intuition," he asserted, "is an ability to verbalize a situation . . . and then in turn create a . . . picture of that event."

That sounded a little inverted to me. I asked where the picture came from in the first place. Curley changed the subject.

According to the *Oxford English Dictionary* the definition of *intuition* is "the immediate apprehension of an object by the mind without the intervention of any reasoning process." A scientific study in 1947 found that the intuited perceptions studied had been absorbed below conscious levels and were based on "sensory observation of the subject." This would seem to rule out anything of a paranormal nature. But that doesn't discourage the occultniks who grasp the vagueness of the term *intuition* and use it to further their arguments.

Curley then began to demonstrate his "intuitive" powers. He selected one young woman from the audience and proceeded to tell her that she was going through a period of turmoil, that she had decided to become independent and not to get involved in new relationships. She was quick to verify the accuracy of his reading. There are two principles of what is called "cold reading" involved here. First, the generalities would apply to almost any young person in today's society. Second, under certain conditions a subject, particularly one who has a tendency to be a believer, will be quick to validate a psychic reading—even if only part of it seems to be accurate.

Up to this point it was good, clean fun. But then Curley proceeded to "read" an elderly woman in the audience, and used the same harmful tactic I've seen repeated many times by so-called psychics. "The lower portion of that left lung," he told her, "is a little out of shape. I do strongly recommend that you . . . have that looked into very shortly. You have some scar tissue there. . . . You do have a little asthmatic problem."

I interjected, "You have lower back pain." This is a standard pronouncement. Who doesn't have it after middle age? After all, I too could have a well-developed intuition.

Strangely, Curley quickly disagreed. "Not at all!" he said.

Brian Gazzard interrupted to ask, "Wait a moment, do you have lower back pain?"

"Sometimes," said the shaken woman.

Curley didn't hesitate. "But not at this time." A quick comeback—the mark of an experienced fortune teller. He continued, "I don't know who talked you into going on a diet, but you forget it, because you're not supposed to be on one."

The woman answered, "I'm not on a diet."

I pointed out to the audience the possible psychological harm that can be done when a person, particularly an elderly one, is fed this type of nonsense about a lung problem—by an unqualified layman. As if to underscore this, when the program was over, a woman who had been sitting next to the subject approached to tell me that her friend was very upset by the reading, and was really concerned about her condition.

Let's wait for cold, hard evidence

People often read what they want to read—not what is written. In other words, one's thinking influences one's perception of what one reads. We hear a lot about "objective" writing. There's perhaps an even greater need for objective reading.

For example, reader Andy Dwornik writes to me: ".Just what did you debunk in your article on firewalking?"

It might be useful to define the word *debunk*. To debunk is to un-mask, to put straight, to clarify, to remove false opinions, to correct, to free from illusion. In the firewalking column referred to, I revealed the scientific explanation of why a person—any person—can stride over hot coal embers under certain conditions. I showed that the people who run firewalking seminars are using this phenomenon to gouge the public by suggesting there is something psychic about it. Is this not debunking?

Regarding telepathy, Dwornik brings up a point that is a favorite with paranormalists. He contests my statement that the brain does not have the power to project its minute electromagnetic or radio waves beyond the skull.

"Who says they have to be radio waves?" Dwornik writes, "They could be of a different nature and science has not yet developed the proper instruments to detect and measure them." Could be, but until these phantom waves have been shown to exist, let's not make wild and speculative claims that telepathy does exist. Science does not make claims that phenomena exist until the cold, hard evidence is established.

Occultists live in a world of speculation and imagination. Imagination can be very useful in helping to devise theories—and indeed it is a powerful tool for the research scientist. But without a hard-headed, factual foundation, imagination in itself cannot support the many claims of the paranormalists. Dwornik defines "paranormal" as "not understood." I would say that many so-called paranormal happenings are understood and have been explained by science—and that many others eventually will be.

Elementary: Computer enhancement solved the case

Here's the trivia quiz for today: What fictional character would you say was the ultimate master of logical thinking? You needn't look at the bottom of the page for the answer; it could only be Sherlock Holmes. We would assume that his creator, Sir Arthur Conan Doyle, was a man of logic, of intelligence, of rational thinking. He was. He also believed in fairies.

In 1921 Doyle wrote *The Coming of the Fairies*—and not as fiction, as his Sherlock Holmes tomes had been. The book states the case for Doyle's belief in the little translucent creatures with gossamer wings. It is still available in reprint.

The England of 1920 is a hotbed of spiritualism. Thousands are visiting spirit mediums, taking part in seances, listening to rappings on tables, consulting Ouija boards. There is a great need to somehow contact the dear ones lost in the Great War. Doyle is a confirmed believer. He is also one of the most respected men in Britain because of his literary contributions. He has been knighted for his accomplishments.

In *Strand* magazine that year, Doyle writes an article entitled "Fairies Photographed—An Epoch-making Event." It recounts the story of two Yorkshire girls, Elsie Wright and Frances Griffiths, who took photographs of each other in Cottingley Glen. Gamboling around the girls in several photos are a number of fairies. Not only that, but a goblin is thrown in for good measure. These pictures will achieve great notoriety. To this day they reside in the Kodak Museum in the United Kingdom.

After receiving and studying the photos, Doyle obtains the original plates and has them examined by experts. They agree—there is no evidence of double exposure. It would take an experienced photographer to fake pictures of that kind. The girls are not capable of this. The pictures are the real thing. Sir Arthur is ecstatic. He writes to his friend Harry Houdini, the great escape artist, "I have something . . . precious, two photos, one of a goblin, the other of four fairies in a Yorkshire wood. . . . It is a revelation." Hundreds of people write to Doyle telling him of the fairies they have seen in their gardens.

Several years later the plot begins to unravel. A thorough investigation of the photographs is launched by Kodak in London. All sorts of clues are diagnosed and lead to the conclusion that a gigantic hoax developed out of what had been a childish prank. The publicity generated by Doyle's endorsement of all this nonsense was the key factor.

In 1971, BBC-TV interviews Elsie Wright, now an elderly lady. She will *not* "swear on the Bible that the fairies were really there." Asked about the photos, she replies: "Let's say [the fairies] are figments of our imaginations." A more revealing interview came from Elsie's mother back in 1920. She told investigators that Elsie was "a most imaginative child, who has been in the habit of drawing fairies for years."

The case was wrapped up only recently. Computer enhancement, a technological device that thoroughly analyzes photographs, did the job. The Cottingley fairies were cardboard cutouts suspended by thread that only modern technology could reveal. Even Sherlock Holmes wouldn't have solved this case with only his intellect and his magnifying glass.

A busy psychic sleuth

I wonder what has happened to Peter Hurkos. The celebrated clairvoyant seems to have completely disappeared from the news. Hurkos was, and perhaps somewhere still is, known as a psychometrist. That is, in psychic language, a person who can tell you personal facts about someone or help find a missing person simply by handling a personal article associated with that individual. A human bloodhound, so to speak.

Born in Holland in 1911, Hurkos did not make the usual claim of having been a psychic as a child. It wasn't until he was thirty-two years old that the miracle happened. Standing atop a thirty-foot ladder painting a window frame, Hurkos lost his balance and fell head-first to the pavement. Regaining consciousness three days later, he felt the powers possess

him. As he states in his autobiography, "I discovered the strange gift that
God had given me."

I have often commented on the many opportunists who write books
and give seminars on how they can bring out ESP powers in almost
anyone. And you know my opinion of these people and their teachings.
But if you really feel the need to be a psychic, I would strongly recommend one of these courses rather than the "falling off a ladder" method.
Peter Hurkos soon found he could do well as a psychic detective—an
occupation that is in great vogue today. He had all the attributes: a great
gift of gab (in an accent that made him sound even more authentic), a
talent for making wild and unsubstantiated claims, and a natural ability
to attract publicity.

For example, when the highly publicized theft of the Stone of Scone
took place in Westminster Abbey in 1950, Hurkos got in on the act. He
rushed to London and drew a map tracing the route taken by the thieves
with their loot. When the gem was finally recovered, through routine
police investigation, Hurkos took the credit, although it was not in the
location he had pinpointed. That was a small detail to Hurkos. His claims
were what the public read.

Probably the most famous case in which this "psychic detective" was
involved was that of the Boston Strangler. Over a period of eighteen
months a vicious rapist-killer had stalked and murdered eleven women in
the Boston area. The city was in a panic. Hurkos was brought in by a
wealthy private citizen to crack the case. The assistant attorney general of
Massachusetts, no less, cooperated with the psychic by supplying him
with objects the killer had used to strangle his victims.

Hurkos put on a virtuoso performance. He described the appearance
of the killer and, provided with a map of Boston, pointed out the spot
where he lived. The next day he was handed a letter that had been in the
possession of a suspect. Hurkos grabbed it, did one of his concentrated
psychometric readings, and confirmed that this was their man. There was
only one thing wrong with the prediction. Hurkos fingered the wrong
man. The police later arrested another individual, Albert DeSalvo, who
confessed and provided the evidence of his guilt. A great many people
who read of Hurkos's involvement are still under the impression that he
helped solve the case of the Boston Strangler. And I have never heard of
his denying it.

Years ago, when I first read of Hurkos's supposed accomplishments,

I thought, well, maybe this guy's got something. Then I saw him on a television program "reading" the contents of a sealed envelope. My illusions were immediately shattered. He was using exactly the same method I used in my "mental" act.

With the seeming disappearance of Peter Hurkos, there may be only one way he can be located. If somehow I could secure some personal possession of his . . .

A hefty tome on experiments in parapsychology

I have always approached books written by parapsychologists with a great deal of skepticism. For the uninitiated, let me explain: A parapsychologist is one who conducts experiments into the possibility of the existence of "psi," or paranormal powers.

Most parapsychologists are strong supporters of the paranormal. Psychologists and others in the scientific community tend to be skeptical of their claims—to put it mildly. There are many reasons for this attitude by mainstream science: poorly controlled experiments, experimenter fraud, hanky-panky practiced by some subjects who hoodwink the experimenters—just to name a few. So I found it quite refreshing to look through *Foundations of Parapsychology,* published by Methuen Publications.

This hefty tome was written by four leading parapsychologists, who explore the field in depth. The publishers claim the book is "designed to be the standard textbook on the subject." Well, to be fair, it might be just that—from the viewpoint of the parapsychologists. But we would also have to take into account the many excellent books written by critics of the subject.

In spite of my skeptical viewpoint, I found a good deal of merit in this book. It isn't often that a parapsychologist hits the news pages, but one of the authors, Robert L. Morris, did just that not too long ago. You may recall the sad demise of noted author Arthur Koestler. He and his wife took their own lives in a suicide pact. Koestler had strong beliefs in the paranormal. He was also a supporter of parapsychology. When his will was probated it was no surprise that he left a generous grant to the University of Edinburgh for a chair of parapsychology. Robert Morris was appointed to this chair.

A chapter in *Foundations of Parapsychology* by Morris, entitled "What Psi Is Not," is a good primer in the art of deception. If you would like to know how psychics operate, read this chapter. Morris seems to have done a good deal of research into the methods of the mentalist-magician—my own specialty. The so-called psychics, of course, use many of the same methods. Would you like to know how psychics can have a large coin placed over each eye, with dough covering the coins, with gauze taped over the dough, with a hood placed over the head—and still be able to read words written on a card held in front of them? Morris lets you in on the method involved in that caper, which enables one to peek around and through all these barriers.

I'll clue you in on a way of stymying the psychic, without going into any technical details. Simply turn the card around, with the writing facing away from the wonder-worker. Presto—a frustrated miraclemonger. This ploy was used some years ago by the late Milbourne Christopher, a noted magician and psychic investigator in the United States, to expose a young lady who had gained notoriety for being able to read with her fingertips while blindfolded. Evidently her fingers lost their vision when he turned the card over.

Foundations of Parapsychology provides an interesting review of many of the well-known experiments in the subject, including the pioneering work of J. B. Rhine at Duke University in the 1930s. And it points out the weaknesses of many of the experiments. On the other hand, many other experiments already shown by investigators to have been either weak or fraudulent are given tacit approval. One of these is the "thoughtography" experiments conducted with Ted Serios in the 1960s. What did Serios accomplish? He merely projected his thoughts onto unexposed film in a camera, after which the developed film revealed the images he was supposedly thinking of. The trickery he employed was exposed by skeptical and knowledgeable investigators, but the authors of this book still aren't convinced Serios was a charlatan.

Lethargic, not stupid

At the 1984 convention of the American Association for the Advancement of Science in New York City, I posed a question to Isaac Asimov, the prolific author and scientist. The answer drew probably the biggest laugh at the meeting.

"Dr. Asimov," I asked, "we know that polls show that tremendous numbers of people say they believe in such things as astrology, ESP, and other paranormal happenings—probably more believers than disbelievers. What is your opinion on this psychology of belief?"

Asimov's reply: "Well, I'm not a psychologist and haven't studied these things, but I think there's a positive correlation between the stupidity of a proposition and the intensity of a belief."

I have great admiration and respect for Isaac Asimov, but I can't say that I entirely agree with his response, which strongly hints that the public is stupid. When it comes to believers in paranormal or occult phenomena I don't agree with the widely held opinion that these people are stupid or gullible. Lethargic? Yes, because the average person will not take the time or the trouble to look into the possible rational explanations for so-called psychic phenomena.

The book market has always been flooded with writings on the occult, as a visit to any well-stocked bookstore will reveal. But it has only been relatively recently that books with counterarguments have appeared on the shelves. Somehow they don't seem to be displayed as prominently as perhaps they should be. Could it be a lack of public interest? Or is the reading public just unaware that these books are available? I am constantly being asked my opinion of the psychic spoon-bending "abilities" of Uri Geller. When I reply, "Haven't you read the Prometheus book, *The Truth About Uri Geller,* in which Geller is exposed as a fraud?"—I usually get a negative answer. When noted British physicist John Taylor wrote *Superminds,* in which he endorsed Geller's feats, the book became a best seller. When later, after being enlightened, Taylor wrote another book in which he retracted his previous views, hardly anyone heard about it.

On the UFO scene, Prentice-Hall published *The Andreasson Affair,* "The documented investigation of a woman's abduction aboard a UFO." It was so successful that it was followed up by a second book, *The Andreasson Affair, Phase Two.*

Methuen Publishing turned out *UFO Sightings and Landings and Abductions.* There are myriad other publications describing UFO sightings and landings and human contacts with UFO occupants—all presented as truthful documentation. The books that try to counter this wave of irrationalism are sparse. Random House's *UFOs Explained,* by Philip J. Klass, is a standard in the field. So is Klass's later book, *UFOs: The Public Deceived,* published by Prometheus.

I do know there is strong public interest in explanations of so-called psychic phenomena. When I mentioned the *Skeptical Inquirer* in one of my columns, I received scores of letters asking about subscription information. If you are interested in the occult controversy, this is the publication to read.

Hormones and psychic powers

My favorite psychic story appeared in the "Anti Matter" column of the October 1985 *Omni* magazine. According to William Roll, director of the Psychical Research Foundation in Chapel Hill, North Carolina, the hormone vasopressin "may somehow trigger the extrasensory talents of the psychic." According to Roll, "Progesterone causes the release of vasopressin, and psychically talented women have been found to have unusually high premenstrual levels of progesterone. Also, mediums frequently report serious emotional shocks in their childhoods—and vasopressin is released during times of stress." Roll says that the impact of the hormones on the nervous system may lead to psychic abilities. Note the word *may*. Roll, incidentally, was an invited speaker at the 1984 annual conference of the Committee for the Scientific Investigation of Claims of the Paranormal held at Stanford University. The committee makes an effort to provide both sides of the issues discussed at its meetings. Noted parapsychologist D. Scott Rogo gives only partial support to Roll's theory. "I don't think the evidence is ironclad," he says. Rogo wrote the book *Phone Calls from the Dead*—in which he "documents" a number of claims of phantom phone calls from the departed. The book is labeled "nonfiction."

Can the mind take photographs?

If you are a camera buff and take regular field-trips and vacations to add to your collection of pictures, you can now stay home and accomplish the same thing. Just think of a scene, gaze into your camera lens, and push the button. The image will impress itself onto the film. What could be simpler?

They call it "thoughtography"—and one man who vouches for it is psychiatrist Jule Eisenbud of Denver, Colorado. Some readers may recall having seen a "Shulman File" television program in which Eisenbud participated. He was the gray-haired gentleman who stubbornly insisted that his tests of psychic Ted Serios were thorough and definitive.

Serios is the Chicago ex-bellboy who claimed he could project his thoughts onto photographic film. Eisenbud, also a parapsychologist and strong supporter of psychic happenings, really put Serios on the map when he wrote *The World of Ted Serios,* in which he describes the many experiments he conducted with Serios over a long period of time—experiments that convinced Eisenbud that Serios was the real thing. There was one small detail, however, that cast a glimmer of doubt on Serios' methods—but not for Eisenbud. To project his thoughts Serios used what he later called a "gizmo." This was a small cardboard tube about an inch long, which he held in his hand and pointed at the camera lens. Why? To help him "concentrate his projection."

Eisenbud put great emphasis on the fact that the film had been sealed and was perfectly normal. Strangely, he downplays the significance of the cardboard tube. "Why," he told me, "anyone could have examined the 'gizmo'—it was just an ordinary cardboard tube." What nobody got a chance to examine was the device Serios concealed inside the gizmo and would later slide out and drop into his pocket. You can make one for yourself. Simply construct a tube to fit inside an outer tube. Into this insert a small transparency of a picture in one end and a small magnifying lens in the other. Point it at your camera and snap the shutter. You're now in the thoughtography business.

Photo experts Charles Reynolds and David Eisendrath from *Life* had a chance to observe the so-called psychic in action. They saw him drop the gizmo in his pocket and immediately bring it out again after he was asked to show it for examination—an old magic trick, the device resting safe and sound in his pocket.

The most interesting and revealing part of this subject to me is the attitude of Jule Eisenbud. Here is a man of science, ostensibly sincere, strongly endorsing a phenomenon that clearly does not fit into scientific law as we know it. Is he doing it for financial gain? His book did sell very well, and is still selling. Is he doing it for recognition? I can't answer that one. I will make one guess: Eisenbud simply will not accept the fact that he may have been deceived.

I tried to put my theory to the test when we lunched together after the television taping with a few of the other participants on the program. I demonstrated a couple of magic tricks to illustrate that anyone, no matter how learned or intelligent, can be deceived by the underground art of conjuring. Everyone at the table was suitably impressed—except the good doctor. Eisenbud, to our surprise, looked straight down at his plate as he ate. He absolutely refused to watch. His only comment: "I'm not interested. This has nothing to do with my experiments."

Is it lunacy to blame the moon?

Did you know that the North American Indian gave the harvest moon its label? Because it furnished extra light for more hours, in order to bring in the crops. According to Ian McGregor, of Toronto's McLaughlin Planetarium, the Indians gave names to all the moons, such as lovers' moon, wolf moon, corn moon, and so on. All of which leads up to my next question—How does the full moon affect you?

Does it stimulate your romantic proclivities? Does it perhaps have a tidal effect on your body fluids, as many paranormalists claim, sending you into some sort of physiological never-never land? Or perhaps the "lunacy" effect drives you temporarily wacky—in a mild way, of course. On the other hand, does the crime rate shoot up all over the continent? Are police stations swamped with emergency calls? Do attempts at suicide proliferate? And, perish the thought, do werewolves swell the population?

All of these effects have been blamed on the full moon for many years. Indeed, many scientific studies have tended to back up the theory of an influential moon, at least to some extent. A recent study by two psychologists and an astronomer, published in the *Skeptical Inquirer* under the heading "The Moon Was Full and Nothing Happened," takes exception to these almost universally accepted claims. This particular study is exceptional in that it is an analysis and review of thirty-seven other major studies on the subject.

It is important to point out that, in science, conducting a series of experiments, or a study, and having a summary paper about it published, does not necessarily establish the truth of a theory. At that point other scientists will analyze and attempt to replicate the study. Only then will its validity be established. This, of course, has always been the problem in parapsychology. None of the many claims for extrasensory perception has ever been replicated and validated by objective and independent observers.

In this latest analysis of the "lunar effect," every one of the previous studies takes a critical beating. First of all, almost half were found to contain statistical errors. One study, for example, had shown that a disproportionate number of traffic accidents occurred during the night hours of a three-day transition period from full to new moon. Analyzing the data, it was found that a large number of these nights fell on weekends. Are there not usually more accidents on weekends than during the week? So, was it the moon or the day of the week that accounted for the increase? If we can't be sure, the claim has not been scientifically established, which puts a dent in that particular study.

Analysis of other studies showed that there was definitely no relationship between phases of the moon and acts usually described as "lunatic." In fact, throughout the relevant literature, for every study that found that people behave more strangely than usual when the moon is full, another found that people's behavior was not affected. The claimed "tidal effect" on human body fluids, a popular theory of astrologers, is an interesting subject in itself, as is the general question of why there is a preponderance of belief in the moon's effect on humankind. There is no doubt that the full moon can have a psychological effect of some kind on impressionable people, but the many claims of all its other effects have no basis in fact. They're just a lot of moonshine.

When the mind fills in the blanks

You have just arrived in a strange city. You have never set foot there before. As the airport bus deposits you at your midtown hotel you glance up the street and suddenly get a very strange feeling. The street, the buildings, the entire surroundings are familiar—you've been there before. But you weren't—it definitely is a first visit.

If you are inclined toward belief in psychic phenomena or some of the Eastern religious philosophies, you may consult some of the relevant literature and come up with explanations that satisfy you. For instance, you could attribute this strange phenomenon to telepathy. Another person could have been in this location and transmitted the scene to you through "mental radio." Why not—if thought transmission is feasible, as many think it is. If you believe in spiritualism there's another possible explanation. Someone who once lived in this town could be sending you the images from the "other side." You, of course, would have to be a medium to be a receiver. A third theory would be that you have the power of prophecy. You really haven't been in this town before, but at one time you unconsciously had a vision that you would be. Now that you are here, your vision becomes reality. The fourth and last possible explanation would be reincarnation—and this is the most popular of the theories for this strange happening, which we all have experienced at one time or another. We must accept that a good part of the world's population has a strong religious belief in reincarnation. The Hindu religion particularly endorses this belief. For me, a religious belief is an article of faith, with which I have no quarrel. But there have been a few people on the fringes of the scientific professions who have attempted to promote reincarnation as a proven fact. With that position I do have a quarrel, because to date there is as much firm scientific evidence for reincarnation as there is for ESP and all the other related psychic phenomena—none.

The strange feeling that I've been referring to is, of course, known as deja vu. The classic Hindu explanation for deja vu is "karma"—karmic traces producing a kind of half-recalled memory from a past life. This is a widely accepted explanation for deja vu. And, believe it or not, a fairly recent Gallup poll showed that more than 20 percent of North Americans accept the theory of reincarnation.

If we turn to science we get an entirely different viewpoint on deja vu. Psychologists classify it as a memory failure or distortion and have labeled it "paramnesia." Some also consider it to be an anomaly, or abnormality, of perception. To put it simply, your perception is your interpretation of something you sense. And your perception of most things is influenced by your emotions, your biases, and your past experiences. A possible explanation for the familiarity with a strange street in a strange town could be that the scene is vaguely similar to a scene you experienced in another location. Or perhaps it is similar to a picture you once viewed. Your memory and your perception have filled in the blanks, and you get this strange feeling of familiarity.

So once more we come up with a phenomenon that has two possible explanations—the paranormal one or the more mundane scientific one. And once again the paranormal view is more interesting, provocative, and exciting. What's the answer? Do we go for the unproven? Or do we side with science?

A personality reading that fits most people

Suppose you have just visited a psychic adviser. She hasn't met you before and knows nothing about you. In order to make an impression, she gives you a character assessment. It goes something like this: "Some of your aspirations tend to be pretty unrealistic. At times you are extroverted, affable, and sociable, while at other times you are introverted, wary, and reserved. You have found it unwise to be too frank in revealing yourself to others. You pride yourself on being an independent thinker and do not accept the opinions of others without satisfactory proof. You prefer a certain amount of change and variety and become dissatisfied when hemmed in by restrictions and limitations.

"At times you have serious doubts as to whether you have made the right decisions or done the right things. Disciplined and controlled on the outside, you tend to be worried and insecure on the inside. Your sexual adjustment has presented some problems for you. While you have some personality weaknesses, you are generally able to compensate for them. You have a great deal of unused capacity that you have not turned to your advantage. You have a tendency to be critical of yourself. You have a strong need for other people to like you and to admire you."

Read it over again. Does it fit your personality? How would you rate it on a scale of one to ten? This is a stock spiel that has been used and studied in university psychology classes for more than thirty years. I used it in my lectures on the paranormal at McGill University—and got some interesting results. With an average of forty students per class, I would distribute a copy of the spiel to each student—each believing he or she was getting a different, personal assessment. The students were then asked to rate the accuracy of the reading on a scale of ten.

The average in each class was a rating of eight or nine. There were usually several tens. This was consistent with the scores obtained across the continent, which means that the most reasonably intelligent people are prepared to accept this assessment as fitting their own character. It was only after the score was toted up that I announced that each student had received the same assessment. They found it hard to believe.

This spiel was first used in 1948 by a lecturer named Bertram Forer. He got most of it from a book on astrology. If you study it carefully you'll see it is full of generalities and contradictions—as are most astrological horoscopes. Many of the statements will fit almost anyone. The real secret is that it is the subjects who make the reading succeed. They actually convince themselves that the reading matches their own character, simply in the way they interpret it. Of course, the psychic has to do a good selling job to make the client believe the assessment is personal. But that is part of the psychic's stock in trade.

Psychology has a term to describe all this. It's called the "fallacy of personal validation." *Psychology Today* published the results of an experiment that tested this fallacy in a different way. The experimenter discovered that when people gave their date of birth, and were told that the assessment was based on an astrological reading, they gave it an even higher rating than usual.

That's food for thought.

How does dowsing score?

I had to chuckle. Usually, anonymous letters get a quick passage to my wastebasket. This envelope didn't contain a letter, though—it held a folded page from the *Toronto Sunday Star*. The lead story was headlined "Diviner of Oil." It concerned a seventy-seven-year-old man named Howard Oliver, in Alberta, who allegedly found oil through the use of a pendulum, often used in water-witching—or dowsing. It wasn't the story that tickled my funnybone, but the penciled message at the top of the page: "Ahem, Mr. Gordon . . . do you ever read the *Sunday Star*?"

Yes, indeed I do . . . and every other paper I can lay my hands on. And my file of clippings of articles like this would fill the Grand Canyon. This particular story recounts Oliver's use of a weighted chain as a pendulum, and how its gyrations indicated an area where his company would strike oil—and in fact did strike oil. Readers may not have noticed a few words to the effect that this company had used his services before and dug several wells that turned out to be dry. This really tells the whole story of dowsing—and of many other claims in the psychic field. The failures are ignored. Only the occasional success is documented.

Most dowsing is done with a dowsing rod, the traditional forked twig shaped like a wishbone. It can be fashioned from wood, or even metal. Hold each end of the forked side very tightly in your fists. Point the single extension forward. All you have to do is walk around and have your dowsing rod find underground water—or oil—or gold—or Aunt Emma's lost earrings. A strike will be indicated by the projecting end dipping downwards. Does it work? Sure it does. In a way.

It works on the same principle as your friendly Ouija board: automatism—the translation of subconscious thought into muscular action. Most dowsers claim that their powers come from two sources: mysterious magnetic waves that emanate from the earth and attract the rod, or an unidentified occult power that guides the rod. If these magnetic waves existed, they could be measured by scientific instruments. Have they ever been detected? Never. Claims of occult powers are impossible to confirm and are therefore ignored by science.

So how do dowsers sometimes find hidden water sources? They often have keen powers of observation. They notice the vegetation, the rock structures, and other relevant signs. They have a fair idea where water might be found. Subconsciously that knowledge translates into a slight muscular movement that causes the rod to dip.

Dowsers are most often honest and sincere. Of course, we also have the charlatans who fake it by deliberately maneuvering the rod. An important point: If the dowser can't make an educated guess as to where the water or oil might be, that wishbone will definitely not dipsy-doodle— unless it's controlled deliberately.

Many dowsers have been scientifically tested voluntarily. Not one has ever passed the test. The fact that Howard Oliver found oil in the oil-rich province of Alberta impresses me as much as the dowsers who find water in areas where there are large subterranean water tables. Now, if Oliver should bring his magic pendulum to Ontario and strike a big oil find, I'll reconsider my opinion. I might even buy stock in his company.

Firewalking can be done—but why?

Yes, you can walk on fire. Now, let's get this straight—I don't recommend firewalking as a hobby. I don't recommend it, period. But it can be done by anybody, and it's got nothing to do with anything mystical. It does have something to do with physics, though, but more on that later.

Firewalking has been around for centuries. Originally it was a ceremony that formed part of the primitive spring festivals designed to ensure a plentiful harvest.

Today this foot-warming ritual is practiced in many cultures and for

various reasons. The shamans and sorcerers in some countries still do it
to impress their followers. To them, of course, it has occult and mystical
meanings. To some it signifies purification through fire. It is sometimes
used as an ordeal to prove a person's innocence.

The firewalk is usually staged by digging a shallow trench and filling
it with burning coals. The walking is done on the glowing embers, often
at temperatures around 1,400° Fahrenheit. The trench can be fifteen to
thirty feet in length. The walker strides quickly, bare-footed, from one
end of the trench to the other. Often there is no effect whatever on the
soles of the feet. Sometimes there's a bonus of blisters.

One of the most famous walks of modern times was made by the
magician Kuda Bux, from Kashmir—also known as "the man with the
X-ray eyes." Bux did his stroll in England in 1935, striding across a
twenty-foot length of glowing embers—not once, but four times.

As I say, anyone can do this. And recently thousands have been
doing it. It seems that some enterprising people have been giving seminars
on firewalking. These self-help "institutes" are demonstrating that their
students can firewalk without damage—and in the process convincing
them that they're getting some sort of "mind-controlling" advantages from
the course. Well, the truth is, anyone who has the guts to indulge in this
ridiculous exercise can do it—without taking any expensive courses.

This point was made just recently by two California scientists. UCLA
physicist Bernard Leikind and UCLA psychologist William McCarthy did
a little investigating. One of them attended a seminar, the other did not.
Both of them then firewalked, and neither experienced harm. Not only
that, but Leikind, in an interview with the *Los Angeles Times,* came up
with a scientific explanation for the phenomenon that seems to make
sense. There have been many attempted explanations over the years, but
they were hardly scientific and were quickly disproven. One was that
moisture on the feet caused a vapor barrier that protected them; another
was that some preparation was secretly applied to the soles of the feet;
still another cited calluses on the feet of people who often walked barefoot.

To quote Dr. Leikind:

The secret is the difference between temperature and heat. Consider a
cake baking in an oven. The air in the oven, the cake, and the cake pan
are all about the same temperature; but, while you can put your hand
inside the oven, you cannot touch the pan without getting burned. The
reason: the air has a low heat capacity and poor thermal conductivity,

while the pan has a high heat capacity and a high thermal conductivity.

In the case of the firewalk, the embers are light, fluffy carbon compounds with low heat capacity. The human body has a relatively high heat capacity, similar to water. When the foot touches the embers, they cool off faster than the skin warms up, enabling one to tolerate a quick walk.

Both Leikind and McCarthy are members of the Southern California Skeptics, one of the many new groups springing up all over the continent to challenge pseudoscience. This group contains a number of prestigious scholars and scientists and advocates clear, critical, rational thinking. The crusade against credulity continues.

The March 1985 *Life* had a spread on the "charismatic kid," Tony Robbins. This twenty-five-year-old made a fortune while hot-footing it to fame—walking on hot coals and enticing others to do so. He practices a technique called "Neuro-Linguistic Programming," a system of self-help therapy that includes having his disciples indulge in firewalking. Robbins has managed to inspire a fad that has swept the continent. His Robbins Research Institute has established "managers," according to *Life,* who have spread the gospel from sea to sea.

Overseas, Robbins hasn't been quite so successful. When he planned to present his seminars in Australia a skeptical group down under bombarded the media with an exposure of the deception in his techniques. Robbins cancelled his firewalking tour. Did he get cold feet?

Another year of paranormality

The year's end always sees a rash of reviews of events on the political, social and entertainment scenes. During 1985 there was no lack of stories in the major magazines on the weird and wonderful happenings in the world of the paranormal.

Omni had a feature on "voices from beyond." It seems that Dr. William Braud of the Mind Science Foundation in San Antonio, Texas, discovered strange sounds being emitted from audio tapes played back on recorders—tapes that had never been recorded on. According to *Omni,* such events are known by parapsychologists as "electronic voice phenomena" and have been attributed to spirits, people from other dimensions, and even the rumblings of our distraught, collective unconscious. Braud says that of course it may not be these things at all. It may just be that "some people are psychokinetically imprinting the sounds."

Omni didn't neglect the UFO scene. It sponsored a UFO contest. Winners would be those who sent in the best answers to the following question: If aliens land in the United States, where will they appear and why will they choose that particular place? The magazine takes care to point out that it doesn't doubt those who claim to have already met aliens, but that such experiences won't count in the contest.

My favorite magazine item of 1985 was a paragraph in *Maclean's*. It was part of an article on the October crisis of 1970 in Quebec. Jerome Choquette, then justice minister of Quebec, was being interviewed by *Maclean's* regarding the government's efforts to trace the whereabouts of minister Pierre Laporte and Britain's James Cross, who had been kidnapped. The question: "How did you search for the kidnap victims?" Choquette's reply: "We considered every angle, every possibility. At one point we sat around a table over the map of the Montreal region while a clairvoyant stood over it with a pendulum, and when the pendulum settled he said, 'This is where they are.' Of course he was wrong, but we did not rule anything out."

Shirley MacLaine is barking up the wrong tree

The 1984 Academy Awards presentation featured Shirley MacLaine, who won the Oscar for best actress.

She had also been grabbing headlines in another field—the paranormal. MacLaine has joined a very long and distinguished list of prominent people who have hopped onto the occult bandwagon.

In her latest book, *Out on a Limb,* published by Bantam, MacLaine takes the trouble to name some of these people. One of the reasons she has been hooked by the psychic salesmen seems to be this lineup of references: Pythagoras, Plato, Carl Jung, Thomas Edison, Walt Whitman, Peter Sellers, William Blake, Abraham Lincoln, Sir Oliver Lodge, William Randolph Hearst—all these and more are dredged up as examples. "If they could believe, why shouldn't I?" asks MacLaine.

In *Out on a Limb* MacLaine mentions her guru, David, as introducing her to occult literature and guiding her along the path to psychic revelation. In a 1983 interview in the *Philadelphia Inquirer,* MacLaine revealed that David is in fact a composite of "four spiritual men" who have influenced her education. Furthermore, she said, they all had relationships with extraterrestrials who came down to earth from the Pleiades star cluster.

MacLaine has swallowed if not digested almost every paranormal subject tossed at her. Reincarnation, visitors from other worlds, spirit mediums, the miracles of Edgar Cayce, the fraudulent fantasies of Erich von Däniken, extrasensory perception, the myth of Atlantis, precognition, out-of-body travel, the wonders of the Great Pyramid of Egypt, she accepts them all without question, or after very little question.

To take just one example, MacLaine mentions Sir Oliver Lodge's research into the spiritual readings of the infamous medium Leonora Piper: "We discussed the case of Mrs. Piper in Boston and how her information always checked out to be infallible." If Shirley had bothered to do a little more reading she would have discovered that Piper was exposed as a fraud, that she used the standard methods of mental mediums, and that she had also duped the great psychologist William James. As with most believers, MacLaine has immersed herself in occult literature without taking the trouble to get a more balanced view.

The question can be asked: "Why be critical of Shirley MacLaine? After all, she has the right to her beliefs. If she believes the moon is made of Swiss cheese, so what?" The answer to that question is this: MacLaine writes a book on the subject; she goes on countless television programs to proclaim her views; she makes dozens of statements during press interviews—in other words, she goes public. By doing that she leads millions of people down the garden path.

I find it interesting to see how gently MacLaine's views on the paranormal are treated by her interviewers. People like Phil Donahue, for example, don't take issue with most of the nonsense she supports—their strongest remarks are something like, "You don't really believe that, do you?"

Sure, Shirley MacLaine is a likable person, a great entertainer, popular with the public, and an expert in her field of show business. But, like other experts, including many prominent scientists, MacLaine gets into very tall grass when she wanders outside her field of expertise.

MacLaine has a strong social conscience, is very interested in self-expression, and stresses open-mindedness. Well, we should all have open minds—but not gaping ones.

Interviewing Shirley MacLaine is a bit like nailing Jell-O to the wall. The talented actress, singer, dancer, and author has been interviewed by Larry King, Phil Donahue, Barbara Frum and many others about her controversial book *Dancing in the Light.* The book is a sequel to her best-selling *Out on a Limb,* and continues along the same theme—MacLaine's complete immersion into the world of spiritualism, mysticism, reincarnation, and almost everything connected with the paranormal.

After viewing some of the aforementioned interviews I felt that the hard questions just weren't being asked. Well, when MacLaine paid a visit to Toronto, I got my chance to have a private discussion with her. I did ask the hard questions, but all I got were soft answers. Soft? Well, maybe abstract would be a more accurate description. Discussing MacLaine's many sessions with a particular spirit medium, and her avid reading of paranormal literature, I asked, "Have you ever made a study of the literature that explains a lot of so-called psychic phenomena?"

MacLaine's tentative "Uh-huh" was followed by: "You see, I really think we're all creating our own reality. I think I'm creating you right here—so therefore I created the medium, I created the spirit entities—so therefore I've created everything."

"But," I countered, "how can you say you created the medium? He does exist—he's a reality to other people who visit him."

"In my dream he is," MacLaine responded, "but I don't know if he's a reality to you."

"But if I ever met him," I replied weakly, "he'd be a reality to me."

MacLaine didn't hesitate: "It would still be in my dream that you met him."

It was then that she hit me with the scientific whammy: "That's what quantum physics is telling us. When the observer is in the laboratory and looking at subatomic particles and watching them change according to the consciousness of the observer, he's creating subatomic particles." When MacLaine takes the scientific road to attempt to bolster her paranormal claims, she's making the same error other paranormalists do. In most cases they know little about physics or science in general, but have soaked up a few standard phrases that seem to lend authority to their arguments.

Without getting technical, a few brief words about quantum physics, which deals with the subatomic world. Physics has discovered a miniature world of moving particles that makes up all matter. Physicists have found certain properties of this world that they cannot yet explain. This is nothing new in science. In time, the explanations usually emerge. These particles sometimes act in a way that defies common sense. It has been established that when measurements are taken of the action of these particles, the measurements themselves seriously affect their position, velocity, or direction.

This, of course, is an oversimplification. The point is that the particles are affected by the measuring instruments—not by the consciousness of the scientist doing the measuring, or the observing. And this is where the paranormalists are off base. They like to stress the involvement of consciousness. This then leads to their theories of unreality. From this point the whole of their arguments becomes unreal. MacLaine maintains the same line, which isn't surprising—it comes from the same sources.

MacLaine devotes a good part of her book to describing her experiences with acupuncture—a controversial subject in itself. But she goes a lot further than the usual claims for cures of bodily ailments. For MacLaine, acupuncture is a means of regressing to former lives. Readers will really have to suspend their disbelief when they get to this section of *Dancing in the Light.*

Most of the media people who talk to, or about, Shirley MacLaine seem bemused by the fact that she expresses a belief in reincarnation. But if you consider that a good number of the earth's population follows religions that have adopted this belief, it isn't that hard to accept. Of course, MacLaine goes a lot further than most when she cites specific anecdotes of her past lives. You could possibly credit this to an overactive imagination.

Perhaps more of a shocker is an incident MacLaine recounts in *Dancing in the Light.* She describes a visit to a Beverly Hills shop in which she lays down her purse only to have it suddenly vanish. MacLaine's explanation? Dematerialization. When I asked her if she really believed in dematerialization, MacLaine answered with a self-conscious laugh, "Yes, until some other explanation comes along." Well, explanations don't come along. You have to look for them. That's the problem with believers in the occult. They want instant answers for strange happenings. It's much easier for the believer to accept a supernatural explanation than to search for a rational one.

I've always been interested in what sets people on the road to mystical beliefs. MacLaine said she'd always had an intuitive feeling for such things, but added, "I've had profound experiences when traveling, in that I felt I'd been to certain countries before." I wonder if she has researched the psychological reasons for "deja vu."

In her book MacLaine writes about a California trance medium, Kevin Ryerson, whom she visits regularly to get in touch with her spirit entities. It's quite evident she's influenced by him and that he has her complete confidence. And how did Ryerson accomplish that? He might have used the standard method of many psychics—secretly securing some personal facts about the client and then revealing them in a mystical manner. MacLaine's own words, from her book: "I can only say that Tom McPherson, one of the entities that Kevin channels, knew intimate details about me and my life which no other human being on earth knew."

I asked MacLaine if she had ever heard of the events that took place after the death of the noted medium Arthur Ford—when files were discovered that revealed that he had amassed information on many of his subjects before he sat for them. No, she hadn't, but that didn't bother her. "I think there are times when mediums must feel the pressure and not let down their clients." This is a stock cop-out for psychics pulling fraudulent stunts.

I finally got down to basics. "You are a public person and a role model for a lot of people. It's quite evident that many are being swept along by what you are saying. Many people are emotionally unstable, and can be affected by your writings and public statements. You are proselytizing, aren't you?" MacLaine's answer, "Oh, I hope not—I'm sharing."

"But," I continued, "when you advise people, as you did on the Phil Donahue Show, to go to the metaphysical bookstores and read the books, why don't you tell them to read the rational books and make a judgment?"

"They can find those books in the metaphysical bookstores," answered MacLaine. They can? In what proportion? If you want to get a clue about the effect Shirley MacLaine's message is having on the public, you needn't go further than watching the faces in the studio audience on the Donahue show, or listening to the call-ins on the Larry King cable television show—every one supporting MacLaine's philosophy.

I know the media people find her books flaky, but also a good subject for a column or an interview. Unfortunately, MacLaine is also helping to energize the tidal wave of irrationality that's been sweeping this continent. The public is getting only one side of the story.

Colin Wilson: A good man, but off base

British author Colin Wilson has written yet another book. *The Essential Colin Wilson* brings the author's output to well over fifty. His novel *The Outsider,* published in 1956, when he was only twenty-five years old, won instant acclaim. Since then Wilson has turned out fiction and nonfiction—on subjects ranging from the occult to philosophy and criminology. A listing of Wilson's books groups those on the occult under the heading of nonfiction. I would argue with that labeling. Wilson's recounting of anecdotal psychic tales, his acceptance of almost everything mystical and occult, are difficult for a rational person to accept.

After reading one of Wilson's later books, *Poltergeist,* I decided to pack it in. No more wallowing in Wilson Weirdness. Stephen Spielberg's film of the same name entertained millions. I doubt that very many viewers took it seriously. But Wilson's book is presented as a serious study of the phenomenon of the poltergeist, the mischievous spirit or ghost. He doesn't equivocate—Wilson has a definite theory about poltergeists. They derive their power from lines of "earth force" that crisscross the surface of the earth. At the intersections of these lines, claims Wilson, occur most of the poltergeist activities. Not only that, but these areas also account for UFO sightings. He produces no evidence, but takes the offensive by charging, "The poltergeist is undoubtedly a reality, and anyone who thinks otherwise . . . is being willfully blind or stupid." Strangely, Wilson even seems to endorse the authenticity of the antics of the Fox sisters, whose mysterious knee- and toe-joint cracking sparked the spiritualist movement in the nineteenth century. Is it possible that Wilson, an authority on the paranormal, is ignorant of the fact that the Fox sisters were frauds—and admitted it publicly?

As I said, I had closed the book on further Wilson reading. But curiosity conquered when I heard of his new book. *The Essential Colin Wilson* is an anthology of some of his major works, compiled by the author himself. The chapter that caught my attention was "Magic—The Science of the Future." It was excerpted from his huge tome, *The Occult,* which has become the bible of the paranormalists.

Some of the references give a clue to the man's gullibility and his complete acceptance of almost any psychic claim. Referring to the so-called clairvoyant Peter Hurkos' Wison writes, "In 1943 Peter Hurkos was working as a house painter when he fell from his ladder and fractured his skull. When he woke up . . . he discovered that he now possessed the gift of second sight." Unfortunately, writes Wilson, Hurkos could not then concentrate on anything. "His mind was like a radio set picking up too many stations."

As an electronics engineer, I have often wondered about the tuned circuits that psychics possess that enable them to sort out the millions of thoughts and signals floating around out there. Or how spirit mediums can pick up a message from one particular entity, when so many billions have "gone over" since the beginning of humanity's life on earth.

Colin Wilson doesn't question anything of this sort. Neither does he seem aware that Peter Hurkos is a proven fraud as a clairvoyant, the "psychic detective" whose claim to fame is having helped the police find the Boston Strangler. Unfortunately, Hurkos fingered the wrong man. Wilson fills this chapter with one unproven anecdote after another—as does so much of the vast literature on the paranormal.

Colin Wilson is an accomplished writer. His philosophical musings offer much food for thought—agree with him or not. His mystical leanings can be understood, even respected. Wilson's complete swallowing of almost every paranormal claim, without critical investigation, however, subtracts considerably from his credibility—in my estimation.

A violinist and the paranormal

It's always interesting to examine the psychology of belief. Why do so many people believe so strongly in the paranormal, in pseudoscience, in psychic phenomena, in mysticism? It is even more interesting to scan a list of the people prominent in the arts and sciences, politics, and the professions who follow these beliefs. People like Arthur Koestler, Sir Arthur Conan Doyle, Victor Hugo, Sir William Crookes, Thomas Edison, Henry Ford, Mackenzie King . . . to name just a handful. One doesn't often get a chance to talk with people of this prominence, even when they're alive. If I were a medium I might get a crack at some of the aforementioned— but I have a feeling my membership card in the spiritual association has been revoked.

Interviewing a contemporary believer of prominence can be a little sticky. He or she will usually be reticent about discussing the personal matter of belief in things that go bump in the night—unless it's Shirley

MacLaine, of course. Give her high marks for guts, candor—and credulity.

So, when I had the opportunity to have this type of discussion with a man I've admired for many years, it was a little out of the ordinary. Yehudi Menuhin recently appeared at Roy Thomson Hall conducting the Royal Philharmonic Orchestra of London. The famed violinist and former child prodigy is a citizen of the world, an urbane, sophisticated man, a leader in his field for the past sixty years.

I had heard of his interest in yoga, of his long visits to the mystic land of India, of the development of his philosophy in that environment.

A review of Methuen Publications' *The Music of Man* reveals more insight into the beliefs of Yehudi Menuhin. He coauthored the book, and it covers the excellent television series of the same name. It's an introduction to the history of music.

In the first chapter of *The Music of Man,* a history of music coauthored by Menuhin, the violinist refers to Kirlian photography as evidence of the existence of the "human aura," and states, "When a new person comes into a room, their aura and that of persons already in the room undergo a change, linked to the emotional states of the individuals." A number of studies have discredited Kirlian photography and shown that there is no scientific evidence whatever that there is such a thing as an aura around the human body.

Menuhin also refers to tests that supposedly showed that flocks of birds in flight keep formation by flashing telepathic messages to one another. I'd be more than interested to see documentation of such tests.

After the concert I spoke with Menuhin, hoping to clear up a few of these points. He did verify his practicing of Hatha Yoga, which is the head-standing, physical branch of that discipline. The meditation part is another branch. Menuhin has stood on his head in the company of other luminaries, including Pandit Nehru and David Ben-Gurion. On the subject of reincarnation, he said, "I'm convinced that there's a connection between places and other times. . . . I know that we've been here already before . . . but I would have no idea of how the theory of reincarnation can be explained." Menuhin reflected thirty-six years back, to a statement made by his four-year-old son—"I do not believe in death. . . . I believe I've always been here, will always be here." Evidently this long-remembered remark has had some effect on the musician's thinking, and perhaps on his belief structure. I could not get a direct answer about statements he made about the paranormal in *The Music of Man.*

My assessment of Yehudi Menuhin? A sensitive man with perhaps a leaning toward the mystical, a great artist with a strong belief in intuitive thinking—like many creative artists.

A lot of gullible listeners still seek psychics' advice

Radio station CKO in Toronto is still at it. The morning talk show featuring John Gilbert is still promoting psychics and astrologers. And the gullible listeners are calling in for advice faster than the switchboard can handle them. The latest program I had the misfortune to hear had a guest host who announced that the theme for the morning would be reincarnation. You would expect that a station in a metropolitan area like Toronto would occasionally have a guest with a skeptical outlook to provide a little balance to the program. Not so with CKO.

The guest on this particular show was Ian Currie, the man who claims to have been hypnotically regressed to past-life memories twenty times. I'm not certain if that means twenty times to the same life or once to each of twenty separate past lives—which could get very confusing. He also claims there are all kinds of evidence for reincarnation.

Currie is fond of referring to Ian Stevenson as a source for proof of reincarnation. It might be useful to reveal a few facts about Stevenson. Born (most recently) in Montreal, Stevenson is a psychiatrist and parapsychologist at the University of Virginia. He has researched and written extensively on reincarnation and traveled to the Middle East, through Southwest Asia and Indochina, to India and Sri Lanka. From these areas he has collected and written about many cases of reincarnation. Most of Stevenson's case histories concern children claiming past lives. It is no coincidence that these are cultures that have belief systems that support reincarnation and where it is not too likely that a parent will readily dismiss a child's claim to have lived before.

You wouldn't think that anyone would take the trouble to investigate Stevenson's vast number of case histories in India, but one person did. British author Ian Wilson came up with some interesting facts after delving into some of these reincarnation claims by children. Written records are rare—most of the details of Stevenson's collection were received verbally. And even these aren't too reliable, since Stevenson was forced to use interpreters during most of his questioning. Translation can be responsible for considerable distortion.

Stevenson seems to have been very impressed by the emotional reactions of the families involved, hardly a scientific way of making judgments. Could there have been a particular motivation for children and their families to make these reincarnation claims? Interestingly, most of the case histories were of low-caste, poor families whose children claimed to have been members of upper-caste, wealthy families in former lives. Some of them even made property claims on their "former" families. Stevenson is a favorite reference of "scientific" reincarnationists—but his mass of case histories is based on very shaky evidence. Quantity doesn't make quality, even when published between hard covers.

CKO has a theme song that is obviously designed to fit its news and talk-show format. It is repeated regularly through the day by a vocal group. The oft-repeated phrase is "You Gotta Listen to Talk." Of course, you don't "gotta" listen if the program insults your intelligence. I've got a suggestion for a new theme to precede the psychic call-in shows: "You Gotta Listen to Nonsense."

The scientific method

You're sitting on a city bus—bored. Your eyes wander over the advertising boards above the windows. Most of them are making strong claims for the product they're pitching. You arrive at the lecture hall you've been heading for. The speaker delivers an impassioned address, asking you to believe myriad facts he's tossing in your direction. You finally get home, tired and perhaps a little confused. You switch on the television set to catch the news. You run smack dab into a furious argument between two talking heads. They are debating the merits and the drawbacks of installing some local public works. The facts and statistics they are quoting are definitely at odds. You don't know whom to believe.

You switch off the box in resignation and turn to a book, these days, often a last resort. Here's something to get your teeth into—it's published by a major company and written by a noted author. The fact that it's about life after death makes it even more intriguing. But wait a minute. As you plow through the first chapter you realize that you're scanning a lot of unverified anecdotes and biased opinions. You put down the book and begin to reflect on the events of the day. How in the world do you know what to believe? How do you separate sense from nonsense? How do you know what is true?

These aren't easy questions to answer, but science seems to be the one discipline that has the right method. In a nutshell—look for evidence. Not always easy, I'll admit. You can't always get a "scientific" answer to every question. But just look at how science works—and I'm referring not only to the theoretical sciences, such as physics and astronomy, but also to the less precise ones, such as sociology and economics.

The initial prerequisite is skepticism. You don't accept authority and you don't take anything for granted. When a scientist comes up with a new discovery or a new idea, he or she will write a paper on it. The idea is to have it published and circulated in the scientific community, not for the satisfaction of seeing one's name in print, but to have it examined and criticized by one's peers. Even that isn't easy. First, a team of referees has to rule whether the paper merits publishing. A scientific statement or claim has a lot of hurdles to hop.

Now, just compare this system to the number of books published on, for example, the paranormal and the pseudosciences. The would-be author has an idea, does some research (usually in other books on the paranormal), writes a manuscript, finds a publisher—and another book of wishy-washy wisdom hits the market.

You might think common sense on your part will enable you to separate sense from nonsense. Not necessarily. It takes more than that. After all, common sense might tell you that the earth is flat, that the sun revolves from east to west around the earth. People believed those things for thousands of years—until science proved otherwise. What is required is a dash of skepticism, a whole lot of curiosity, and the initiative to search for information and evidence. That's the way science operates. The scientific method does not establish the ultimate truth. But, at this time, it's the best method there is of searching for it.

Sifting myths, fallacies, and lies from truth

To debunk—what does it mean? The dictionaries tell us, "To unmask, to reveal nonsense, etc." I suppose you can distill it to "telling truth from falsehood"—and if you want to get it all in a nutshell by all means get the book *How Do You Know It's True?*, subtitled "Sifting Sense from Nonsense."

Very readable, this book by David and Marymae Klein lays down simple guidelines that are invaluable. It lists a plethora of myths and falsehoods that we have always accepted as truths—but it also points out many things we haven't accepted that are very likely true.

We all have mind sets; that is, we have a tendency to see only one side of an issue, or we misinterpret what we see and hear. This includes the many false perceptions of so-called paranormal events. Here's a true or false question in the book that illustrates a mind set shaped by the media: "Lawyers who make dramatic courtroom appearances earn more money than those who spend most of their time in their law offices." Research has shown that the majority of people answer "true" to this statement. In fact, the statement is false. Newspapers and television programs usually show dramatic criminal trials. We get the impression that successful lawyers spend most of their time in courtrooms haranguing a jury. But there are relatively few prominent criminal lawyers—most defendants can't afford legal fees. Most successful lawyers manage to settle cases out of court.

The Kleins note the myth of the rags-to-riches story—that almost anyone can start out poor and wind up as a millionaire if they try hard enough. This belief, though quite inaccurate, was what attracted hordes of immigrants to this continent, according to the authors. I would qualify that by saying it was just one of the reasons. However, most historians agree that the majority of immigrants arrived poor, lived poor, and died poor. Many did improve their standard of living, and some did get rich—but this was the exception, not the rule.

Another thing you can't always trust too readily is statistics. People are more inclined to believe facts if they are backed up by numbers. Over the many years of parapsychological research, for instance, statistics have frequently been used to make a case for the paranormal. But it has been shown over and over again how statistics can be misleading. A good general example of this fact is the common conclusion drawn from the statistical reality of the high incidence of divorce in our society. Statistics do show a divorce rate higher than ever. Most people therefore assume marriages are mostly unhappy these days. But there are other factors involved. Divorce is accepted much more today than it was thirty years ago, and more people expect their marriage will be happy nowadays—they're more willing to break up a shaky one and hope for better luck next time. So the divorce statistics don't necessarily mean that marriages are less happy than they were many years ago.

The Kleins also mention a method of sugar-coating that is often used to deceive the public: the euphemism, a pleasant word or phrase used to describe an unpleasant reality. From a *New York Times* article on military euphemisms they quote: "The more gruesome the weapon of destruction, the more sanitized the terminology by which it is described . . . what do we call our [destructive weapons]? Intercontinental ballistic missiles and medium range tactical cruises and multiple warhead missiles [MIRVs, or multiple independently targetable re-entry vehicles], and the MX. MX sounds as if it were a sports car, and MIRV a new Atari game." And, of course, in the event of nuclear war we won't die—we'll just pass away.

It's not easy to cope with the variety of deceptions that inundate us. When we were kids we were taught to believe in Santa Claus and the tooth fairy. We've learned better. Or have we?

PROPHECY

Two Nations Will Go to War, But Only One Will Win

The individual who gives a personal reading and predicts the future now eschews the label "fortune-teller." The current term is "psychic."

Among the many dangers associated with accepting the predictions and advice of a fortune teller is that of the self-fulfilling prophecy. Just listen to the psychic on an open-line radio show telling a gullible woman at home that there is trouble ahead on the marital scene for her and her spouse. Listen to the uncertainty in her voice as she asks for advice for the future. And think of the possible conflict between her and her unsuspecting husband that may result from this meddling.

This type of personal probing into the future poses far more dangers than do the annual predictions of the *Enquirer*-type precognition pack. In 1984 Indian Prime Minister Indira Gandhi was assassinated; an African famine killed millions of people; an Irish Republican Army bomb almost wiped out the British cabinet, including Prime Minister Thatcher, in Brighton, England; Konstantin Chernenko became the new leader of the USSR; two American passengers were killed in an airplane hijacking in Teheran. In 1985 the Columbian volcano Nevado del Ruiz blew up, causing a gigantic mudslide that wiped out 25,000 souls; a Japan Air Lines flight went down in the mountains north of Tokyo, killing 250; an Air India 747 went down in the Atlantic, an apparent victim of terrorism, and 329 lives were lost; another new leader took over in the Soviet Union— Mikhail Gorbachev. In 1986 the space shuttle Challenger blew up in full view of millions on television, with the loss of its entire crew.

Strangely enough, *none* of these major news events was reflected in the crystal balls of the prognosticators whose predictions clutter up newspaper pages at the beginning of each year. Among the thousands of fuzzy predictions of disaster, general warnings of possible doom, statements of political foresight—not one precise prediction of any of the aforementioned was made. Anyone with the time and inclination can trace back, year after year, and the same pattern will emerge. And yet the public still hungers to look into the future and demands that the media satisfy it. The papers will accordingly continue to publish the nonsensical prophecies of the publicity-hungry precogs. After all, who bothers to doublecheck the predictions of a previous year? Only the skeptics who are trying to make a point, a point the public largely ignores.

It is doubtful that any of the modern-day prophets will occupy the historical niche carved out by Nostradamus. Even today, countless thousands believe that his prophecies have enjoyed significant accuracy, unaware of the many interpretations that can be placed on his quatrains.

To compare the modern, publicity-prone prognosticator to the ancient prophets of the Bible (a comparison I'm often asked to make) is nonsensical. The ancient prophets had messages for their times. Predicting inevitable events was their vehicle for criticizing the social and political order, and for calling people to the service of God by using the threat that dire things would happen if they did not respond.

The precognitive dream probably inspires more belief in the paranormal than does any other personal "psychic" experience. The world of dreams has always been a never-never land of mystery, so the prophetic dream fits very nicely into the category of the paranormal. If the books explaining the meaning of dreams were arranged in one pile, they would probably reach halfway to the moon. Is it not strange that the expert dream interpreters, including Sigmund Freud, have never written any books explaining the precognitive dream? Modern psychology has come up with some explanations on the subject, and these are covered in this chapter.

So the business of predicting the future continues. The practice of reading the entrails of dead chickens is rapidly declining, and even crystal balls, tarot cards, and palm-reading are now struggling in the face of deadly competition from computerized fortune telling. But a rose by any other name remains the same, and so it is with the scam of precognition.

Prophets: Future imperfect

The high priestess of the Oracle at Delphi in ancient Greece used to climb on her throne and, chewing on narcotic leaves, fall into a mantic ecstasy. Then, speaking through her, the oracle would freely dispense predictions for the future, always cleverly cloaked in generalities.

Perhaps the best example of how the Delphic Oracle was interpreted is the famous story about Croesus, the king of Lydia. He asked the oracle if he should attack Cyrus, king of the Persians, and the oracle, through the priestess, answered: "If you go to war you will destroy a great empire." Naturally. Croesus marched off to fight the Persians. His army was destroyed. The prophecy was correct. He had destroyed a great empire—his own.

Prophecy, fortune telling, seeing the future, call it what you will, the practice dates back thousands of years to the ancient oracles, when the gods were supposed to speak to humans through the mouths of priests or priestesses.

Things haven't changed much. The same rules apply today. The palmist holds your hand, reads the lines, forecasts your future. The tea-leaf reader analyzes the contents of your cup and does the same. The tarot card expert furrows her brow and predicts dire happenings. The crystal ball gazer fantasizes and forecasts. The only real difference today is that with the help of modern communications fortune telling has become a thriving commercial industry.

But how accurate are today's seers, such as Jeane Dixon, who make predictions for every new year and have them published in their syndicated columns across the continent? A little research shows they're not very accurate at all. Here's how the scam basically works: The fortune teller makes a vague prediction and after an event has taken place fits it into the generalization of the original prophecy. It's as simple as that. Once you are aware of this basic fact you will recognize it in almost every psychic reading or forecast.

Modern seers, known as "precogs" (from *precognition,* or advance knowledge), like to cite the biblical prophets as examples of the art of prediction. Some of the precogs even claim to get their messages from God, just as the ancient prophets did. But the primary purpose of the great Hebrew prophets was religious instruction. Ezekiel used poetic imagery that one could interpret as one chose—the message was redemption, not prophecy. Jeremiah, in predicting the fall of Jerusalem, was merely making an informed judgment, just as today's futurists do.

The most famous precog of all was Michel de Nostre-Dame, a physician and scholar in sixteenth-century France. Better known as Nostradamus, the man's prophecies were published in the form of quatrains, four-line poems. I would defy anyone who reads one of these quatrains to explain what it is that is being predicted. Then how can they be interpreted? Nostradamus predicted aircraft dropping bombs on civilian populations. Uncanny. But long before that, Leonardo da Vinci had published blueprints with designs of flying machines and bomb-like devices. Quite likely the crafty prophet applied some logical thinking and made a few guesses. Our science-fiction writers have been making wilder guesses than that for years—and many of them have come to pass.

In the 1930s, Edgar Cayce, the sleeping prophet, claimed to be a psychic physician. He would go into a trance and prescribe remedies for the ailing while he seemed to be asleep. Some of his remedies did indeed help. He borrowed from homeopathy and regularly prescribed tasty potions like "oil of smoke" and "bedbug juice" and treatments like "bamboo oil massage" and "fumes of apple brandy." These "medical treatments" were his specialty, but much was made of his prophecies, which were very precise.

It is strange that his followers, who today number in the thousands, never seem to question even the most absurd of Cayce's prophecies. To list just a few:

—From a religious Russia will come "the greater hope of the world."

—There will be a full-scale revolution in the United States.

—Earthquakes will destroy New York, Los Angeles, and San Francisco.

—The waters of the Great Lakes will empty into the Gulf of Mexico.

—The mythical lost continent of Atlantis will rise from the oceans in the 1960s as a result of these catastrophic upheavals.

Without a doubt Jeane Dixon is the premier precog of the present scene. She has a daily astrology column in many newspapers. She's written several books. Her lectures are in great demand. When she issues her annual forecasts they're given wide coverage. As with all seers, her "hits" are given great publicity. Her misses are ignored. Does anyone keep score? Dixon is a master of the technique of vague predictions. In 1968 she was credited with predicting a scandal for Richard Nixon. Here's the actual wording of her prediction: "A wiretapping scandal is yet to come. It will involve Richard Nixon but will show him as a sincere man and will help his public image. I saw a ball going round and round in what seemed to be a roulette wheel. The ball seemed to stop on a double O. It seemed to indicate a name which I could not interpret. A tall dark man seemed to be involved. The entire matter will affect Nixon favorably."

Dixon's crystal ball must have been a little cloudy that day. Here are some of her other major predictions:

—The Soviet Union will move into Iran in the fall of 1953.

—A world war will take place in 1958.

—By 1964 one man will rule the combined countries of the Soviet Union and China.

Dixon came into prominence when she was supposed to have predicted President John F. Kennedy's assassination. Did she really put it in those terms? The prediction was published in 1956 and read as follows: "As for the 1960 election, Mrs. Dixon thinks it will be dominated by labor and won by a Democrat. But he will be assassinated or die in office." Seven years later Kennedy was shot. Let's take a look at this statement. Many elections have been influenced by a strong labor vote, and usually in favor of the Democrats, of course. And after eight years of Eisenhower it was reasonable to assume that a Democrat would take over. Is this a psychic prediction or an educated guess?

The death of a U.S. president while in office is not as improbable as it may seem. There have been precedents. Assassinations have taken place, in addition to several unsuccessful attempts, including those on Roosevelt, Truman, and more recently Ronald Reagan. Dixon's guess was later exploited, and with a few twists here and there the public was convinced she had named the date and place of the event.

The *National Enquirer,* a weekly tabloid bought by more than five million people, is big on predictions. It said that 1982 would be a year when Reaganomics would bring prosperity to the United States, when space scientists would make contact with alien creatures, and when a new source of magnetic energy would end the world's dependence on Arab oil.

Here are some predictions for 1982 from the *Enquirer*'s top ten psychics:

—The Loch Ness monster will wallow ashore in Scotland and be captured with nets.

—A giant tidal wave will smash the Hawaiian Islands in August, causing great loss of life.

—The skeletal remains of an incredible creature, half-man, half-fish, will be discovered in the Indian Ocean.

It's interesting to observe how most prophets function. They're always predicting calamities—assassinations, sickness, international problems, natural disasters. If they predict enough of these—"the shotgun effect"—some are bound to take place.

In 1973 Professor Gary Fine conducted a study at Harvard University. Ten students were asked: "Imagine you are a well-known psychic who believes in his or her power to predict the future. You are asked for predictions about the coming twelve-month period. What events do you expect to occur? Include approximately six predictions in your forecast."

These predictions were recorded and then compared with those of ten professional psychics whose forecasts had been featured in the *Enquirer*. After careful analysis the results of this controlled study were published. According to Fine, the students scored better than the psychics.

In July 1979 "psychic" Pat St. John made headlines with her prediction that a retaining wall would give way above Niagara Falls. The rushing waters would capsize the Maid of the Mist, the boat that takes tourists to the base of the falls. A large number of children would drown. The fatal date, July 22; the time, exactly 4:56 P.M. On that date the viewing areas at the falls were jammed with the curious. The media coverage was generous. Nothing happened. St. John had displayed a lack of psychic professionalism by predicting the exact time of the event. But she had an out. When questioned after the nonevent, she said the falls would collapse at 4:56 P.M. —but on some other day. The crowd didn't stick around.

I'd like to make a prediction of my own. The precogs will continue to flourish as they have for millennia—and many people will continue to flock to psychics and continue to support the phony profession of precognition.

Nostradamus's predictions are vague

John Picton recently wrote an interesting, entertaining, and very readable article for the *Toronto Sunday Star* about the quatrains, or verses, of Nostradamus. But to accept his predictions as accurate is to go far out on a limb—with all due respect to Shirley MacLaine. It will take more than one of these columns to fully expore this complex subject, but I'd like to analyze at least a couple of the references in the aforementioned article.

The following verse by Nostradamus is quoted as surprisingly on target:

> The assembly will go out from the castle of Franco;
> The ambassador not pleased will make a separation;
> Those of the Riviera will be involved,
> And will deny entry into the great gulf.

This quatrain was supposed to forecast the meeting of Spain's General Francisco Franco and Italian dictator Benito Mussolini on the Riviera during World War II. And Franco, of course, refused to allow the Axis powers to pass through Spain to Gibraltar. Much was made of this prophecy. A little research reveals that the first line of the quatrain was wrongly translated from the archaic French. It should have read, "Out of Castelfranco will come the assembly." There are several cities in Italy named Castelfranco and one named Riviera. There is a Castelfranco near Modena, less than a hundred miles from Riviera. Nostradamus was probably writing about cities, not people and regions. The entire verse now takes on a different meaning, even though it is still obscure. But when it is interpreted hundreds of years later, the facts are made to fit the prediction. This is exactly the way today's phony prophets operate.

The trick is to search for similarities between the vague predictions and events that have already happened, and to match them up. It's a game anyone can play. The endurance of the Nostradamus myth is explained by the vagueness of his prophecies, by the many different translations of his writings, and by the many different interpretations of his quatrains by the cultists who profit by perpetuating the myth. It's amusing to see how one particular quatrain can be interpreted in four different ways by four different people. An interesting sidelight is that, during World War II, both the Allies and the Nazis used some of the old seer's quatrains for propaganda purposes—sometimes using the same verse and interpreting it differently to serve their own purposes. My favorite quote about Nostradamus—by French author Jean de Kerdeland—characterizes his prophecies as "an inexhaustible magic hat from which modern presti-digitators can pull innumerable rabbits." That says it all.

Wouldn't it be cheaper to buy fortune cookies?

The psychics have gone scientific. They have become computer oriented. This was the most noticeable fact of the third annual Psychics, Mystics and Seers Fair, recently held at Toronto's Exhibition Place. The faithful and the curious were out in droves. This supermarket of the occult attracted ten thousand people last year. Judging by the crowds I fought my way through last Sunday, they probably topped that mark this year. At four bucks to get in, and with fees running from $2 to $50 at each booth, I would assume a fair amount of money changed hands.

What impressed me was the number of computers that have invaded the mystic world. At booth after booth the gurus sat at their microchipped monsters, looking for all the world like IBM programmers. No more the verbal or handwritten prognostications—the prophetic printout has taken over the big time. That is not to say that the good old-fashioned psychic talking head has disappeared. It was there in abundance—the tarot card readers, the palmists, the crystal ball gazers, the horoscope readers, the aura specialists. But if you scanned the hall it was easy to see where the computer-generated readings were operating—you just looked for a long line of eager customers waiting their turn, their dollars already clutched in their hands.

One of the business displays featured an impressive array of equipment about twenty feet long. Huge reels were whirling, hundreds of colored lights were blinking on and off, and two exhausted-looking people stood in front of this "computer" display trying to take the money of the endless line of customers. For $2.50 one could get a handwriting analysis or a horoscope reading. All that was required was to write one's name and birth date on a card. It was shoved into a slot and a printout immediately emerged and was handed to the subject. The analysis or horoscope reading contained such gems as: "Be sure any change you make in buying and selling will improve your monetary affairs"; "You tend to mind your own business and expect others to do the same"; "Most of your success in life stems from originality and shrewdness"; "This year will be happy and exciting for romance and love"; and "Be concerned but not worried about your health."

So you can see, the major questions that people ask of psychics were covered—money, sex, and health. But honestly, wouldn't it be cheaper and more nourishing to buy fortune cookies?

Another long line attracted me to a computer palm-reading display. Clients held their palms in front of a camera lens and saw them displayed on a monitor. A moving vertical line passed over the images, which gave the illusion that the palms were being scanned. An instant printout gave the customers their readings. I can't see this method being a permanent success. There's no substitute for the personal warmth and understanding of a charming, dark-eyed fortune teller holding one's hand. Technology is going too far.

The people I spoke to were certainly intelligent enough to realize that most of the nonsense on the printouts was a series of generalities. But almost everyone admitted that there was at least one observation that hit the nail on the head where he or she was concerned. This is what psychics always strive for—the one big hit. This is what turns people into believers.

Prophecy—or mere coincidence?

The *Titanic* is a hot news story again. The discovery of the wreck, and now the actual exploration of the sunken giant, has grabbed the public imagination. So it's probably more than coincidence that Prometheus Books has published Martin Gardner's *The Wreck of the Titanic Foretold?* This is more than just another book describing the circumstances surrounding the 1912 marine disaster. It probes the provocative subjects of prophecy and coincidence as well.

In 1898, Morgan Robertson, a former sailor who specialized in writing sea stories, penned a short novel entitled *Futility*. In it he told of the sinking of a huge liner, the *Titan*. The matching of details between this story and the actual tragedy of the *Titanic* is incredible. Gardner compares these details point by point and takes a hard look at the possibilities— coincidence or precognition? He also provides a reprint of the original Robertson novel so that readers can perhaps form their own judgments. Incidentally, the original story was republished in 1912, after the *Titanic*

sinking—this time under the title *The Wreck of the Titan; or Futility.*
Good commercial publishing practice.

Here are some of the similarities between the novel and the actual
Titanic disaster, as outlined by Gardner:

—The *Titan* and the *Titanic*—the names of the ships.

—Both ships were all steel, with three propellers and two masts.

—Both ships were considered unsinkable because of their many water-
tight compartments.

—Both were called the largest passenger ship ever built.

—Both ships had far too few lifeboats.

—The two ships were going at approximately the same speed when
the sinkings occurred.

—Both ships hit an iceberg near midnight, at spots just a few hundred
miles apart.

—Both ships began their fatal voyages in April.

—Both ships were owned by British firms headquartered in Liverpool
with branch offices off Broadway in Manhattan.

—The principal stock owners of both ships were Americans.

These parallels are so startling that it is easy to understand why the
purveyors of the paranormal have seized on them to argue that precognitive powers do exist. Gardner takes another view. From a scientific perspective, he says, one must look at probabilities, and consider the possibility of coincidence. The problem with this comparison, says Gardner, is
that it is not what mathematicians call "a well-formed problem." There is
"no way to estimate, even crudely, the relevant probabilities."

Furthermore, he points out, if you imagine yourself in Robertson's
shoes when he wrote this novel, it is not too surprising that so many of the
details are similar. For example, what could sink a monstrous liner except
a monstrous iceberg? It was a common happening in those days. And
would it not be more dramatic to dub a huge ship "unsinkable" for the
purposes of the story line? And to have a dearth of lifeboats? An intriguing argument—on both sides. Take your pick.

Meanwhile, for those who are within visiting distance of the Ontario
Science Centre in Toronto, there is a huge scale model of the *Titanic* (over
five-and-a-half meters long) on display. This model, accurate in every
detail, was constructed in Belfast, and is on loan from the National
Museum of Science and Technology in Ottawa.

Some simple secrets of the psychic trade

It's not just elderly housewives who consult clairvoyants, but people from all walks of life, including hard-headed businessmen. Many business and political leaders consult these fortune tellers (a title they deplore). A Toronto so-called psychic who advertises widely claims to make a good living as a businessman's psychic. His rates for the average Joe are a mere $75 to $100 an hour. But for business consultations, by his own claims, he gets up to $1,000 an hour.

How can intelligent, rational people be taken in by this nonsense? The answer is—easily. A person can be clever, rational, a leader in his or her field of expertise—and still get hopelessly lost in the murky swamp of the paranormal.

A paranormal event is one that is claimed to be unexplainable in terms of known scientific laws. Never mind that the answers are usually available. Who wants to bother studying psychology, physiology, or anthropology? Most people start off by being curious. To that curiosity add a smidgen of belief. After one visit you're hooked. Here's how.

Psychics give the visitor the impression of knowing more than they do. Once they disclose a "true" fact that it seems they couldn't possibly know, the visitor will believe everything. After that the subject will open up and confide in the psychic.

The trick for a good psychic is to get that key first item of information. This is done through expert interviewing and pumping for information without seeming to do so. The subject can be tricked into giving information without realizing it. When the information is fed back later in the sitting, he or she is overwhelmed.

A second method is to covertly obtain information about the subject prior to the sitting. In the case of a prominent person this is obviously simple. Another standard practice is to study surveys, polls, or other readily available statistics. The psychic, knowing something about the client such as education level and other general information, can make some pretty accurate guesses—and sometimes make a direct hit. When they read the tarot cards, gaze into the crystal ball, or examine the palm, psychics are accomplishing two things. First, they are creating a mystical atmosphere that lends authenticity to the reading. Second, they are gaining a greater opportunity to stall for time and devise convincing phrases to add to the spiel.

Skeptic meets psychics

It had been two years since I last appeared on the television program "People Are Talking" for the Westinghouse Group stations in Baltimore, Boston, and Philadelphia. So when they asked me to do the three-city tour again, I gladly accepted. After all, how can a dedicated skeptic turn down the opportunity to lock horns with two or three so-called psychics in front of a studio audience packed with believers, not to mention hundreds of thousands of home viewers with mixed opinions? Three one-hour TV debates in three different cities on three consecutive days can be just a bit hectic, but the subjects are similar—and so is the quality of the opposition. Whether investigating faith healers or psychics, the basic rules are similar: Get there early and keep your eyes open. Among other things, one of the standard scams is to have "plants" in the audience.

Waiting in the Green Room (the traditional performers' waiting room) at Philadelphia's KYW-TV, I took in the opposition: three psychics, two female and one male. Evidently one of the women was a tea-leaf reader, the other specialized in tarot cards. The man used no particular props. He was just a plain, everyday psychic who could read minds and tell the future and the past—just an ordinary individual gifted with supernatural powers. He did seem popular, because he had several visitors, all of whom seemed familiar with him and very friendly.

It came time for the show to begin. The three miracle-workers were introduced and did their stuff. The tea-leaf reader interpreted the muck at the bottom of host Richard Bey's cup, telling him all kinds of detailed information, including the prediction that his house would be robbed.

"You can see all that in the cup?" asked the incredulous Bey.

"Sure," replied the psychic.

"Do people think you're crazy?" asked Bey.

I couldn't catch the mumbled reply, but it was obvious the woman was not disturbed. I have often observed this reaction. Most psychics have developed a thick skin. They've learned to shrug off criticism. They have enough faithful followers to give them all the support they require.

The tarot reader then scanned her cards as she did a reading of a member of the audience. This reading included a series of questions, such as, "Do you have a child? A girl—how old is she? Having any problems with her? Is your marriage getting a little fluffy?" For this you need tarot cards?

But the real blockbuster came when the male psychic, asked to read someone in the audience, selected a woman and proceeded to tell her something about herself that he couldn't possibly have known about a stranger. Bey was truly amazed. "Have you ever seen this man before?" he asked her.

"Never," answered the woman, whom I had seen talking with the psychic earlier in the waiting room.

When I finally got on camera I was asked my opinion of the preceding phenomena. With suitable humility I commented that reading tea leaves was tidier than reading the entrails of a dead chicken, and that tarot cards were just a prop to lend a mystical atmosphere to a standard, generalized psychic reading—similar to the use of crystal balls, people's palms, head bumps, and, yes, tea leaves. I also pointed out that one of my investigations had revealed that tarot readers will sometimes give three different interpretations for the same selection of cards. But I'm sure they have a justification for that one.

When Bey asked me how I could explain the male psychic's miracle, I was in a bit of a dilemma. How could I charge these two people directly with outright collusion, on public television, and still maintain a relatively friendly atmosphere? I managed to wriggle out of the situation by subtly implying that psychics sometimes use "plants." The message seemed to get across.

California and its psychic storefronts:
An unnerving trip

It seemed like a good idea for the both of us: My wife and I were on our way to the 1986 conference of the Committee for the Scientific Investigation of Claims of the Paranormal, in Boulder, Colorado. Why not start out with a side trip to Southern California? After all, my long-suffering spouse had for many years shared with me the bouquets and brickbats tossed at a debunker of psychics, palm readers, astrologers, precogs, and all the various and assorted occultniks that afflict our society. At the conference we'd be immersed for two solid days in paranormal affairs—a change of pace was in order. Nothing but good scenery, good food, and interesting places to visit in Los Angeles, San Diego, and points in between.

But I had failed to take one thing into account. We were visiting California. So here's the picture. We land in L.A., rent a car, and head for the San Diego Freeway. Half a block from the car-rental agency, we see a storefront with a huge sign—SPIRITUAL READER—PALMS READ—NO WAITING.

Well, not to worry. Just one of those coincidences I like to write about. But a couple of blocks farther along we spot another storefront with a huge overhead sign and two verticals at either side—TAROT CARD READER—HOROSCOPES—PSYCHIC ADVISER—PALMREADER. I drive down the freeway, my brain spinning, not concentrating on the carefree California drivers darting from lane to lane in front of me. Is this my vacation? Did I come to the wrong state? Am I being hounded? Did someone set up false storefronts to drive me bananas? Am I really in the land of the Twilight Zone? But this, my friends, was only the beginning.

A quick trip to Tijuana revealed several of these establishments in a short stretch of the flea-market area. I was beginning to accept the inevitable. Back up the coast to Los Angeles, and there they were. The psychic storefronts were everywhere. On business streets, in outlying areas—everywhere. But the real clincher was this. Right next door to our hotel in Hollywood—*next door*—were signs reading SPIRITUAL ADVISER, PSYCHIC READINGS, TEA LEAVES READ. I immediately went into a deep depression. Then I began to think a little more rationally. What to do? Should I visit the emporium next door, sit for a reading, and then expose the charlatan in the local press? But what would that do to Canadian-American relations? And how about the fee for the sitting? I would have to pay in U.S. dollars, and that ain't hay. A similar reading in Canada would be easier on the bankroll. Then and there I made up my mind. I would just ignore the whole thing. Besides, with my constant harping on the subject, my wife was beginning to look at me strangely.

What has really upset me about this whole experience is this: I have had many encounters with psychics who claimed prophetic powers. And we have had many friendly conversations, despite my debunking approach to their business. Now you would think that one of my acquaintances with these powers would at least have given me a friendly warning. Not once, mind you, not once, had anyone predicted I would run into these unnerving experiences in California. I would have switched our vacation to Haiti.

Biorhythms, like the Blue Jays, struck out in the division finals

If you were following the *Toronto Star* sports pages the year the Blue Jays and the Royals met in the playoffs, you couldn't have missed the biorhythm column offered before each game. Biorhythms were used to predict how well each player would perform during a game. The theory is that from birth all humans have cycles, up and down periods of performance. Each person is supposed to have three cycles: a 23-day physical cycle, a 28-day emotional cycle, and a 33-day intellectual cycle. The curves of these cycles are plotted on graphs. When a particular curve is high, a person is considered to be at his or her best. Beware of critical days, when the cycles are changing.

The playoff biorhythm charts made a series of predictions about the performance of certain players in each game, based on their personal cycles.

Here's a rundown on how well the charts did:

Game One: "Dave Stieb moving upwards on all cycles. Should pitch well and have a complete game"; right on. "Leibrandt of the Royals could be in trouble, cycles down"; also right on. "Tony Fernandez on down cycles—a critical day"; Tony got 2 hits for 3 at-bats, playing flawless ball. "George Brett down on all cycles"; George got 3 hits for 4 at-bats. "Royals most positive factor is Pat Sheridan, who is up in all areas"; Sheridan went 0 for 3.

Game Two: "Jimmy Key not at his best. Emotional cycle high, intellectual cycle down"; Key was sent to the showers in the fourth. "Brett still down in all cycles"; Brett went 0 for 4. "Lamp is down"; he pitched 4 hitless innings. "Balboni on the up cycles"; he went 0 for 5 at the plate. "On up cycles for the Jays at bat—Bell, Garcia, Iorg, Johnson, Barfield"; their respective performances—0 for 3, 0 for 5, 1 for 3, 2 for 3, 1 for 4.

Game Three: "Doyle Alexander up on physical and emotional cycles"; Doyle was knocked out in the sixth, gave up 9 hits, 5 runs. "Saberhagen has identical rhythm to Alexander (cycles are up)"; he was knocked out in the fifth, also giving up 9 hits and 5 runs. "George Bell is not only down, but critical—his most dangerous day of post-season play"; Bell got 3 hits for 4 at-bats. "George Brett on down cycles"; Brett was the star of the game—4 for 4. "White, Sheridan, Wilson and Balboni all on up cycles"; their respective records—0 for 3, 0 for 3, 2 for 4, 1 for 4.

Game Four: "Dave Stieb is on even better rhythms than he was for the opener, being completely up in all areas"; Dave walked 7 men, including 1 run. "Henke should still be below his normal form"; the Terminator took over in the last couple of innings, to contain the Royals. "Charlie Leibrandt's rhythms are down"; he pitched 5 scoreless innings.

Game Five: "Danny Jackson up on his cycles—Jays are in for a tough night"; right on—Danny pitched a full-game shutout. "Moseby and Upshaw are both up on their rhythms today"; Moseby hit 0 for 4, Upshaw 1 for 4. "Bell on the downside"; he hit 2 for 4.

Game Six: "Doyle Alexander down on both physical and intellectual cycles"; Doyle gave up 5 runs in 5 1/3 innings. "Gubicza should be pitching well"; he gave up 3 runs in 5 1/3 innings. "Lamp is down"; he allowed 1 hit and no runs in almost 4 innings.

Game Seven: "Dave Stieb is high on 2 cycles . . . should pitch well, should contain them"; Dave gave up 6 hits and 6 runs in 5 2/3 innings. "Acker is in the down column"; he allowed 2 hits and no runs in almost 4 innings. "Tony Fernandez is on an up cycle"; Tony went 1 for 4. "Moseby on an up cycle"; Moseby got a goose egg for 5 at-bats.

If you read the daily astrology horoscopes and biorhythm columns, the pattern is the same. They're packed with generalizations and contradictions. If you question the contradictions, you'll find the analyst has covered his tracks—he can't be wrong. Some examples:

"The fact that George Brett is playing through a down cycle doesn't seem to make him less dangerous." Then why are biorhythms being used to predict player performance?

"Saberhagen is on an up intellectual and down physical rhythm." Where are we? Is he up or down? What's the bottom line?

"Both Fernandez and Oliver have demonstrated an ability to play through down cycles with above average performances." How does that explain a lousy performance during an up cycle?

"Jimmy Key is still down on his vital and intellectual rhythm, although his physical and emotional cycles are up." So how's he going to pitch?

You'll notice that a few of the game-to-game predictions were right on the money. That is according to the law of averages. What have biorhythm curves got to do with the whole thing? Absolutely nothing.

In 1975, a thorough study was conducted on the major leagues—checking the performance of certain players on each team, throughout the season, against his biorhythms. The result was that there was no significance at all to the biorhythm theory. If you're going to bet on a baseball game, forget the biorhythm predictions. First, make a thorough study of the two teams, player by player, position by position. Then toss a coin.

Psychics on radio shows

Radio stations carrying talk shows, particularly those with a call-in feature, learned something a long time ago. If they want to hype their ratings, they get a psychic on the show. CKO Radio in Toronto is no exception. With talk shows all but eliminated from local airwaves, except for CBC's solid "Radio Noon," CKO has the field to itself. Veteran broadcaster John Gilbert has expanded his daily CKO morning talk show to include an open-line format, and once again the paranormal is polluting the province.

A short time ago I received a couple of phone calls from irate listeners complaining that CKO had aired a feature on the Bermuda Triangle that was ridiculous and misleading. What could I do about it? Not much, I told them, except to present the actual facts about that mythical area in this column. But Gilbert is now getting into the heavy psychic stuff. A couple of weeks ago he had a so-called psychic on his program—gave him a platform to expound his views and to dispense "psychic" advice to callers. All this for two solid hours, as compared with the limited time accorded other guests. Not only that, but Gilbert touted this man as a true psychic: "We accept that you certainly do have the gift of psychic power," he said. Does "we" include all of the thousands of listeners tuned in, or is Gilbert using the word in the editorial sense? And on what evidence does he make this statement?

Having been on the air with Gilbert several times in the past few years, and having listened to him many more times, I know that he has been tremendously impressed by readings he has received and by psychic anecdotes he has heard. He freely admits this. But, like many people, Gilbert hasn't bothered to devote the time, as far as I'm aware, to study the subject of the paranormal from both sides, to investigate the art of cold reading, to study the history of psychic anecdotes. If he has, he shows no evidence of it. Like many others he has, perhaps unconsciously, closed his mind to rational explanations for psychic phenomena.

Some time ago I wrote about Shirley MacLaine and how her high profile enabled her to spread her way-out paranormal beliefs among her admiring public. A broadcaster like John Gilbert has the same capability—plus the responsibility to maintain a balanced presentation in his programming.

The psychic on this recent broadcast was a pleasant-sounding fellow by the name of Tommy Roberts. He uses every trick in the cold-reading trade. Just by having callers say a few words he immediately gets "impressions" from the sound of their voices and reads all. He spouts generalities, asks questions and then agrees with the answers, and fishes for information, while backtracking and changing directions.

You have to admire the skill of some of these soothsayers. Psychic they're not—clever they are. An example: Roberts tells a male caller he has a money situation he's worried about. (Who hasn't?) The man answers, "That's what I want to ask you about."

Roberts: "You will consider improving the situation." (This is psychic?)

Caller: "I'm starting into a new business—I don't know how it's going to turn out." (Who does?)

Roberts: "Yes, I know . . ." (So do thousands of listeners by this time). He then gives some ill-founded advice on the subject, followed by "I'm getting something that has to do with travel."

Caller: "No, not right now." Roberts then responds by saying he meant travel some time in the future. (Heads I win, tails you lose.)

A woman calls in asking about her son's health.

Roberts: "He feels like a low energy." (That figures, when health is in question.)

Caller (impressed): "Right."

Roberts: "He's very sensitive to viral influence. . . . I feel it's going to be stabilizing."

Caller (reassured): "Okay, that's good."

Another woman asks whether there will be an improvement in her mother's health.

Roberts: "Does this have to do with the chemistry of her body?" (What else?)

Caller: "Yes."

Roberts: "Okay, that's where I see it. There's a very strong potential for improvement here."

Another caller says, "Hello, Tommy," and Roberts immediately replies: "I get the impression . . . you're going to have a good day . . . somebody's coming to visit."

Caller: "No, I'm not expecting company."

Roberts: "That's why I said it's going to be a good day." (He skates well enough to play for the Maple Leafs.)

Another call.

Roberts: "Emotional situations around you seem to come and go . . ."

Caller: "That's certainly true."

John Gilbert (triumphantly): "Tommy, you're dead on this morning."

Still another call.

Caller: "I would like to move—if you can say something about that?"

Roberts: "Is this something about a house?" (Wow, is there no limit to this man's psychic talents?)

You might say, so what, it's a lot of fun—what harm is there in all this? Let's take a look at two more calls. An obviously troubled woman asks for help. She has had some frightening "psychic experiences." The psychic tells her she must learn to live with her fears, to ignore them. My advice would have been to visit a professional psychologist or psychiatrist for proper guidance—rather than listen to a radio broadcaster and a questionable psychic. Another troubled woman is told by Roberts that her husband (a man Roberts has never met) is not supportive of her. Can you imagine the domestic controversy this can cause when an impressionable person is fed this line by a "psychic" who has been publicly promoted as "dead on this morning."

In the foregoing examples you'll notice the constant use of questions and generalities—and the sheer inanity of the whole exercise. I'd like to help John Gilbert test his faith in the psychic abilities of Tommy Roberts. I, and others associated with the Committee for the Scientific Investigation of Claims of the Paranormal, will set up a series of scientifically controlled tests to verify Roberts's paranormal powers. If he meets the standards, his success will be well publicized. If he fails, that too will be made known. How about it, John?

How do those clairvoyant dreams really happen?

A strange experience. That's the way it usually begins. I'm often asked why so many people believe in ESP, life after death, fortune telling, and all sorts of psychic happenings. One reason is that some seemingly unexplainable personal experience triggers something in a person's psyche that can lead to irrational thinking.

The most often repeated questions give me a good clue as to the experiences that exert the strongest influences on people. At a recent lecture at Dawson College in Montreal, the first thing I was asked was to explain the precognitive or the clairvoyant dream. This is the dream that seems to paint an image of an event that eventually does take place, or an event that is actually happening at the time of the dream. There's no doubt this is one of the most common of so-called paranormal phenomena. There are several possible explanations for it. Take the case of a person who dreams about the death of a relative and discovers on the following day that the sad event has actually taken place. First, it is quite likely the relative had been ailing for some time. The thought had been preying on the dreamer's mind for weeks, perhaps unconsciously. In that case it would not be uncommon for the thought to surface as a dream. Second, there's a good chance the dreamer experienced the same dream several times previously, and nothing had happened to the relative. When this occurs, we have a tendency not to notice, or to completely forget the dream. When the event does take place, however, we have a tendency to interpret the coincidence of dream and reality as a paranormal event. Completely forgotten are the previously unfulfilled dreams. Third, if we look at this phenomenon statistically, we can perhaps place it in a better perspective.

Science has been able to provide us with some insight into sleep and dreaming. Research has shown that dreams usually correspond with the rapid-eye-movement stage of sleep, known as REM. We also know that REM sleep and dreams occur about two hours every night—and that many of these dreams are on the negative side. Experiments have indicated that when people are awakened after monitoring has revealed REM sleep, they often report having had bad dreams, involving accidents or death. It's assumed we have a solid hour of this type of dream nightly. If you then consider how many hours in a year the population experiences these dreams, and the relatively few numbers of times a so-called psychic dream occurs—statistically it would stack up as nothing but coincidence. And another thing—the recountings of past experiences are often distorted by false memory. Add to that the hazy quality of dream recall, and you're treading on shaky ground. I'll say this—if I were to add four more explanations for the psychic dream to the four I've already stated it would make little difference to the true believer. Rational reasoning seldom convinces.

I would be remiss covering the subject of dreams without a brief mention of dream analysis. The books on dream analysis, if piled one on the other, could probably reach to the moon. The Freudian literature on the subject is a dream analyst's dream and deserves a column of its own. The fact is that dream analysis has never been proved to be scientifically valid. As pop psychology, the literature is always in demand—but it should not be taken too seriously.

In the meantime, as Perry Como would put it, "Dream along with me."

A crystal ball is useful—as a prop

It's as predictable as death and taxes. The new year always has everyone gazing into their crystal ball, pontificating on things to come. The question is—why a crystal ball? The practice of staring into this supernatural sphere originated way back in antiquity. It was called "scrying," from the ancient English word *descry*, meaning "to make out dimly, to succeed in discerning, to perceive things at a distance." The original crystal balls were composed of polished rock crystal. Today, most of the crystal balls sold on this continent are made of glass. If made of crystal they would be prohibitively expensive. Most of the "crystal" balls we see on dealers' shelves are made in Czechoslovakia or West Germany.

Much of the scrying done today (as in ancient times), does not even make use of the crystal ball. Any shiny or polished surface can be used. The ancient Greeks were fond of gazing into pools of water. A polished metal mirror was also popular. The Egyptians favored a pool of ink, or even blood, for this divinatory diversion—certainly more economical than the cost of a crystal ball. The Islamic world endorsed and practiced scrying for centuries. In certain parts of the Arab world gazing into reflecting surfaces was believed to be a cure for illness. Even concentrating on a fingernail was part of the practice. The Romans, for some reason, did not indulge very much in scrying. In England, one of the most dedicated users of the crystal ball was John Dee, official fortune teller to Queen

Elizabeth I. His crystal, he claimed, was given to him by the angels. Dee himself never looked into the ball. An assistant did this while Dee recorded the visions. Who knows how many state decisions were influenced by these readings? After its great popularity in the Middle Ages the practice languished, but it experienced a revival in the nineteenth century that continues to the present among occultists.

There's a definite set of rules governing the use of the crystal ball. It should be at least the size of a small orange. It should never be handled by anyone other than the owner—that will "mix the magnetisms and destroy their sensitiveness." The ball can be "remagnetized" by passes made with the right hand for about five minutes at a time. This gives it more power. Passes made with the left hand add to its sensitivity. I wish I could be more helpful to you crystal gazers and give more details about these passes. Nowhere can I find out if they should be back and forth or circular. And, if circular, whether clockwise or counter-clockwise.

There is, of course, nothing supernatural about crystal gazing. It does have an effect on some people but has nothing to do with the crystal itself. The action of concentrating on the reflecting surface will cause some individuals to hallucinate or will help produce a form of mental imagery. This imagery is sometimes so vivid that the subject actually believes he or she is seeing a certain scene. The effect can be quite remarkable in children. It has absolutely nothing to do with prophecy, with seeing into the past, or with clairvoyance—it is simply a product of the subject's imagination.

In the early 1900s the societies for psychical research, forerunners of today's parapsychologists, tried to find a link between these hallucinations and the magic of telepathy or clairvoyance, but without success. Today the parapsychologists look down their noses at the crystal ball. But the true occultists and fortune tellers haven't given up on it. It's a useful prop that adds to the mysticism associated with a psychic reading. I think that the one thing that might convince me that the crystal ball works as a medium of divination would be if two people would gaze into a crystal ball at the same time and come up with identical visions.

Hazards for the gullible believer

I had a recent encounter with Earl Curley at a taping in Montreal of the "Brian Gazzard Show." Curley is not really a psychic; intuition is his bag.

He gave a "reading" to an elderly lady in the audience, and he implied that she might have a serious illness. Now this is one of the tricks of the trade of the purveyors of the paranormal that packs all sorts of hazards for the gullible believer. How many times have I heard the radio talk-show psychics tell eager listeners that certain dangers lay in their future; that marital breakups were on the horizon; that other domestic problems were in the stars. The self-fulfilling prophecy is still with us. It can affect people's lives—particularly those who are easily influenced.

Earl Curley does not claim to be a prophet, but he does forecast future events. Not only does he forecast them, he can alter them. How? Simply by, as he puts it, "changing reality." For example, he claimed to have forecast an attempt on the life of Vice President George Bush, causing a change in Bush's movements that aborted the assassination. That's Curley's claim, the evidence for which I have not yet seen. Believe me, I requested the evidence on the program—I pleaded for it. I'm still waiting. Curley also seems to have the capacity to solve a problem that has been challenging some of the world's greatest intellects for some time: the eradication of the threat of terrorism. In his words, "We now have a group of people who work on possible threat situations with world leaders. . . . We have the capability of projecting an exact scenario . . . down to the exact time, the exact date and the exact individual [who may be threatened]." These obviously world-shaking facts should not be confined to a mere syndicated television program. This, I think, is something for the United Nations to act on. Curley also claims that after the tragic Air India disaster over the Atlantic he was actively involved in locating the aircraft and was even able to describe how the plane broke up. Fascinating. But we have to ask: Why was this engrossing story not picked up by the world press?

There is one problem that always comes up when I face off with a psychic. The claims of prophecies and psychic feats fly thick and fast, but my requests for documented evidence fall on deaf ears. Now, who has the time or the inclination to follow up on all these wild claims? They sound great to the uninitiated listener or viewer. I can't possibly refute them on the spot. But when I do find the time to check on the odd claim at a later date, I get the strangest answers.

Curley made one very definite claim: Back at the time of the investigation of the Atlanta child murders, Curley advised us that he gave a composite drawing and a profile of the unknown killer to the FBI. He

strongly implied that, as a result of his input, Wayne Williams was appre-
hended four and a half days later. Nothing fuzzy about this claim. A
couple of phone calls to the FBI in Washington soon cleared that up.
Here's the direct quote from the FBI's Press Information Office (and yes,
I do have the evidence): "Mr. Earl Curley contacted our Atlanta office
(voluntarily) in 1980 and 1981. He sent in some kind of writeup of what
he thought the subject would look like, and he sent in some sort of a
drawing. However, there was no impact on the case as a result of what he
sent in."

Hand it to palmists, they've got their job down to an art

"To believe is to perceive—either by the senses or the soul." The author of
these words of wisdom is Cheiro, the world-famous seer of the 1920s and
1930s. He took his name from the Greek word for "hand"—*chiro*. Cheiro
was probably the world's greatest authority on palmistry, one of the most
ancient of the arts of divination. Note the word *arts*. Palm reading to tell
fortunes is certainly not a science, as some would claim—any more than
is tea leaf reading, tarot card reading, or crystal gazing.

"Psychics" who call themselves scientific palmists are using the term
scientific very loosely. True, the study of the fingers, the fingernails, and
the hand is useful in medical practice. A doctor will often use these
observations to help in diagnosis, and certain indications concerning lines
on the palm are related to some cases of mental retardation. These creases
are there to help you use your hands. If nature did not provide them we'd
have a heck of a time flexing our fingers and hands. Cheiro's writings are
still considered gospel by palmists. He separated the art of palmistry into
two sections. One branch deals with the shape of the hand and fingers.
The other, chiromancy, is the study of the lines and markings of the
hands. Cheiro claimed that interpreting the lines alone gives a very in-
complete reading. Everything must be observed—the lines, the shape of
the fingers and hand, the bumps and lumps, the skin, the fingernails, even
the hair. This makes the subject more complicated, which is a favorite
ploy of occultists. The more complications, the thicker the books that can
be written, the more convincing they are to the believer.

So now you can guide your life by studying your hands. Do you have a square hand with short fingers? You are materialistic, stubborn, plodding, practical. Sorry about that. A square hand with long fingers? You are logical, highly intelligent, probably headed for a scientific career. A square hand with spatulate fingers? You're going to be an inventor or mechanical engineer. Cheiro often refers in his writings to the square hand with mixed fingers—one long, another short, another square-tipped, and so on. A mixed bag, so to speak. If you have a friend with hands like that, you've got a pal who is very versatile. Or maybe he's just mixed up.

I'm told that the Chinese study the soles of the feet. And why not? The soles also have lumps, bumps, lines and many other individual characteristics. This art is probably called footistry. Our feet are usually covered. Doesn't this give them a greater aura of mystery? Just thought I'd mention it as a footnote.

The back cover of *The Secrets of the Hand,* by Maria Gardini, modestly states, "Palmistry, like astrology, is an ancient method of divining hidden facts, and [this book] provides all the information you need to peer into the future or gain a new perspective on the past and present." Looking into the future by studying the hand can present some problems, as the author indicates. She asks, "If we know the future, can we change it? . . . The power of a palmist to change what fate has already decided is minimal." She goes on to say that all the subject can do is to prepare spiritually for what is to come by accepting the inevitable.

I'd have to question that assumption. Suppose I visited a palmist and he or she predicted that, because of certain characteristics of my hand, I was going to be struck down by an automobile within ten days. Suppose then that I left immediately for the countryside and settled down to camp in the bush for a couple of weeks. No cars, no accident, no fulfillment of the prophecy. What then? If the future can be decreed, can it be changed? And, if it can be changed, what about the signs on my hand? These are questions that always come up in debates about prophecy. I've never heard an answer that satisfied me.

Palmists like to claim scientific respectability for their practice, sometimes referring to the medical profession's study of parts of the hand when making diagnoses—and to the use of fingerprint technology by the police. Neither of these practices is concerned with divination. Medicine is interested only in the physiological indications that the hand, fingers, and fingernails sometimes reveal. The police aren't interested in the meaning of the swirls and sworls on the tips of the fingers—only in their singularity.

Have you ever considered how many other crease lines you have on your body? On your eyelids, on your elbows, on the soles of your feet, and many other places? Why do the "scientific" palm readers ignore them? If someone took the trouble to assign a certain symbolism to each one of them, they could double the occult literature overnight. Wouldn't it be fascinating to go to an occultist to get the backs of your knees read?

The analysis of the hands and palms of great figures of the past is an ongoing exercise. My favorite analysis is one performed by the famous nineteenth-century French palmist, Henri Rem. He analyzed the shape of Shakespeare's hand. How he was able to know the shape of the Bard's hand intrigues me. ESP, I would guess.

A computer center for psychic readings?

Harry B. Mingail, president of Newcom Management Systems, is a computer consultant, an expert in his field. He has an idea. Computers, he says, work through the use of logic. Psychics claim they work by intuition and from images they receive from they know not where. "Why not," suggests Mingail, "program a computer to be a psychic? After all, if, as you claim, psychics have no magical powers and practice their deceptions through logical methods—why can a computer not use the same methods to give psychic readings?"

Harry, you have opened a whole can of psychic worms. I find the idea so appealing that there's a good chance it may become an obsession with me. Can you imagine a true believer visiting a psychic computer center, dropping a donation into a money slot, sitting down to a keyboard and typing in his or her problems? The screen would ask the usual, seemingly innocent questions, and the subject would key in the appropriate answers. Finally, the machine would disgorge a detailed printout that would guide the subject's life for the next twenty-five years. This plan is not to be confused with the simple computer horoscopes furnished at the psychic fairs. I'm talking about a full-fledged psychic reading, giving the troubled subject details of past, present and future.

The idea isn't as far-fetched as it seems. The computer industry is already developing "expert systems" that can presumably handle this subject. "Expert systems," according to Charles Ed Sherman of Victoria,

British Columbia, "can assess probabilities and make inferences. Those now being used in medical diagnostics will ask for more information and give probabilities on the condition of the patient." This is exactly what a psychic adviser does. I can see the picture now. With the proliferation of microcomputers, soon there will be a psychic in almost every home. Never again will you have to listen to the banal utterings of the fraudulent psychic advisers on the open-line radio shows telling you where to find your missing cuff links, or how to get rid of your spouse, or what to do for your lower-back pain. No more scanning the newspaper pages searching for predictions of the coming earthquakes in California.

And how about our old friend Nostradamus? Just press a button and you'll pick up any of his predictive quatrains in a millisecond. Press another button and you'll get an explanation of that quatrain. Not only that, but press three more buttons, and you'll get three more (and different) explanations for the same quatrain. Why buy expensive books to get this priceless information? Why, it's like having your own private genie.

I'm really getting excited about this whole thing. Is there a computer manufacturing company around that is interested in getting in on a sure thing? This ingenious plan for a psychic computer will serve as a double-edged sword. It will not only hype the computer industry—it will put all the phony psychics out of business.

Astrology

When astronomy enabled humanity to measure the immense distances to the sun, the planets, and the stars, and to measure their masses, it became clear that their radiation or gravitational forces had an insignificant effect on human beings. The mass of the book you are now holding exerts a stronger gravitational effect on you than all the stars and planets out there. At the moment of birth the obstetrician has immensely more gravitational pull on an infant than has the planet Mars.

Andrew Franknoi, an astronomer and the editor of *Mercury,* has a few questions for astrologers: If there is some unknown force emanating from the planets that affects humans at birth, why does it not decrease with distance, as do other forces in the universe? After all, Mars is sometimes close to the earth and sometimes it's on the other side of the sun. And why are our charts drawn up relative to the moment of birth? Why

not to the moment of conception? Thousands of years ago the birth
process was not understood. The instant of birth was thought to be a
magic moment of some kind. Astrologers still base their assumptions on
this old magical thinking. Thousands and thousands of astrological charts
were drawn up before the discovery of the planets Uranus, Neptune, and
Pluto. These planets were not taken into account. Were they all wrong?
Again, the astrologers proceed along the ancient, established pathways.

Then there's the matter of precession, the shift over time in the direction of the earth's axis or rotation. The constellations are no longer where
they should be in the astrological scheme of things.

In 130 C.E., on March 21, the sun was "passing through Aries." On
that day in 1986, the sun was in the path of the constellation Pisces. The
fact is that in the past two thousand years, each sign has shifted westward
in relation to the earth by thirty degrees. This has created quite a problem
for the astrologers, but they have surmounted it. They created the solar
houses, and claimed that the constellations were "born" in these houses,
making their current positions irrelevant.

This gobbledygook would take too much explaining in this limited
space. But it works—for the astrologers. It's understandable why the
astro-merchants choose to ignore the scientific facts. Why undermine a
lucrative industry?

Lois Mulhall of London, Ontario, wrote a letter to the *Toronto Star*
taking me to task for my recent critical columns on astrology. It is some-
what ironic that she calls my comments "outdated" when that term can be
applied to the entire pseudoscience of astrology.

She refers to quantum mechanics, a favorite ploy of the paranormalists, most of whom don't understand that science at all, and suggests that I
read a little about it. Well, I've read a lot about it, have interviewed
several leading physicists on the subject, and have just attended a lecture
on quantum mechanics by Nobel laureate Murray Gell-Mann. And as
even many physicists do, I have to admit a distinct haziness on that complicated discipline. It is that haziness, of course, that makes it a favorite of
the occultists, who thrive on uncertainty. Mulhall writes, "Astrology
works best from the moment of birth. Why? Wouldn't we all like to
know." Yes, we sure would. She then goes on for two pages about the
intricacies of the brain—the neuron structure, the DNA molecules involved, the brain's electromagnetic properties—somehow obliquely tying

this in with the credibility of astrology. Mulhall's questionable expertise in quantum theory and neurology, and the arguments she presents, leaves me even hazier than do the theories of quantum mechanics. Mulhall keeps referring, throughout her treatise, on keeping an "open mind." Well, "open" is fine—but not "gaping."

Astrologers, Mulhall writes, are working hard to research and prove the case for their "science." But, "no wonder astrologers have been slow to prove anything; the 'bad press' makes it difficult to gain any cooperation." Does science require good press to prove its theories? Mulhall's letter is strewn with such conjectures as, "What if . . . the position and motions of Mars, interlacing with other planets, cause certain neurons to migrate to and proliferate in that area of the brain where aggressive tendencies will be?" That's a very big "what if." With that sort of reasoning, we can make a case for any kind of crackpot theory.

Mulhall uses the well-worn argument of other defenders of the paranormal by likening misunderstood astrologers to Galileo. But they always seem to overlook the fact that Galileo proved his point. Can astrologers make that claim? Mulhall goes on, defensively, "Can you prove psychology, psychiatry, sociology, acupuncture? Should we stop the research [on astrology]?"

I would venture that psychology and sociology are proved or accepted sciences. The controversy on psychiatry continues. Acupuncture often seems to have an analgesic effect, but otherwise there is considerable controversy about it. As for research on astrology—I have a question for Mulhall. If, as you say, research is still being done in an effort to prove the credibility of astrology, why do its practitioners seem to accept the fact of astrology and use its dubious methods to advise gullible and impressionable people about how to conduct their lives? Mulhall fails to note in her letter that she is a professional astrologer, which might have a slight bearing on her arguments. She concludes, "But let's face it, bashing people via the press is a very lucrative industry, isn't it?" Not quite as lucrative as the practice of astrology.

The pseudoscience of astrology is thriving and has been for millennia. It has had its low and its peak periods. Right now, according to various polls, a large proportion of the population believes in its authenticity. If one takes the trouble to investigate it scientifically, this ancient belief does not stand up to scrutiny. Astrology is perhaps the oldest of the arts of divination. It all began when man began to scan the heavens and wonder about the wandering planets as they moved about in their various constellations.

The Babylonians named the planets after their gods; the Greeks gave the constellations their names, borrowing from their mythical heroes and creatures like Sagittarius the centaur and Aries the ram. The magical powers of these creatures were supposed to emanate from the skies and influence the character and destiny of humans from the moment of birth. The ancient superstitious beliefs that grew from those early days have persisted into the twentieth century—into the era of computers, space travel, and advanced scientific thinking.

Astrology today is a huge, high-growth industry. Horoscopes are not only available in newspapers, magazines, and books, but they are also spewed out of computers and available by telephone. The syndicated astrology columnists have acquired followings in the millions. The astrologers who give personal readings charge fantastic hourly rates to dispense their devious divinations. The big question is, why? Why, in this enlightened age, do people feel a need for all this nonsense based on a superstitious system forged thousands of years ago?

I suppose we can immediately account for a good number of people who look on astrology as entertainment, a fun thing, a source of amusement and light conversation among friends. Quite understandable. We need some relief from the stress of everyday living. But how about the countless others who take this pseudoscience quite literally, who base their day-to-day decisions on their horoscopes? To many of these people life is quite unpredictable. The future seems to hold all kinds of uncertainties. They're looking for something more definite, and that's what the astrological chart provides—a definite prediction of what lies ahead. Somehow this provides a sense of security, particularly when the astrologer tells the subject what he or she wants to hear. The fact that the information is founded on quicksand is usually of no concern to the believer.

Carl Sagan made a point in his television series and the resultant book, *Cosmos*: "Astrology flourishes because it seems to lend a cosmic significance to the routine of our daily lives. It pretends to satisfy our longings to feel personally connected with the universe."

Swiss psychoanalyst Carl Jung, who had some way-out theories about things that go bump in the night, had a rather more hard-headed theory about astrology. He came to the conclusion that humanity was not affected by the stars, but by the symbolism of astrology itself.

SPIRITS
Don't Bury a Man in Bright Argyle Socks

The beginnings of modern spiritualism can be traced to the capers of the Fox sisters in Hydesville, New York, in the nineteenth century. From this foundation, I believe, came the spinoffs that evolved into the present beliefs in all kinds of so-called paranormal phenomena.

Spiritualism itself has branched off into two directions. We have the proliferation of spiritualist churches, a move into the mainstream of religious fervor. A glance at the religion pages of the weekend newspaper will reveal a sizable number of advertisements for these institutions. Having attended services at some of these churches, I must confess some skepticism about the sincerity and methodology of some of the demonstrations I have witnessed. Some "ministers" perform a standard mentalist-magician's mind reading act that reveals to some parishioners intimate facts about themselves—a typical psychic reading.

And then, of course, we have the seance, in which the spirit medium allegedly brings back messages from the great beyond. This practice hit its heyday in the early part of this century; but, contrary to popular belief, it still flourishes today. Sadly, it will not die out as long as people feel the need and nourish the hope to make contact with loved ones who have died.

The big difference in today's seances is that the physical medium no longer predominates. In our more sophisticated age the floating spirit trumpets, the ectoplasm emanating from body orifices, the ringing of bells and tipping of tables, all these have been largely eliminated. The mental medium has taken over. Today it is sufficient to have the medium go into a trance, assume the voice of a spirit contact, and relay messages from the departed. The visitor is impressed when the spirit voice relates certain details that they feel only the departed would know. It is the standard ploy of the psychic reader.

The belief in spirits spills over into sightings of ghosts and apparitions, which is far more common in this day and age than is popularly understood. Whenever I appear on an open-line radio broadcast with ghosts as the subject, the calls come flooding in. Most of these people are certainly not on the lunatic fringe. I have been contacted personally by many prominent, rational, intelligent individuals who ask me either to investigate or to explain some of their ghostly experiences.

A surprising number of people hire themselves out as ghost busters. They will visit a haunted house, or the residence of someone who calls them in, for a fee, to exorcise a ghostly visitor. After the usual mumbo-jumbo, they collect their loot and leave a sometimes impressed client.

I, too, have done my share of ghost busting, but with a slightly different approach. After listening to a tale of woe, I try to explain, rationally, the probable reason for the claimed sighting. No fee. Whether my method leaves a convinced customer, I cannot say. It's hard to shake the strong believer.

The really active spirit will not be content to merely make an appearance as a ghost. Being shy as well as spirited, it will avoid being seen, but will instead cause havoc by throwing around dishes, telephones, furniture, and various and assorted household appliances. The only kind of spirit to earn a moniker of its own, the poltergeist has acquired enough nerve and ego to continue its destructive ways and crash the media for big news stories at regular intervals.

Here again the "psychic investigators," usually self-proclaimed psychics or psychic supporters themselves, are called in to "investigate" and drive out the poltergeist. Representatives of the Committee for the Scientific Investigation of Claims of the Paranormal are almost always barred entrance to a domicile in question.

Is it possible that the occupants of some of these houses are contentedly wallowing in the publicity generated by their pet poltergeists, and that they don't want a natural explanation that would deflate the mystery surrounding their intriguing, noisy spirits? Or is it possible that knocking the props from under some of these stories will kill the chances of publishing a book about hair-raising experiences?

The spirit world and the world of fun and games joined forces when the Ouija board was invented. After sixty years it is still a steady seller. Because of its tie-in with the spirit world, it will probably continue to be available long after most of today's games have disappeared. The Ouija board can be an entertaining pastime on a long winter's evening—but, make no mistake, it can also instill fear in the mind of the impressionable believer. Whenever I make reference to the Ouija board in my writings or broadcasts, I get lots of mail. And some inevitably convey real fear of this innocent little board game. It's not the board itself that inspires this paranoia, it's the possible direct link-up with the spirit world.

The belief in spirits persists, and always will. There is too much need for this belief by too many people for it ever to die out. So, as Woody Allen once said, never bury a man in bright argyle socks; he'll never live it down in that other world—and he'll never forgive you for his embarrassment.

How modern spiritualism was established

The belief in modern spiritualism has been with us for more than a hundred years. There are many who still believe that spirits from the "other side" can contact us through a communicator, or medium. It all began with fakery. In 1848, in Hydesville, a hamlet in upper New York, two young girls named Margaret and Kate Fox started it all by frightening the wits out of their parents, and later their neighbors. The Foxes would hear loud knocking sounds coming from their daughters' bedroom at all hours of the night. They assumed these sounds were coming from a disembodied spirit that was haunting the house. The girls soon devised a code, so that the knocks would answer questions through a series of numbered signals.

Before long, outsiders were brought in to witness the phenomenon, and the word spread. Over a period of years the Fox sisters took to the road and became world-famous. Other mediums set up their own presentations and through their travels spread the phenomenon to Britain and Europe. Modern spiritualism had been established.

The literature on the subject does not deny these facts about its beginnings. But, strangely, very little has been published about the explanations for the effects accomplished by the Fox sisters. Have you ever cracked the finger knuckles of your hands? Try it with your toes. Not so easy, perhaps. But the Fox sisters were very good at it, so good that they started a new religion. They actually produced knocking sounds that baffled everyone. What began as childish mischief developed into a very commercial proposition. Of course, when they hit the lecture circuit they added other effects to their act to make it entertaining as well as mysterious—as any good magician would do. After many years Margaret Fox blew her cover. She publicly confessed to the deception. And, strangest of all, very few believed her. Thousands still preferred to believe in spiritualism, and still do.

When the commercial spirit mediums took over, they added psychokinesis to their effects. Floating trumpets, ectoplasm oozing from body orifices, bells that rang by themselves, ghostly voices and apparitions—the spirit seances took over. With World War I, the popularity of the seance hit its peak, particularly in Britain. So many lives had been lost, so many families were bereaved and longed to contact their loved ones, that the charlatans had a field day.

Today they are still thriving and still preying on the bereaved. The market will always be there. The seance still exists. It is important to remember that belief in the possibility of communication between the deceased and their survivors has existed since recorded history began. The difference between that belief and modern spiritualism is this: Modern spiritualism claims to have scientific evidence to bolster its claims.

Spiritualist fakery persists

In this enlightened age, in this modern world of advanced technology and scientific exploration, belief in the supernatural is spreading at an unprecedented clip. A recent survey reveals the astonishing fact that 40 percent of respondents think it possible to communicate with the dead. In the old days, the physical mediums prevailed. They produced ectoplasm from body orifices—actually luminescent gauze skillfully concealed beforehand. They made spirit trumpets float in the air by using long, invisible extensions attached to the luminous horns. This was done in semi-dark rooms, of course.

Today the methods are more sophisticated. The mental mediums flourish. They make spiritual contact with the dead and simply pass along information verbally. I have always found it incredible that a medium could contact a spirit in seconds. When you realize how many billions of souls are floating around out there—how do they do it? Ask that question of any psychic and you'll get a stock answer—"I don't know, it just happens."

During one of my recent investigations I visited an Ottawa psychic. After he went into a trance, and began speaking like Peter Sellers in a Pink Panther movie, I asked him if he could contact my dead sister. It took him all of fifteen seconds to locate her spirit. It was now embodied in a person "helping underprivileged children in Belgium," he said. I was underwhelmed. I never had a sister. This startling communication cost me $75.

The average patron does not usually question the medium's message. Now why is that? When old Uncle Harry, long departed, speaks through the medium and says, "Charlene, I've missed you so. And remember your little dog, Oscar, which you loved when you were a child? He's with me now. And he misses you too . . ." Is it any wonder that the gullible person is impressed? When the medium comes up with information he could not possibly have known through normal means, he has his follower hooked. He has made the big breakthrough. That is the basic working principle of all mediums, of all psychics.

Strange as it seems, psychics and mediums have always been able to prey on the gullible through such nonsense as psychic toe-cracking, spoon-bending, and feeding back trivial information. Those who pay their dollars to these people are always fair game—be they bishops, scientists, ordinary, everyday citizens, or a prime minister.

"Spiritual science": A contradiction in terms

Open-line radio shows featuring psychics are no rarity, but recently one of these programs was a little different. For the first time in my memory—and I've heard, taped, and participated in these programs for years—the host of the show was asking critically probing questions of the psychic guest.

David Schatsky, host of CBC's "Radio Noon," was featuring Hilda Martin, who was introduced as being a trance medium, spiritual healer, and former detective with Scotland Yard. She is now pastor and president of a spiritual church in England, and claims to be the first medium invited to perform in the Soviet Union. She also claims to have contacted spirits while in Australia, New Zealand, Sweden, Finland, South Africa, and the United States.

Schatsky asks: "Is what you do religion or science?"

Martin: "A combination of both."

Schatsky: "Scientists don't accept what you do. They say it's bunk, it's fraud."

Martin: "Oh, no, no, no—not on the metaphysical side."

Then Martin sidesteps: "In Russia they're so advanced . . . [their scientists] don't disbelieve it."

Now here's a standard cop-out. Corner a psychic and he or she will immediately switch to the Soviet psychic scene—knowing that it is difficult to check the facts on occurrences behind the Iron Curtain. Nonetheless, it so happens that Martin is off base on her last statement. The scientists in the Soviet Union are no less critical of the occultniks in their bailiwick than are Western scientists of our own oddballs. Sure, they, too, have their fringe scientists who like to speculate on the possibilities of far-out phenomena. But that's universal.

At this point in the program Schatsky is beginning to sound more than a little skeptical. "Hilda, how do you contact people who are dead?"

Martin doesn't hesitate: "It's mental." (What, no touching?) She continues: "Because they dispose of the physical body doesn't mean they have lost their minds or their consciousness or their intelligence or their knowledge. So we just tap in . . . to help us with information."

Schatsky: "So it's like a big computer memory bank?"

Martin: "Yes."

When the calls from listeners came in, they were no different from any other psychic talk show. Almost every caller supported the psychic. Schatsky hinted, almost pleaded, that perhaps some listener with a scientific viewpoint would like to take on Martin. In the entire hour only one skeptic responded, and he was later criticized by two other callers for his rational viewpoint. This is not a new situation. Most scientists and scientific thinkers have never wanted to get involved in the paranormal morass. It has been only in the past few years that several have begun to speak out.

One caller, obviously troubled, asked how he could help a very sick loved one. Martin told him that the illness was terminal, but advised him to think "pink" and the person would be healed. The sad part was that the caller asked how he could later get in touch with the psychic.

One believer inadvertently gave a good reason why so many believe in the paranormal when he said, "I think what makes life interesting is the unknown, and as soon as you find out about something it loses its interest."

In response to a call referring to the lack of proof for certain scientific claims, Martin answered that she had once actually seen an atom.

"Where?" asked an incredulous Schatsky.

"In Russia."

Painting from the beyond

Ostensibly, one Matthew Manning executes art work while in a trance. Drawings and paintings in the style of Bewick, Rowlandson, Beardsley, Klee, Matisse, Picasso, and other great names began to appear over the walls of his rooms and then all over the ceilings. He was visited by the spirits of these greats—according to Manning.

In an article in the *San Francisco Examiner,* Manning claimed that an art expert with Sotheby's gallery in London had said that one of the Picasso's he had drawn looked like an original, and that Sotheby's would have vouched for that if they hadn't been told that Manning had done it. Fellow skeptic and psychic investigator James Randi decided to follow up on this story. He wrote to Sotheby's. A reply by a Sotheby's official declared the claim "absolutely not true." He wrote that the various drawings done by the "spirits of various artists" had all been rendered by the same hand, and that they were very clever but not very convincing forgeries of existing works.

Manning made another claim in the *London Daily Mirror.* He had made a drawing of a monkey "while in a trance," and published it in his book, *The Link.* It had caused great excitement at the Rijksmuseum in Amsterdam, he said. It was similar to a Savery original that was in their vaults and had never been published. Randi sent another letter. A reply from the museum cleared up the matter. The drawing had been published, first in 1905 and again in 1965. It was still available. And the original was on display to the public, not locked up in a vault.

These are only two items that were investigated. How many people will take the time and the trouble to check upon the myriad claims made by phony psychics? It is so much easier to sit back and say, "Hey, isn't that fantastic? This guy works miracles." It's more exciting, more out of the ordinary—makes for more stimulating conversation. It's also a lot of hokum.

The immortal debate

There are few subjects of more interest and concern to mankind than the question of immortality. What happens to us after we die? There are also few subjects that have been more greatly exploited by spirit mediums, psychics, and purveyors of the paranormal. So, when I participated in a recent debate on the resolution "People Survive Bodily Death" at the University of Guelph, I wasn't surprised to see the assembly hall jammed. A couple of hundred students were turned away at the door for lack of seating space.

Even more significant, but also no surprise to me, was the result of an initial vote on the audience's belief. The audience was polled before the debate—did they support the positive or the negative side of the resolution? They were polled again after the debate. The winner was the debater who swung over more votes by helping to change people's minds. The debater taking the positive side would have to provide strong evidence for post-mortem survival—whether through the existence of ghosts, contact through spirit mediums, or whatever.

When the initial vote was taken I would judge that approximately 80 percent of the audience, mostly students, voted positive. As I said, no surprise. For years most polls taken among university students have indicated a strong belief in astrology, UFOs, ESP, and other things of an occult nature. I, of course, was arguing the weakly supported (by the audience) negative side. In my view, belief in survival after death is purely an article of faith and hope. I have not yet seen any firm scientific evidence to support that theory.

The enthusiastic participant on the positive side was Ian Currie, a sociology lecturer at the University of Guelph and an author of a book that supports lots of theories on the existence of ghosts, apparitions, poltergeists, reincarnation, and life after death. I shouldn't neglect to mention that he also claims to de-haunt houses. Currie's arguments may seem way out to some, but his grasp of the subject is thorough.

I find one basic weakness in Currie's arguments: His "evidence" is based on personal anecdotes and eyewitness testimony. To accept such evidence you have to agree that most people are reliable witnesses, that they have perfect memories, and that they can trust the evidence of their senses. It's an illusion to believe this. There have been a great number of psychological studies done in the past few years on the subject of eye-witness testimony. It is flimsy. It is often undependable. Apart from what these studies have revealed, it is also well known that eyewitness testimony has caused tragic errors to be made in some court cases.

How about your memory? Do you store things away and then re-trieve them as a tape recorder or a computer does? Do you see things and file them in your brain as you would file a picture from your camera? It just doesn't work that way. Your memory is influenced by many other factors. It's no exaggeration to say you can't trust it. How about trusting your senses? When you see, hear, touch, taste, or smell something, is it always what you think it is? No. You are often deceived by your senses.

On a cheerier note, from my viewpoint, is the fact that I won the University of Guelph debate, although by a narrow margin. This gives me some cause for optimism. Perhaps our young people, even while they adhere to their religious beliefs, will learn to separate faith from claims of scientific evidence.

People can hallucinate in groups

I agree that many, many people think they have seen apparitions. Under-line the word *think*. Because, according to the findings of several research-ers in psychology, there are natural explanations for these so-called sight-ings. The most common psychological explanation for seeing ghosts is that of hallucination. A hallucination is a false perception. It is a mental image that only seems to be real. One needn't be mentally ill to experience a hallucination. It can happen in a dream, while falling asleep, when awakening from sleep, even while daydreaming.

What causes a hallucination? Why would someone swear they had seen the ghost of a dear departed relative or friend? It's well known that this can be induced by the power of suggestion, particularly if the person is suffering from fear or anxiety. If the subject expects to see an apparition, the image will appear in his or her mind's eye.

This leads to another point. In a recent debate I had with Ian Currie, a believer in life after death, Currie argued that you couldn't attribute a ghost sighting to hallucination when, as he claims, more than one person has seen it at the same time.

How can several people hallucinate the same image at the same time? The fact is, once again, that studies have shown that collective hallucinations do take place. And the power of suggestion is the explanation. Some good examples are the mass sightings of flying saucers, with descriptions of circular metallic craft with lighted portholes. When investigation of one famous sighting in the United States revealed that it had been the re-entry of debris from a space satellite, some of the witnesses were still not convinced. The belief produces the hallucination. The hallucination confirms the belief. For the rationalist, it's a no-win situation.

The sensing of ghosts in a so-called haunted house can have natural causes. Various investigations have revealed very ordinary reasons for very spooky happenings. For instance, one report of a ghost seen moving from window to window in a haunted house turned out to be the reflection of moving car lights from the street. The mystery of an electric clock that stopped every Tuesday and Thursday was cleared up when it was found that the cleaning woman unplugged the clock to plug in her vacuum cleaner on those days. In one haunted house a wild shrieking sound coming from the attic turned out to be a child's whistle plugged in a knothole. Then we have the well-known slamming-door phenomenon—caused by a broken latch, a loose top hinge, and a broken window with the wind entering the room.

In occult literature there are literally thousands of books incorporating countless ghost stories. Some of them have become classics. One of the most up to date is *The Encyclopedia of Ghosts,* by Daniel Cohen, who has turned out a number of books on monsters and other delightful things. The book consists mainly of a retelling of many standard stories, with some new ones, to me, thrown in. It makes for great campfire storytelling.

Poltergeists: Child's play

A few years ago considerable international coverage was given to the Columbus, Ohio, family of John and Joan Resch, who were being plagued by objects mysteriously flying about their home. Lights and appliances were going on and off without switches being activated. A shower turned on by itself. A stereo suddenly began to blast forth without benefit of human control. Scary stuff, but an old story. For those who have read *The Amityville Horror,* or seen the film, the Columbus story is a mild rerun. For myself, it is interesting to note the claims and descriptions—they are facsimiles of poltergeist tales I have been investigating for many years.

The Resches have a fourteen-year-old daughter, Tina. In almost every poltergeist case ever described there has been one or more adolescents in the residence. Where it has been possible to pin down a human culprit, the teenager has almost always been involved. So what happened in this case? A hidden TV camera recorded Tina's hand surreptitiously pulling a lamp off a table. This would seem to indicate some culpability, wouldn't it? Well, not exactly. An employee of the TV station came up with the standard psychic cop-out. According to his story, "This one instance of recorded fakery does not explain the other bizarre happenings witnessed at the house." How many times have I heard this rationalization about Uri Geller and other psychic fakes—"Sure, he was caught cheating once or twice, but the other times it was for real." Is it barely possible the TV station wanted to keep an attention-getting story alive? This same person, Drew Hadwal, was quoted as saying, "I was seated at the kitchen table with Tina and all of a sudden the chairs spread out. . . . I don't see how she could have sent them out in three directions like that." Now, if Hadwal would come to Toronto and enroll in the adult magic course I conduct, I would be pleased to show him how to use a length of thread in such a manner that a tug on one end will cause a number of chairs to spread out in all directions. I will even show him how to secretly dispose of the thread after the fact.

How about the other phenomena described—lights and appliances going on and off around the house at the same time? Eureka!—I have an idea. Switch on the lights in several rooms, and perhaps a stereo, ahead of time. Go downstairs and disconnect the fuses controlling the rooms. When you wish the spirits to manifest themselves, simply control the fuses.

See how simple it can be? You, too, can haunt a house.

Keep one basic fact in mind: What people think they see and what they

actually do see are not always precisely the same. How else could stage
magicians survive?

Poltergeists trigger speculation

On the Track of the Poltergeist, by D. Scott Rogo, is one of the many
books tracing the activities of the "invisible energies" that make a variety
of strange sounds and cause the movement and breakage of household
articles. I would label this book "recommended" reading for those interested in the imagination-stretching and naivete of an author who, like so
many others, assumes the role of "psychic investigator"—the proper title
would be "purveyor of the paranormal." Rogo describes several anecdotal
cases of poltergeist activities that drew considerable public attention. He
cites three theories that have been advanced over the years to account for
this phenomenon—all by paranormalists, of course. Somehow, the general
theory agreed upon by informed skeptics seems to have been lost in the
shuffle. Not a mention of it in the book.

One of the theories Rogo mentions is attributed to W. G. Roll,
project director of the Psychical Research Foundation in Chapel Hill,
North Carolina. He credits Roll with being "one of the friendliest researchers in the field." I wouldn't dispute that statement for a moment.
Roll's theory? "The typical poltergeist is somehow created by a force
housed in the brain and body of the agent himself. . . . The force probably emanates from two places on the agent's body that take on the
function of the 'rotating beams' of force." Another theory, that of Dr.
Hans Bender, noted German parapsychologist: If you lower the temperature of a room by one degree, a tremendous amount of energy would be
conserved. "The poltergeist agent physically draws [this] energy . . . and
redirects it to producing the weird antics of the poltergeist." Dr. Nandor
Fodor, a Hungarian psychoanalyst, is, according to Rogo, a little more
speculative. Says Fodor: "The poltergeist may be masterminded by some
portion of the agent's unconscious mind that has physically detached
itself from the host's brain, psyche, and body, and has developed a primitive intelligence of its own."

All these people take the typical occultist's obfuscating, complicated,
speculative approach to these phenomena—completely ignoring the simple, straightforward, and rational explanations offered by objective and

knowledgeable investigators. Every investigation conducted by a magician versed in the art of deception has shown that poltergeist activity usually takes place at a residence occupied by a troubled adolescent and that this youngster is usually physically responsible for the hanky-panky that takes place.

In the home of John and Joan Resch, it was soon clear that young Tina Resch was somehow involved. It took investigators from the Committee for the Scientific Investigation of Claims of the Paranormal to prove that Tina was pulling the "schtick"—that it was a hoax.

Rogo's explanation? Sure, she performed a few sly stunts. But how about the other things that happened (where she wasn't caught)? If D. Scott Rogo is on the track of the poltergeist, I feel that somewhere he's been shunted onto a siding. Not that I have any doubts about his credibility as an expert on the paranormal. After all, how can you question an author who has also written such books as *The Haunted House Handbook, ESP and Your Pet,* and *Phone Calls from the Dead*?

Why do poltergeists even rate a question mark?

Arthur C. Clarke—the man is a paradox. He is a longtime scientist, a scientific visionary, and one of the world's greatest science-fiction writers. On the other hand, he lends his name and his writing talents to a book and a television series packed with very questionable information on the paranormal.

John Wiley and Sons have just come out with a fascinating "scientific autobiography," a book entitled *Ascent to Orbit*—covering the technical writings of Arthur C. Clarke. Most of us know Clarke as the author of *2001: A Space Odyssey* and *2010: odyssey two.* But this latest publication reveals a side of him long hidden from the public. Did you know that in 1945, in his now-famous article in *Wireless World,* Clarke first predicted the use of satellites in electronic communication? So when you watch TV and see an event that is being transmitted live from the other side of the world, you can credit the theoretical wizardry of Arthur C. Clarke for this modern miracle. For good reason he is now recognized as the "father" of satellite communication. *Ascent to Orbit* also reprints a number of Clarke's early writings on rocketry, astronomy, and spaceflight. Clarke is a scientific pioneer and visionary—no doubt about it.

So it's quite a shocker to compare *Ascent to Orbit* with *World of Strange Powers*—based on the television series "Arthur C. Clarke's Mysterious World." Here Clarke deserts the world of science and science fiction and dabbles in fictional science. *World of Strange Powers* covers the whole range of psychic phenomena. It includes poltergeists, mind over matter, dowsing, life after life, reincarnation, and clairvoyance. The series and the book were written by British TV producers John Fairley and Simon Welfare, with Clarke contributing commentaries on the subject matter. True, he writes skeptically about many things, but at the same time he seems to accept many other farfetched anecdotes—a little surprising from a hard-headed scientist.

A good example is the chapter entitled "The Noisy Spirits." The authors quote case after case of poltergeist hauntings in many countries. In those cases that had been properly investigated and a fraud exposed, the authors quite properly describe the exposures. Other cases are left with a big question mark. The reader is left wondering when, at the end of the chapter, in answer to the question "Is there such a thing as a poltergeist?" Clarke winds up with, "We still do not know." This is standard paranormal sales technique. If we "do not know," let us stop planting the idea of "maybe" until we have evidence.

The point is that there is a lot that we do know. We know that every case that has been thoroughly investigated by a knowledgeable magician familiar with the art of deception has ended in a revelation of hanky-panky. Either that or the poltergeist has usually mysteriously vanished after a competent investigator visited the premises.

If anyone ever offers me evidence of a poltergeist that I can feel, hear, see, smell, taste, or measure—I'll buy it. Speculative theories are for the birds. True enough, they help sell books and television programs—the public must be titillated. *World of Strange Powers* does make for interesting reading, and I will admit that it has better balance than most books publicizing the paranormal. But I don't think that a man of Arthur C. Clarke's stature needs this sort of association with the murky world of the occult. Since his long retirement in Sri Lanka with the proceeds of his movies, he doesn't need the bucks.

I find Clarke's summary of the book amusing. "At a generous assessment," he says, "approximately half this book is nonsense. Unfortunately, I don't know which half." I would be less generous. I would include both halves.

The secret behind the Ouija board mystique

The woman in the green dress places the fingertips of both hands on top of the small board. It begins to move around slowly, as if guided by some unseen force. One side of the board is pointed. This point moves toward various letters of the alphabet painted on a larger board beneath it. Eventually a word is spelled out. This word is the answer to a question I had asked. It is correct. Once again the old reliable Ouija board has proved itself.

If we translated the French *oui* and the German *ja* into English we could call it the yes-yes board. It's been around for more than a hundred years, since the French invented it and called it a *planchette*. It was about six inches long, heart-shaped, mounted on tiny wheels. A pencil was inserted, point down, at one corner. Two people would each place the fingertips of one hand on the board. A question would be asked, the board would move around—the pencil writing out the answer. The friendly spirits were at work.

Baltimore toymaker Isaac Fuld used his Yankee ingenuity to develop the idea into a tremendous commercial success. He marked the letters of the alphabet on a large baseboard, added numbers from zero to nine, and fashioned a small, pointed "planchette" to slide along as an indicator. Sales took off. Many who had lost loved ones in the carnage of World War I wished to contact the spirits of the departed. The spirit seance proliferated—and the Ouija board became a popular instrument of communication with the dead. The U.S. government slapped a 10 percent tax on sales of the board, classifying it as a game. Fuld fought the tax all the way to the Supreme Court, claiming that the Ouija board was a scientific instrument. The government won.

The board might be labeled a game, but believers in psychic phenomena will argue until they are blue in the face that it's no game, that it is a device through which unseen forces can manifest themselves. Well, there is an unseen force, but there's nothing paranormal about it. In psychology it's called "automatism." In their very readable book, *Anomalistic Psychology,* authors Zusne and Jones explain that automatism is a motor behavior, or muscular action, to an unconscious thought, "as when doodling while talking on the telephone, aware that the hand is writing something . . . but unable to control it." Your consciousness is divided.

When the Ouija indicator moves toward various letters and numbers you are actually guiding it without being aware you are doing so. But the control is still coming from your own brain. Some people have a greater aptitude for this than others. Some cannot do it at all. Then, of course, we have the frauds—those who merely push the indicator to the correct places, consciously. It's not easy to separate the forthright from the faker.

The scene with the woman in the green dress took place at McGill University, in a class I was teaching on the paranormal. My psychological explanation of the working of the Ouija board hadn't satisfied her. She claimed that spirits were guiding the planchette. There was only one way I could prove my point. I placed a piece of brown wrapping paper over the Ouija board, with the planchette resting on top of the paper. Then I put her to the test again. Whenever the planchette stopped we lifted the paper and noted the letter it pointed to. At the finish it spelled out nothing but gibberish.

A new scientific discovery—spirits cannot see through brown wrapping paper.

The ubiquitous Ouija board keeps surfacing. Now there's an entire book written about this little spirit game—*The Most Dangerous Game*, by Stoker Hunt. Whenever I pick up a book on the paranormal (and I've picked up enough of them) I always look for some balance in the presentation. Does the author dwell only on the supernatural side, or does he or she toss in a modicum of rational explanations for the so-called phenomena involved?

Well, bouquets to Hunt's book. He does refer to automatism, which is the psychological explanation for the workings of the board. Automatism, as I've pointed out frequently, is the involuntary muscular action produced by subconscious thought. But, I hasten to add, the fairly brief references to this explanation are practically buried by an avalanche of the usual psychic anecdotes, explanations, and references to questionable authorities. It still makes for interesting reading if you can separate the wheat from the chaff. You'll need a fairly large shovel, maybe even a bulldozer, for the chaff.

Hunt has a chapter on Jane Roberts, the highly successful author of the "Seth" books on ESP and other occult matters. It seems that it all started with a Ouija board. Roberts wanted to write a book on ESP but knew nothing about it. Her trusty Ouija board gave her the answers. Through the board she made contact with the spirit of Seth. He had died, he told her, in Elmira, New York, in 1942. Seth returned in the next Ouija session to communicate that, as a soldier in Turkey in the sixth century, he had known both Jane and her husband, Robert.

To quote from the book, "As the Ouija board experiments regularly continued . . . Jane began noticing that, even as questions were being asked of her Ouija board, answers were formulating themselves in her mind." Jane Roberts converted herself into a trance medium to pass along Seth's words of wisdom. Not for her to simply conduct seances. She put these messages into book form and became a cult figure. The Seth books have sold in the millions. And it all started with the innocent Ouija board.

Another Ouija-board authority quoted in Hunt's book is Barbara Honegger, former White House official and later with the U.S. Department of Justice. You may recall that she quit the Reagan administration years ago in a storm of controversy, accusing the president of reneging on his promise to change laws discriminating against women. Honegger is revealed as having some way-out theories regarding telepathic communication between brains. Lots of surmise, no evidence. She evidently also has a strong belief in our links with the spirit world.

The thrust of Hunt's book is to point out the dangers involved in getting hooked on a belief in the Ouija board. This also goes for unfounded belief in the wisdom of psychics, fortune tellers, astrologers, and occultniks of any kind—whether they use the props of their professions or not. Those who are emotionally unstable are particularly vulnerable.

So why blame the poor old Ouija board? It's just another in a long list that includes crystal balls, tarot cards, pendulums, pyramids, and astrological charts.

SUPERSTITION
Vestigial Fears

It all began with superstition. All the occult beliefs, all of the many paranormal and pseudoscientific irrationalities of the twentieth century have their roots in superstition. It is fostered and cultivated from childhood; in some countries and in some homes such an upbringing can be pronounced.

Superstition and magic are intertwined. Superstition is based on fear, and magic is the practice of power that uses superstition as its *modus operandi.* There are many definitions of superstition: a blindly accepted belief not based on fact; something we think will change our luck; a belief based on fear of the unknown. In all cases, an irrational way of looking at cause and effect.

I am often asked the difference between superstitious belief and religious belief. Thomas Hobbes had an answer to that way back in the seventeenth century: "Fear of power invisible, feigned by the mind or imagined from tales publicly allowed [is] religion; not allowed, superstition."

A rational (perhaps a better word is "rationed") amount of superstitious belief can sometimes be useful. The lucky charm will often give confidence to the athlete and aid in better performance, or will settle down the anxious student writing a difficult examination paper. But a deep belief in old superstitions, such as the evil eye, for instance, can be seriously harmful. There is no harm in knocking on wood or crossing your fingers or keeping your umbrella closed indoors. These are part of our cultural heritage.

I always observe a definite perking up of the audience whenever I lecture about superstitious practices and their beginnings. It's easy to understand why. The audience relates. We all practice these little fetishes in one way or another, at one time or another.

Superstition cuts across a wide variety of subjects. There are almost no categories you can think of that do not have an attached list of superstitions. Almost all countries have their own particular ones. And some countries, such as the United States and the United Kingdom, have particular areas that harbor their own brands of superstition. Then there are the superstitions attached to the professions and day-to-day living—the theater, sports, marriage, death, birth, holidays, seasons, various animals, the home, the garden, the body, clothes, work, travel, the sea, food, sneezing, spitting, broken mirrors, numbers, colors, cutlery, playing cards, horseshoes, and on and on and on.

Superstition attached to numbers—numerology—is of particular interest. Numerology really cuts across two fields: superstition and the controversial topic of coincidence. *Coincidence* probably has as many definitions as *superstition,* but statistician Percy Diaconis probably says it best when he defines *coincidence* as "a set of events which are perceived as meaningfully related, but which have no apparent connection to each other."

Get into an argument about coincidence with a believer in the paranormal and you will soon be drawn into the world of Carl Jung and synchronicity. I would advise studying Jung's theories before getting trapped in that quagmire.

It is perhaps worth keeping this in mind: Surveys conducted in the United States during the past forty years have indicated that a large majority of the population is influenced to some degree by superstition.

And remember, too, the immortal words of that great iconoclast Woody Allen: "I have my superstitions—I would never go to see *Gone With the Wind* with a slave."

Cross your fingers—It's Friday the thirteenth

Today's the day to stay in bed, quietly. It's the safest place. Walking across a busy city street can be a hazard at any time. But on Friday the thirteenth? That's pushing your luck.

Is this merely superstition, or is there really some supernatural power governing the strange happenings associated with this date? Superstition probably began with earliest humanity. When people saw a rock tumble down a mountainside, when thunder rumbled, when lightning flashed, they had an explanation: the spirits, the gods, resided in the rock, caused the thunder, controlled the lightning.

Today we're worldly and sophisticated. We don't have these ignorant, superstitious beliefs. Of course, we may carry around the odd good-luck charm or knock on wood if we say something boastful. Strange, they did that thousands of years ago. The Druids, ancient Celtic priests, advised their followers that spirits resided in old oak trees. When the trees were cut down to provide shelters, the occupants of the houses believed the gods still lived in the wood. Thus knocking on wood was conceived to appease the gods, or to keep them from hearing the spoken words. It seems hard to believe we still do it today. At least the ancients knew *why* they were doing it.

Superstition can be separated into two categories. We have the organized cults, led by people who are mainly interested in power. The late Jim Jones and his followers are a prime example. Then we have the superstition of the individual, the person who practices his or her beliefs defensively— such as not walking under ladders, tossing salt over the left shoulder, and saying "bless you" when someone sneezes. The ladder superstition is interesting. If you lean a ladder against a wall you form a triangle—the ladder, the wall and the ground. This is supposed to symbolize the Holy Trinity. It is considered a lack of respect to walk through it, resulting in bad fortune. A British university psychology class conducted an experiment a few years ago. They set a ladder up against a wall on a busy London street teeming with traffic. The foot of the ladder was put at the curb. The students observed the area for hours. An astounding 70 percent of the pedestrians stepped off the curb into traffic rather than walk under the ladder. Being a skeptic, I walk under ladders regularly, but I keep my fingers crossed.

Crossing fingers is another one. We're performing the sign of the cross, for protection, but it has nothing to do with the crucifix. The superstitious symbol for the cross was known and observed thousands of years before

Christ. It probably dates back to the use of crossed sticks to produce fire.

Remember, if you spill salt, toss some over your left shoulder. Salt was always used as a preservative. It symbolized life and good fortune. If it was spilled you had to appease the devil. And he's always on your left side, the sinister side ("sinister" is Latin for "left"). So let him have it.

For the origins of Friday the thirteenth, we must consider triskaideka-phobia—the fear of the number thirteen. The number thirteen hasn't always been considered unlucky. The ancient Egyptians didn't think it was. To them, life was symbolized by a ladder with twelve steps. Each step represented a path on the road to knowledge. The thirteenth step led to eternal life. It was something to be looked forward to, not feared. But if we look back into history, particularly in the literature of numerology, we find this number associated with all manner of dire events. Its occult significance is partly derived from black magic. A coven, in witchcraft, consists of thirteen witches or twelve witches and the devil. The tarot card of death is number thirteen. The thirteenth of the ancient gods was supposed to have died of violent causes.

There are several organizations that observe Friday the thirteenth religiously. The Thirteen Club in London, England, was founded in 1890. A club of the same name was established in New York in 1884. The National Society of Thirteen is still active in the United States. It meets regularly on every Friday the thirteenth. The members enter their clubroom under ladders, carrying open umbrellas. They have a bed in one corner, on which they lay their hats. There are a few mirrors in strategic positions which the members take great delight in smashing. They dine exactly thirteen to a table. There's a lot of accidental salt spilling, but no over-the-shoulder tossing. Dinner is not served until the ancient clock in the corner strikes thirteen. Their reason for existence? To combat superstition, preju-dice, and fear. It seems to be a reasonable attitude, but as philosopher Sir Francis Bacon observed: "There is a superstition in avoiding superstition."

Probably the strongest reason for the perpetuation of thirteen as a number of ill fortune is the fact that the Last Supper took place with thirteen at the table. United States President Franklin D. Roosevelt's long-time secretary, Grace Tully, once wrote, "The boss was superstitious, par-ticularly about the number thirteen—on several occasions I received a last minute summons to attend a luncheon or dinner party because a belated default or a late addition had brought the guest list to thirteen." Think that's odd? Well, in France a professional fourteenth guest can be hired for parties.

Sometimes superstition will collide head-on with science. In 1970 the National Aeronautics and Space Administration (NASA) took a bold gamble. It launched the thirteenth Apollo space mission, believe it or not, at 13:13 central time, from pad 39 (three times thirteen). The first names of the astronauts were James, John and Fred. Add up the number of letters in their names. On April 13 there was a major problem with the craft's oxygen supply and the mission was aborted. Bad luck? Rarely will you find a hotel with a floor labeled "13," with a room numbered 13, or an airline with a flight 13. In Paris, you'd have to look hard to find a house with the unlucky number.

The year 1985 was blessed with only one Friday the thirteenth. The year before, we had three, which is the maximum the calendar can produce in a non-leap year. There are only two more of these triple whammies in the balance of this century—1987 and 1998. What does this mean? Nothing. Taken over a 400-year period, the thirteenth of the month comes out most often on a Friday—688 times. Sundays are a close second—687 times.

Yet with all the shakes and shivers about the number thirteen, there are those who consider it lucky. In the numerology game you can look for the bad—but you can also look for the good. It is all a matter of how you want to rationalize it. The greatest booster of thirteen was an old friend by the name of Jack Walsh. Jack was a Canadian who lived in Los Angeles and worked for one of the large movie corporations. He was an enthusiastic amateur magician. Fondly known as Canada Jack, he had a strange fascination for the number thirteen. If he had to line up, he would make sure he was thirteenth. He claimed to be the thirteenth of thirteen children. He was born on the thirteenth day of the month. He once confided to me that he regretted that there were only twelve months in the year—he was certain he would have been born in the thirteenth. When the Magic Castle, the famous gathering place for magicians, was founded in Hollywood, Jack Walsh made sure he was the thirteenth member.

Jack's favorite story was about the day he made a fateful bet at the Del Mar racetrack. It was the thirteenth of the month, so, naturally, he went to the races. There were thirteen horses in the thirteenth race, so Jack was attracted as if by a magnet. Standing thirteenth in line at wicket number thirteen, he noticed that horse number thirteen was a long shot in the betting. So he bet thirteen hundred hard-earned dollars on number thirteen. The horse came in thirteenth. I think I'll take that story with a grain of salt and throw it over my left shoulder.

After all this, if you do stay in bed on Friday the thirteenth, it's understandable. But be careful—people have been known to fall out of bed.

Sneezing at superstition

Do you consider yourself superstitious? Of course not. We're much too well educated and sophisticated in this modern age. No longer do we knock on wood, avoid walking under ladders, dodge black cats crossing our path, keep umbrellas closed indoors, avoid stepping on cracks in sidewalks, believe that smashed mirrors bring seven years' bad luck, cross our fingers, toss spilled salt over our left shoulder, or wear lucky charms. Belief in all this nonsense is a thing of the past. Or is it?

Do you ever say "God bless you" when someone sneezes? Many people do, but I'll bet they don't know the origins of the benediction. The sneezing ritual is a good example of a superstition that has persisted through the centuries. There are several stories associated with it. We read in Genesis, "And [God] breathed into his nostrils the breath of life," as the description of the birth of Adam. If the breath of life went into the nose, then a sneeze might drive it out. And so we have the blessing of a departing soul as you sneeze.

Way back in the fifth century B.C.E., the Greeks believed that sneezing was a symptom of plague, and that some kind of supernatural protection was needed when one sneezed. Supposedly, the "bless you" custom began when Pope Gregory the Great, in the sixth century, recommended its use during an outbreak of plague in Rome.

A sneeze was sometimes seen as evidence of diabolic possession—it was believed that demons entered the body by way of body openings, especially the nostrils. For this reason the nostrils were often protected, and still are in some societies, by magical nose rings. The ancient Chinese used to plug their nostrils with pieces of jade. A Brahmin touches his ears when he sneezes—spirits are supposed to enter the ears at these times. Seventeenth-century England had a polite custom when someone sneezed; companions were supposed to raise their hats. I can't explain that one. Incidentally, at that time in England, sneezing was thought to be a sign of good health. People were discharged from the hospital if they sneezed three times. It indicated they had recovered from their illness.

An old Scottish superstition was that babies remained under the control of the fairies until their first sneeze. In Japan, many people believe that one sneeze means you are blessed, two sneezes mean you are guilty, and three mean you'll be ill. So try to kill that second sneeze on your next trip to the land of lotus blossoms. And talking about trips, if you are really superstitious and want to use sneezing to good effect, here is an important tip: When starting out on a vacation jaunt, it's a good sign to sneeze to the right, a bad one to sneeze to the left—so be ready for a quick twist of the neck.

Don't gamble on it

If you have superstitious beliefs, even though you are a rationally thinking person, those beliefs will persist—you will continue to practice your little superstitious rituals. This point was emphasized by Dr. Graham Reed, a psychology professor at York University, at the 1984 convention of the American Psychological Association in Toronto. "We can know an answer is rational and still adhere to irrational ideas," he said.

A good example of this, Reed noted, is the gambler's fallacy. Even if you are aware of the fallacy, you will likely ignore that knowledge when the occasion presents itself, Reed said. If you are likely to take a flyer at the Las Vegas or Atlantic City casinos, a knowledge of the gambler's fallacy might be very useful. The fallacy is the belief that if a chance event has had a certain consistent run in the past, the probability that it will occur in the future has been altered. An example is the tossing of a coin. If you toss a coin ten times and come up with heads each time, you would likely bet that the odds are good that you'll get a tails on the eleventh toss. It isn't so. Each toss is a chance event in itself—one chance in two. The eleventh toss is no different. This applies whether you are tossing coins, rolling dice, or winning—or losing—at poker.

The gambler's fallacy doesn't apply only to gambling. Consider the case of parents who have four sons and are satisfied with the size of their family. But they would love to have a daughter. They would probably assume that the chances of having a girl would be much better on the next attempt. Wrong assumption. The chances are still fifty-fifty. What Reed is arguing is that a rational person, knowing of the gambler's fallacy, will nonetheless ignore it when engaged in a game of chance.

A story that bears out this point about superstitious belief describes two scientists who were dining together. For about an hour they had an animated discussion about superstitious nonsense and the lack of rational thinking by the general populace. Toward the end of the meal one of the men accidentally tipped over the saltshaker and spilled some salt on the table. Without hesitation, and without interrupting the conversation, he grabbed a few grains of salt and tossed them over his left shoulder. It's not easy to discard beliefs ingrained since childhood.

To quote Leonard Ashley from his *The Wonderful World of Superstition, Prophecy and Luck*: superstitions are "interesting for what they reveal of human nature." Ashley writes of the "stubborn insistence of people believing in the fantastical even when it has been proved it *ain't true*. Faith welcomes miracles. Superstition is a sort of faith."

Cicero called superstition a parody of religion, saying that it poisons and destroys all peace of mind. The great political philosopher Edmund Burke called it "the religion of feeble minds." Perhaps that's going a little too far. The sort of little rituals we all practice at one time or another can be harmless—although I personally can manage quite well without them. Knock wood.

Is showbiz superstitious?

Superstition seems to spread into every phase of human endeavor. The home, the marketplace, the building trades, the high seas, the sports scene, the wedding ceremony, and especially the gambling profession—each category has its own set of pet superstitions.

Some of the most superstitious people are those in the world of entertainment. Showbiz people don't attempt to hide their idiosyncrasies. Good and bad luck play a large part on the everyday scene. For those who might have occasion to be in a performer's dressing room, here are a few hints on what not to do. Please, don't ever whistle. Don't even pucker up. Whistling means "whistling up" failure for the upcoming performance. Don't look over a performer's shoulder into his or her mirror. Bad luck, without a doubt. I don't know where the whistling superstition originated, but the mirror *faux pas* stems from the old "evil eye" belief. If you look into a performer's makeup kit, don't tidy it up. Messy means good luck. Maybe that's why Junior keeps his bedroom that way. When actors or actresses are making their first entrance in a play, they will often listen to their shoes. No, the shoes are not prompting them on their lines. They just want to hear if the shoes squeak. If so, they can expect a good reception from the audience. Whether a performer is a cat lover or not, the cat is definitely a good luck omen in the theater. But backstage only. If a cat saunters across the stage during a performance, bad luck. But don't kick a cat. That alone is bad luck. Sometimes you just can't win.

Shakespeare's *Macbeth* is considered to be a very unlucky play by those in the acting profession. Those who are really superstitious can relate many strange incidents that have taken place during performances of *Macbeth* over the years. Many actors won't even refer to this play by name. Its lines, they say, should never be spoken offstage; the "Witches' Song" in particular should never be sung except onstage.

Speaking of singing, one of the most superstitious of performers was the great Italian operatic tenor Enrico Caruso. I couldn't begin to list all his superstitions. To name just a couple: he would not travel or wear new suits on Friday. He also had a great fear of hunchbacks and would do anything to avoid them. In addition to a host of personal superstitions, Caruso also shared all those common to actors and musicians, which adds up to quite a bundle of phobias. You probably know that actors like to peek out at the audience from behind the curtain before a performance. But do you know that it's bad luck to peek out from one particular side? And sometimes showbiz folk don't agree as to which side it is. So the problem is usually solved by the management—they place the peephole dead center. By the way, if you send flowers to an actor or actress, send orange, red, pink, or any other color—except yellow. Yellow is an unlucky color in the theater, probably because it was worn by the actor playing the Devil in medieval plays. You'll seldom see a play open at the end of the week. That, too, is considered unlucky. And of course no play opens on the thirteenth of the month. As in many superstitious beliefs, any kind of congratulations or good wishes are often taboo. Hence the expression "break a leg" instead of "good luck" when an actor begins a performance. As they say, "that's entertainment."

Sports rituals

When is a superstition not a superstition? When it is practiced by a baseball player. Athletes are notorious for being superstitious, and baseball players probably have more good luck charms and indulge in more rituals than any other athletes. The strange thing is that baseball players usually deny being superstitious. After a few minutes of conversation, however, they will admit to an odd quirk or two in their habits. Is it superstition? Of course not. "Just a little thing I do now and then."

The Toronto Blue Jays' first baseman, Willie Upshaw, for instance. "I don't believe in luck. . . . Oh yeah, Alison [The *Toronto Star*'s Alison Gordon] gave me a lucky coin to carry but it got washed away. . . . I just rub dirt off my bat when I go to the plate, that's all." I'll take your word for it, Willie, but isn't it strange that at the end of every inning in the field, when you trot in from first base, a ball is tossed out to you and you carry it into the dugout? That wouldn't be a little "good luck" maneuver, would it?

Outfielder Dave Collins doesn't mind admitting to a few superstitions. "I never change bats when I'm hitting well, neither will I change my batting gloves. And I always stretch my legs before I get into the batter's box." I tried to get Dave off the hook by commenting that the leg stretching is just a normal practice. His honest comment was, "No, that's a superstitious thing I do." The Montreal Expos players have learned one thing—never sit in pitcher Steve Rogers's place on the bench or there will be fireworks. Phil Niekro of the New York Yankees, the oldest pitcher in baseball, has accumulated the wisdom that comes with passing years. Apart from his highly developed knuckleball, Niekro has also developed a certain philosophy. "About the only superstition I have now is not letting myself get superstitious," he says.

Yankees manager Yogi Berra can't remember all the superstitions he had as a player, but as a manager he admits to not changing his clothes, his sweatshirt, or his underwear when on a winning streak. This is standard practice with many athletes. When asked about some of the idiosyncrasies of the greats he played with in the glory years of the Yankees, Berra readily recalled one that stuck in his memory—"Phil Rizzuto used to park his gum on his cap." How about DiMaggio? "Joe always made sure he was the last one to leave the ballpark after a game."

In his hilarious book *The Umpire Strikes Back*, Ron Lucian tells of the ballplayer who carries out the following routine when coming to bat: he walks to the first-base line and takes three practice swings; he returns to the plate and digs a hole in the batter's box with his left foot; he wipes the perspiration over his upper lip with his left elbow; he tugs the right shoulder of his uniform with his left hand; he pushes down on the top of his helmet with his right hand. Finally, he reaches behind his back with his left hand and pulls up his pants from the center. Now, if he gets a hit, he will go through the entire routine again the next time he's up. If he doesn't, he'll develop a new routine. Finally Lucian delivers the clincher: "While [the hitter is] going through the routine, meanwhile, the pitcher is on the mound touching his cap, banging his spikes against the rubber, pulling up his pants and tapping his belt buckle twice."

Tennis players are no exception when it comes to the superstitious ritual department. At the 1984 Players International Tournament in Toronto, former Australian great John Newcombe told me that as a youngster he would wear a certain cap in all tournament play. Wouldn't take it off for years. He finally lost it, then swore off all superstitions, except "I wouldn't change my sweatband on a winning roll, even when it was saturated—it was a bit stupid."

Vitas Gerulaitis admits he used to walk around the entire court when changing ends so that he wouldn't step over the lines, but says he doesn't do it anymore. Watching him get wiped out in the finals by John McEnroe, it occurred to me that perhaps he should resurrect that ritual. McEnroe? "I'll keep on doing the little things I do while I'm winning." John does a lot of winning. He must be doing something right. Watch him get angry if a ballboy tosses him the same ball with which he has just lost a point. He'll toss it right back.

Christmas customs

Many of you may not be aware of the various do's and don't's associated with the holiday season, or even of the reasons why some of the traditions were established. For instance, by stealing a kiss under the mistletoe you are carrying out a punishment once meted out to that plant parasite. You see, the mistletoe once perpetrated an evil deed, and the gods condemned it to look on forever while all the smooching went on. Mistletoe was once considered profane and was banned by the church in Britain. But, just as the banning of smoking meets with determined opposition today, the public responded by hanging it in their kitchens. In England there are still regions in which the people believe that if a woman is not kissed under the mistletoe before her marriage she will not bear children. And be sure to remember that mistletoe must be burned before Twelfth Night, January 6, or all the couples who kissed under it will be enemies before the end of the year.

If you're going to use holly for decorations, remember that it must be picked before Christmas Eve or your enemies will dominate you for the following year. Holly's name is derived from the word *holy* and symbolizes three different things. The red berries remind us of the Crucifixion—its prickles fend off the evil spirits—and its evergreen leaves represent eternal life. A bit of advice to young, unmarried females: walk backward to the nearest pear tree (you can recognize it by spotting a lonely partridge perched on its branches), circle the tree nine times, and you'll see an image of your future husband.

If you're going to burn a yule log in the fireplace on Christmas Eve, you can't stop at one. There must be as many logs as there are inhabitants of the house. If you have a large family, be prepared for a warm living room. The use of the yule log goes way back to the ancient days of tree worship, when Druid priests taught that the gods resided in the trees.

The recent appearance of Halley's comet raises an interesting point— was this the mysterious Star of Bethlehem? It has been calculated that this celebrated comet came into view from earth around 11 B.C.E. Allowing for some discrepancy in the recording of the date of Christ's birth, some astronomers assume that Halley's comet might have been the "Star in the East." This theory would seem to make some sense. In those days comets were considered harbingers of great events, and the coming of the Messiah had long been prophesied. Another theory holds that Jupiter and Saturn were in close proximity in 7 B.C.E., and they could have appeared as one exceptionally bright star.

Like many other holidays and festive occasions Christmas is just packed with superstitious beliefs and customs. Many of the things we do are deeply rooted in the past, their origins sometimes buried in the misty myths that have developed over the centuries. These customs are practiced in this enlightened age without, in most cases, any knowledge of why.

A fascinating book published by Prentice-Hall, entitled *A Dictionary of Superstitions,* informs us that the anniversary day of Christ's birth actually replaces the pagan feast of the winter solstice. The fir, which was the sacred tree of the Celts and the Germanic tribes, was celebrated on this day. Hence the use of the Christmas tree. French authors Sophie Lasne and Andre Pascal Gaultier warn that the tree must be burned before the twelfth night after Christmas, January 6, or there's a risk of a death in the family. This may pose a problem for those with plastic trees. January 6, incidentally, was supposed to be the original Christmas Day.

Did you know that the decorations that adorn the house and the tree also serve as talismans against demons? For the purists let me define the difference between a talisman and an amulet, just to clarify their meanings in the murky machinery of magic. Both are objects supposed to be endowed with magical powers to ward off evil. Both can be worn on the person or posted in the home. An amulet is an artifact that has general protection value—call it an insurance policy. A horseshoe hung over a cabin door is an amulet. A talisman is more specific. It has a one-shot function, to guard a specific area, object, or person against a particular unseen force.

Another book that gives us an insight into Christmas customs is General Publishing's *Knock on Wood*, by Carole Potter. Potter informs us of an interesting fact: the abbreviation *Xmas*, often supposed to be sacrilegious, is not. It comes from the Greek letter χ, chi. Years ago *X-mas* was used as a sacred symbol because it associated the cross with the holiday.

Potter explodes another myth. She writes that although we think that gift-giving at Christmas started with the gifts of the Magi, it actually started much earlier, during the Roman holiday that commemorated Saturn and the beginning of the planting season. What about Santa? The fat little man who gets stuck in chimneys was introduced in a series of Christmas cartoons published in *Harper's Weekly* from 1863 to 1866. Santa was based on Saint Nicholas, who lived in Asia Minor around 350 C.E. The legend of Saint Nick was combined with that of Kris Kringle, the nineteenth-century German character who brought gifts for the kids. The custom of sending Christmas cards was introduced in the middle of the nineteenth century. As Potter tells us, "It didn't become popular in the United States [or Canada] until a printer named Louis Prang took up the idea and marketed the cards, making a bundle of money for himself and creating havoc for the postal service." The association of the poinsettia with Christmas began when Dr. Joel Poinsett, a U.S. minister to Mexico, brought back the plant in 1828. The story goes that a poor little Mexican boy found the plant magically blooming at a spot where he had knelt to pray, and he immediately gave the plant to the statue of the Christ child. By the way, if you've read Dickens's *A Christmas Carol,* fear not—ghosts never, but never, appear on Christmas Eve.

Easter superstitions

Easter probably has more superstitions connected to it than any holiday other than Christmas. The eating of hot cross buns is a custom that originated when spiced bread was consumed at pagan spring festivals, in order to bring a year of good luck. When Christianity developed, buns came to represent the unleavened bread eaten by Christ and his disciples. The cross represents the sign he made over each piece. If you bake buns on Good Friday, hang on to any overstock. They'll never get moldy, and they'll prevent your kids from getting whooping cough.

Have you ever wondered how the bunny rabbit became a symbol of Easter? Well, the story goes that the ancient Teutons believed that rabbits laid eggs at Easter time. The egg has a long, long association with many superstitious beliefs. It has always been a symbol of new life and has also been used as a fertility charm. The ancient Egyptians and Romans used to give eggs as presents to symbolize resurrection and continuing life. The early Christians adopted the egg as a symbol of the resurrection of Christ, and painted them red in memory of his blood. This was the beginning of the custom of decorating Easter eggs.

Good Friday is a day associated with many superstitions. Flies can be eliminated from the house for the balance of the year by hanging a herring from the ceiling. Almost every variety of flower is surrounded by superstition. The lily has always been regarded as a symbol of purity and virginity. The Easter lily attained popularity on this continent at the end of the last century and is still the most representative flower during Easter.

We're all familiar with the Easter parade, when new clothing and new styles are on display. This custom originated from the time when one didn't change his or her clothes until the end of Lent. Getting rid of the old worn and tattered duds at Easter time gave people the excuse to purchase new regalia.

A final superstitious warning: if it rains on Easter, it will rain for the next seven consecutive Sundays. This prediction does not come from the weather office. It comes from a more reliable source—antiquity. Don't question it.

Magic was born in superstition

The word *magic* is one of many in the English language that have a variety of meanings. We speak of the magic of a beautiful sunset and the magic of a child's first, shaky footsteps. Then we have the magic created when we sit in a comfortable seat in Toronto's Roy Thomson Hall and hear the sound produced when Andrew Davis waves his magic wand over the Toronto Symphony Orchestra. All of these happenings produce an undefinable, "magical" feeling we all experience at one time or another.

I suppose the word *magic* produces an instant image to most of us in this realistic world we live in—the image of the stage conjuror levitating a woman and sawing her in half, or producing a shower of coins from the empty air. (Does air always have to be empty?) But the real meaning of *magic* is that of the magic of the occult and the superstitious, which dates back to the beginnings of man and is still with us. The practice of magic is, and always has been, a power trip. It is supposed to be the discovery and mastery of the forces of nature. But why is it occult, or hidden? The occultists will tell you that they want to preserve their mysteries, but that to guard them totally would be to spoil the enjoyment of them. Better to reveal them in obscure ways—through symbols, hints, and allusions. This is how the vast literature of the occult was produced and established. It was based on one basic premise—do not trust reason. Appeal to intuition, imagination, insight, and inspiration—all the intangibles.

There are a variety of theories as to when magic began. One is that it started with the animal hunters back in the Stone Age. The long sticks and spears with which these hunters accomplished the kill became the symbol of magic—the magic wand. The strange red liquid that spurted from their prey was the mysterious force of life. Even today magical ritual is symbolized by blood and sacrifice. Many animals were worshipped as gods, which made the spilling of their blood even more mysterious and magical.

One of the varieties of magic is sympathetic sorcery. One happening is related to another. A pin is stuck into a voodoo doll representing a person one wishes to harm. That person is sometimes affected by this practice, providing he or she is aware of it. The effect is psychological, but to the believer it is magical. Sympathetic magic can be traced back to prehistoric times. Paintings of animals adorn the walls of ancient caves discovered in many lands. Small gouges mar many of these drawings. Archaeologists have deduced that these gouges were caused by spears being stabbed into the drawings. This ritualistic practice might have ensured that the hunters would be successful in slaying real animals during the hunt.

People of prehistoric times, ignorant of the laws of nature, were forced to rely on magic ritual to earn their daily food. But when knowledge developed, some of those who became leaders learned to use magic to keep the population under control. This, of course, soon developed into religion. The ancient priests learned to practice magical effects. With the arsenal of methods under their control they influenced the masses for centuries.

The numbers game

They call it numerology—the occult significance of numbers. I call it the numbers game. For thousands of years humanity has been fascinated with the numerical system of divination and prophecy. The Bible is filled with numerical connotations—the Forty Days and Nights, the Seven Seals, the Twelve Tribes, the Fourteen Stations of the Cross, the Ten Commandments, and many others.

Probably the most devilish biblical number of all is 666, the number of the Beast, the Antichrist. Revelation 13:18 declares, "Here is the wisdom. Let him that hath understanding count the number of the beast: for it is the number of a man; and his number is six hundred threescore and six." Many biblical scholars think 666 is a cipher that stands for an ancient name. The Greeks and Hebrews often used the alphabet as numbers at the time Revelation was written in the first century C.E. Each letter was given a number, and the name of Nero, the tyrannical emperor, was matched by the number 666. Many believe it is Nero who is referred to in Revelation. On the other hand, the early Christians were able to fit that number to the names of many of their persecutors.

Here's a reference to the Bible that might shake you. Many numerologists believe that William Shakespeare worked secretly on the King James version of the Bible. Why? Because the forty-sixth word in Psalm 46 is "shake," and the forty-sixth word from the end of Psalm 46 is "spear"— and when the translation was completed in 1610 the Bard was forty-six years of age. The most familiar psalm is the twenty-third—and twenty-three is half of forty-six.

So it goes to this day. Numbers are used to justify all sorts of opinions and to fit all kinds of mystical theories. For example, the Great Pyramid of Gizeh in Egypt, also known as the Cheops Pyramid, was one of the Seven Wonders of the World. The occultists attribute several numerical "truths" to its dimensions. If you divide the height of the pyramid into double the length of one of its sides at the base, you'll get the figure 3.1416. This figure is known as pi, the ratio of the diameter of a circle to its circumference. It is also claimed that if you divide the base of the pyramid by the width of one of the outside stones, the result would be the number 365, the number of days in the year. If you multiply the height of the pyramid by ten to the ninth power, you get the approximate distance from the earth to the sun.

The number seven has long been regarded as a lucky, or unlucky, number. It has been used in many ways: in dice, you roll a seven to win; there is significance to the seventh son of a seventh son; you get seven years of bad luck for breaking a mirror; on the seventh day God rested; and there are seven virtues and seven deadly sins.

In 1968, just before Christmas, the numerologists had a ball with a forthcoming space flight, wrapping it in mystical connotations. It was the Apollo 8 mission, and the occultists pointed out that Santa Claus has eight reindeer. The three astronauts were compared to the biblical three wise men.

The numerologists noted that the number four was important to the American hostages in Iran. They were captured on November 4 and were in captivity for 444 days. They were released during the inauguration of the fortieth president. In the abortive rescue attempt eight were killed trying to rescue fifty-two. Subtract eight from fifty-two—you get forty-four. And, of course, *Iran* is a four-letter word. It's easy to see that if you take a whole assortment of numbers and juggle them enough, eventually you can find correlations. This is a game that anybody can play. That's why I call it the numbers game.

You simply must read about Dr. Irving Joshua Matrix, the greatest numerologist of all time. Dr. Matrix was concocted in the fertile imagination of Martin Gardner—author, mathematician, puzzle expert, philosopher, magician, and an old acquaintance of mine.

Gardner wrote about the adventures of Dr. Matrix in his "Mathematical Games" column in *Scientific American* for many years. Prometheus Books has now published a complete collection of these columns as

The Magic Numbers of Dr. Matrix. It is incredible what Dr. Matrix has
discovered about numbers. Remember the computer that goes mad in the
film *2001: A Space Odyssey*? It was called HAL. How was it christened?
Dr. Matrix explains: simply shift each letter of *IBM* back one letter in the
alphabet.

But this is just a minor numerological event. The famous "letter from
Dr. Matrix" to Martin Gardner after the assassination of President John
F. Kennedy is one of the classics of numerology and coincidence. Just
read this: "The two most dramatic and tragic deaths in American political
history were the deaths of Abraham Lincoln and John Fitzgerald Kennedy. . . . Lincoln was elected president in 1860. Exactly 100 years later,
in 1960, Kennedy was elected president. Both men were deeply involved
in civil rights for Negroes. Both men were assassinated on a Friday, in the
presence of their wives. Each wife had lost a son while living at the White
House.

"Both men were killed by a bullet that entered the head from behind.
Lincoln was killed in Ford's Theater. Kennedy met his death while riding
a Lincoln convertible made by Ford Motor Company. Both men were
succeeded by vice presidents named Johnson who were southern Democrats and former senators. Andrew Johnson was born in 1808. Lyndon
Johnson was born in 1908, exactly 100 years later. The first name of
Lincoln's private secretary was John, the last name of Kennedy's private
secretary was Lincoln. John Wilkes Booth was born in 1839. Lee Harvey
Oswald was born in 1939, 100 years later.

"Both assassins were southerners who held extremist views. Both
assassins were murdered before they could be brought to trial. Booth shot
Lincoln in a theater and fled to a barn (warehouse). Oswald shot Kennedy
from a warehouse and fled to a theater. *Lincoln* and *Kennedy* each has
seven letters. *Andrew Johnson* and *Lyndon Johnson* each has thirteen letters. *John Wilkes Booth* and *Lee Harvey Oswald* each has fifteen letters.

"The digits of 11/22 (November 22) add to 6, and Friday has six
letters. Take the letters *FBI*, shift each forward six letters in the alphabet,
and you get *LHO*, the initials of Lee Harvey Oswald. He was, of course,
well known to the FBI. Moreover, Oswald has six letters, and he shot
from the sixth floor of the building were he worked. Note also that the
triple shift of *FBI* to *LHO* is expressed by the number 666, the infamous
number of the Beast."

There's more in this letter. I suppose these matchups could go on indefinitely. But that's the nature of numerology. You've got to admit—it's entertaining. Do you believe in coincidence?

When hockey's hallowed Montreal Canadiens were on the verge of winning yet another Stanley Cup in 1986, several sports writers were quick to point out that they had won the trophy in 1946, 1956, 1966, and 1976. And, by golly, they did win it again in 1986. One writer phrased it this way: "Is this an omen?" At the risk of seeming to be skeptical, I'd call it merely a coincidence.

This numerological nonsense comes off a poor second when compared to the American presidential numbers game. That's the one about the presidents who have died in office. Every year since 1840 each president elected at twenty-year intervals has died while occupying the White House. Take a look at the record. The following U.S. presidents died while in office: Benjamin Harrison, elected 1840; Abraham Lincoln, elected 1860; James Garfield, elected 1880; William McKinley, elected 1900; Warren Harding, elected 1920; Franklin Roosevelt, elected 1940; and John Kennedy, elected 1960. It's a little depressing to note that Ronald Reagan was elected in 1980. Is all this mystical or coincidental? We'll never know—but it does leave a lot of room for argument.

Numerology is tied in with names and letters, in addition to numbers. Thanks to Martin Gardner, mathematician-philosopher-author, there are many interesting examples of this subject. Take the first moon landing in July 1969, for instance. The flight that accomplished this feat was Apollo 11. *Moon landing* has eleven letters. The liftoff was from Cape Kennedy. Guess what? It has eleven letters. In mathematics, eleven is the smallest prime factor of the number 1969. The landing was in the moon's Sea of Tranquility. *Tranquility* has eleven letters.

Neil Armstrong's immortal first words from the moon were, "That's one small step for man, one giant leap for mankind." You guessed it— exactly eleven words. Gardner facetiously comments that Armstrong later claimed he had actually said "for *a* man," but that "so strong is 11's power that the message was received without the *a*." When the three astronauts aboard Apollo 11 splashed down in the Pacific, they landed eleven miles from the recovery ship, the *Hornet*. When they were taken aboard the ship they were presented with buttons to wear, inscribed "Hornet + Three." Add the letters in *Hornet* and *Three* and you get the magic eleven once again.

Now if you look at the number eleven, you can also consider it as a pair of ones, which adds up to two. Two men were the first to walk on the moon. And *a* is the first letter of the alphabet. Isn't it strange that these men were Neil Armstrong and Edwin Aldrin, both of whom have surnames that begin with *A*? *NASA* also has two *A*'s. And if you write "Neil Arm Strong, Astronaut"—take the capital letters, and what do you get? *NASA.*

Whew! Are you getting breathless? But wait, that's not all. Edwin Aldrin has eleven letters in his name. And his youngest child, Andrew, was eleven years old at the time of the landing. And the boy's first and last names begin with the letter *a*. And how about this: Edwin Aldrin's mother's maiden name was Moon. And remember Michael Collins, who remained in the command module and kept circling the moon while the other two landed? Well, *Mike Collins* has eleven letters. And his last name, the word *command,* and the name of the command ship, *Columbia,* all begin with the letter *c*.

Had enough? Do you believe in coincidence? Perhaps you can now see why I'm not too impressed by the 1946-to-1986 feat of the Montreal Canadiens.

The occultists always come out of the woodwork after a tragic event. Just a few days after the shocking explosion of the *Challenger* space shuttle, a person telephoned me to point out the mystic properties of the number seven—and that there were seven astronauts aboard the ill-fated *Challenger.* The shuttle exploded on January 27, a date that includes the magic number. I suppose if you took the trouble to analyze various data associated with the mission, you could find a way to fit the number seven into seventy different places. That's the way numerology works.

Of course, the occult significance of numbers has its lighter side, too. The mystic number seven has figured in occult thinking for millennia. The Bible is crammed with references to the number seven—the seven years of famine and the seven of plenty; the seventy years of bondage; the seven pillars of wisdom; the seventy children of Jacob; the seven acts of creation; the seven thousand righteous in Israel; the seventy judges of the Sanhedrin; the seven days during which Joshua and the Israelites marched around Jericho; and the seven days in which the world was created, if the Sabbath is counted. The superstitious believe that a seventh child is lucky—and the seventh son of a seventh son will not only be doubly blessed but can also cure disease. If your birth date is divisible by seven you'll also be lucky. No doubt many married men and women have heard of the seven-year itch, or even experienced it.

The ancient Greeks and the Babylonians claimed that there were seven planets and that the sounds they made as they traveled across the sky were the seven tones of the musical scale—the music of the spheres. The Babylonians were great believers in the number seven. They divided the lunar month into four weeks of seven days. They believed there were seven gods and seven devils and that the world was divided into seven zones.

The mystic seven is still with us. After all, did Snow White have six dwarf pals, or eight? No, seven of course.

I wonder if we still believe in faith, hope, charity, prudence, justice, temperance, and fortitude—the seven principal virtues. There's no doubt that anger, envy, sloth, covetousness, lust, gluttony, and pride are still with us—the seven deadly sins.

SCIENCE
Creeping Irrationalism

Dozens of reputable scientists from the middle of the nineteenth century right up to the present day have been known to believe in the occurrence of paranormal phenomena. Such names from the past as Sir William Crookes and Sir Oliver Lodge, and such present-day scientists as Charles Panati, David Bohm, Jack Sarfatti, Russell Targ, Harold Puthoff, and other luminaries, dot the horizon as far as one can see. In most cases these illustrious people are quite sincere in their beliefs. Many scientists of the nineteenth century made strenuous efforts to investigate the fake spirit mediums who predominated in their day. Strenuous but futile. The intelligence and specialized knowledge of these well-meaning scientists were no match for the skill and subterfuge of the charlatans who masqueraded as mediums. The reader might reason that, well, it was another era—less sophisticated, more naive. Even intelligent people were more easily duped.

One need only look to the past decade to get an answer to that theory. Noted scientist John Taylor, professor of mathematics at King's College, London, was completely taken in by the "psychokinetic" deceptions of Uri Geller. He was so impressed that he wrote an entire book, *Superminds,* in support of the "Geller effect." According to Taylor, "There . . . appears to be control of physical processes at the atomic level. . . . In my view, the whole question of deception, either intentional or unconscious, can be dismissed as a factor." In a subsequent article in a scientific journal, Taylor was forced to admit that he had erred.

John Hasted, professor and head of the Department of Experimental Physics at Birkbeck College, University of London, wrote a book entitled *The Metal Benders.* He goes into great technical detail regarding the effect on the structure of metals exerted by the mental powers of Geller and other masters of deception. Hasted tested the ability of young children to bend metals with the mind—often allowing them to take the objects home in order to accomplish the miracle! One had to overcome the "shyness effect," as Hasted termed it, that took place when the subject was being observed. The professor was impressed by the final results.

Hasted endorsed the authenticity of teleportation, human levitation, poltergeists, and the thought photography of Ted Serios. Indeed, almost every paranormal phenomenon seems to have made a strong impression on this prominent scientist.

One might wonder about all this—the gullibility and self-delusion exhibited by these and other men of science. Well, not to wonder. As a professional magician with long experience in the field, I can tell you that no one is easier to deceive with trickery than a scientist, not even a child. The reason is simple. The scientist is trained to think in a straight line. Magic, or conjuring, is an underground art. Nature does not practice deception; the scientist simply cannot cope in this unfamiliar world.

One of the ploys of the occultists, of course, is to hang onto the coattails of science. They seize on every advance in science, on every facet of technology, attaching paranormal trinkets to the Christmas tree of rational deduction whenever possible. Actress Shirley MacLaine and magician Doug Henning, for instance, can give a speech at a moment's notice on the strange wonders of quantum mechanics, despite knowing very little about that complex branch of science. After all, quantum physicists often make the admission that they don't quite understand all the ramifications of discoveries in the field.

I've had many an argument with occultists who tout the wonders of auras produced by Kirlian photography, and it is almost always obvious that they have no knowledge of the natural forces that help produce the Kirlian photographic effect.

Some of these occultists, when confronted with evidence for the many cases of fraud in parapsychology, take great delight in detailing the fraud perpetrated in traditional science. That argument can easily be demolished by taking a look at it statistically. Just compare the limited number of major experiments in parapsychology with the countless number of those in traditional science, then check the percentage of fraud in each category. No contest.

It is important in this age of still-widespread belief in the paranormal to distinguish between science and pseudoscience. By pseudoscience I mean that grey area where scientific respectability is questionable. It includes not only many of the usual paranormal beliefs, but such controversial subjects as polygraph testing and handwriting analysis. If solid evidence for the viability of a discipline has not been established beyond a doubt, it surely cannot be called science.

One point should be stressed. It is a mistake to write off all paranormal claims as nonsense. The number of intelligent and educated people who believe in these phenomena is surprisingly high. It is necessary, however, to provide natural explanations for the grab bag of questionable and irrational beliefs. These explanations are available for those willing to seek them out.

Margaret Mead and the paranormal

Although she died in 1978, renowned anthropologist Margaret Mead's name is still embroiled in controversy. In his book *Margaret Mead and Samoa,* Derek Freeman takes issue with Mead's early field studies in Samoa. The book stirred up controversy in scientific circles. Freeman attacks Mead's methods of gathering and evaluating evidence, but basically he concentrates only on this aspect of her career. What the public is probably not too aware of is that Margaret Mead was very much interested in the paranormal. We might even say that she was rather supportive of things that go bump in the night.

In her studies of isolated peoples Mead seemed convinced that psychic abilities were quite common among them. In an interview she did with *New Realities,* an occult publication, Mead claimed that many children in isolated regions had psychic gifts but were taught to conceal them. In a column written for *Redbook* in 1977, Mead refers to the mushrooming public interest in astrology, numerology, and other occult matters. "On this growing edge of knowledge," she writes, "scientists are devising experiments that may—almost certainly will—give us, in time, new insights into the powers attributed to seers and clairvoyants, to those who have the power to 'see' auras, to communicate with plants, to dream or visualize events outside the bounds of time. . . . We are living on the edge of the unknown." In another column Mead answers the question, "Do you believe in UFOs?" with a resounding "yes." There is no question, she claims, that there are waves of visits of UFOs. One of Mead's arguments to support this claim is the standard one: "Sure, there are many UFO hoaxes, but that doesn't mean that some of the sightings aren't authentic." But why are the UFOs just buzzing around our planet all these years? Mead answers, "The most likely explanation, it seems to me, is that they are simply watching what we are up to . . . keeping an eye on us to see that we don't set in motion a chain reaction that may have repercussions far outside our solar system." Perhaps we needn't worry about the little green men landing and taking over, Mead continues, because the UFOs "may well be unmanned vehicles controlled from elsewhere in space." Nowhere in Mead's interviews or writings is there any indication of strong evidence to prove these claims.

In 1969, when she was president of the American Association for the Advancement of Science, Mead used her clout to have the Parapsychological Association accepted as an official affiliate of the AAAS. This resulted in a dispute when, ten years later, Dr. John A. Wheeler asked that august body to reconsider its decision. Wheeler felt that the psychic researchers were being given a respectability they didn't deserve. Wheeler comes with good credentials—he is one of the world's leading theoretical physicists and has enormous prestige in the scientific community. He really hit hard at the psychic researchers when he called parapsychology a "pretentious pseudoscience" and urged "everyone who believes in the rule of reason to speak up against pathological science and its purveyors."

Referring to the many claims about telepathy, spoon bending, dowsing, levitation, and other paranormalities—in short, the claim that where there's smoke there's fire—Wheeler declared, "Where there's smoke—there's smoke." The parapsychologists are still an affiliate of the AAAS.

A psychologist's naive view

When a scientist has written more than thirty-six books and seven hundred papers and articles, one has to have more than a little respect for his opinions. Such is the case with British psychologist Hans J. Eysenck, but my opinion of this leading social scientist is lowered when I read some of his writings on the paranormal. Eysenck has great prestige in the academic world. He has written and lectured extensively on the controversial subject of intelligence testing, and he stresses the need for strict controls in psychological testing. I can't understand how he reaches his conclusions when it comes to subjects such as ESP and astrology.

In *Explaining the Unexplained,* co-written with parapsychologist Carl Sargent, Eysenck takes a strong stand in defending many experiments in parapsychology that claim to have proven the existence of ESP. His viewpoint is incredibly naive. Many of the experiments he cites have long been shown to be scientifically unacceptable by informed skeptics. Eysenck credits Helmut Schmidt, a darling of the purveyors of the paranormal and not to be confused with the German opposition-party leader, with experiments that prove the existence of ESP. Eysenck fails to mention that Schmidt's experiments have not been fully replicated by other scientists—an absolute necessity in scientific research. He also fails to note that Schmidt has carefully guarded his data—has not made it available to other researchers. Schmidt, by the way, is the man who claims that cockroaches have psychic powers.

In his book Eysenck supports the case for psychokinesis, mind over matter. He refers to the psychic, metal-bending prowess of France's Jean-Paul Girard. Again, he ignores the fact that Girard was thoroughly tested by members of the Committee for the Scientific Investigation of Claims of the Paranormal, that he completely failed the tests, and that he has since retired from the psychic scene. These are just two examples from this book.

Penguin Books has published an interesting book co-authored by Eysenck, entitled *Astrology: Science or Superstition?* In this tome he tries very hard to stress the scientific viewpoint. Still, he fails to convince me of his objectivity. Eysenck agrees that astrological predictions are based on generalities, faulty human perceptions, and human gullibility. At the same time he states, "Of course, this does not mean there is no truth in astrology; it merely makes it harder to discover." After thousands of years the truth in astrology has not yet been discovered. But skeptical students of the subject have made a strong case that astrology is not a science but a pseudoscience—that it is based on a system of magic devised by the Babylonians and later developed by the ancient Greeks into a complicated, scientific-appearing mumbo jumbo of symbolism. Eysenck refers to this criticism of astrology but fails to pronounce his support for it. He does conclude that, at this point in time, "astrology is largely (but not entirely) a superstition." So, on the astrology issue, Eysenck sits on the fence.

I have to agree when Eysenck says, "We should not be dogmatic." Science never is dogmatic, it is constantly self-adjusting. But I must say this: In every book (and there are others) that Eysenck has written on the subject, he has supported and promoted belief in the paranormal. Many other scientists have done this. The public tends to accept the opinions of these scholars. The public is being misled.

Psychic detectives

The *Toronto Star* received several phone calls during the summer of 1985 asking why the police didn't bring in psychics to help locate Nicole Morin, the eight-year-old who vanished from her Etobicoke, Ontario, home in July of that year. The misconception persists that psychics have helped find missing persons. Despite all the publicity grabbed by these people over the years, there is still no documented evidence to back up their many claims. If there is, I'd like to see it.

Staff Sergeant James Jones of Metro Toronto's homicide squad, who is heading the investigation into Nicole's disappearance, discloses there have been calls by psychics to the police department offering their services. Do the police intend to use the clairvoyant bloodhounds? Jones only says that it's too early in the investigation. "I don't think it makes an awful lot of sense to bring in psychics at the moment," he says. Actually, it doesn't make sense at any time. Sure, when all else fails, desperation takes over.

There are negative aspects to the police following the directives of a psychic "investigator"—and many police departments have done so, although they are understandably reluctant to talk about it. The authorities become preoccupied with false clues and waste precious staff hours and public money following up useless leads. The families of missing persons are fed false hopes and suffer jarring letdowns.

Has there ever been a case in the Toronto area where a psychic has actually aided the police in finding a victim? Staff Sergeant Robert Strathdee says the police have frequently had offers of help from psychics, and "they've had theories" but never anything definite to act upon. Retired Ontario Provincial Police Commissioner Harold Graham recalls that the provincial police used a psychic back in the 1950s—but without success. In forty-one years with the OPP, Graham adds, "A psychic never to my knowledge has solved a case." Says veteran reporter Jocko Thomas, "In the fifty years I've been on the police beat for the *Star* I've never heard of a psychic helping to solve a criminal case."

There was an interesting case in the Toronto area over fifty years ago. Ambrose Small, a millionaire gambler who owned a chain of vaudeville theaters, walked out of his Rosedale home one cold December day in 1919 and was never seen again. For years there were rumors of foul play, but no body ever turned up. A Toronto detective in charge of the case, Austin R. Mitchell, brought in a psychic from the United States to help crack the case. Even back then, it seems, the home-grown product wasn't considered adequate. The psychic used a dowsing rod in the Rosedale ravine and claimed to have located the missing body. Steam shovels dug up acres of Rosedale. Ambrose Small is still missing.

The psychic detectives operate on a fixed formula. They will usually make a statement to the police that includes all sorts of vague generalities —many different possible locations, many unconnected details, a mass of information. When a case is solved the psychic can usually find that one or two of his prophecies seem to fit the facts of the solution. These will be added to the psychic's publicity brochure to help influence other gullible authorities to use his or her services.

The psychic bloodhounds are in the headlines again. The latest case of police consulting a psychic to locate a missing person is the one taking place in Florida and Alabama. This is the case involving beauty queen Beth Kenyon, last seen on March 5, 1984, in Coral Gables with mass-murderer Christopher Wilder. Wilder, you will recall, met his death during a shoot-out with New Hampshire state troopers in April of that year.

After a massive police search for the missing woman came up with no results, a phone call to the anguished parents in the Buffalo, New York, area stirred new hope. A psychic who refused to reveal her name claimed to have had a vision of Kenyon being held in a cabin in rural Alabama. On the strength of that call, the desperate father, William Kenyon, a businessman wintering in Pompano Beach, Florida, set out on an intensive search of the area described by the psychic. Buddy Aldridge, the presiding sheriff of the county involved, launched his entire department, plus a number of volunteers and a helicopter, into the hunt. After a fruitless week the psychic suggested another area. The search was switched to the new scene. To date, no results.

The odd thing about this story is that no one, in all the wire stories and radio and television coverage, ever questioned the legitimacy of the psychic. Why did she not wish to reveal her identity? Could it be that she would gladly have done so had the victim finally been located as she had predicted? A lonely cabin is a good educated guess. The psychic could still eventually be vindicated.

Judging by the questions I am asked at my speaking engagements, much of the public seems to be under the impression that psychics have helped solve many cases. Well, I'm busy on a search of my own. I'm still looking for documented evidence that a psychic has solved one case—just one—anywhere on this continent, at any time. My letters to various police departments have reaped no positive results in this respect. As a matter of fact, the Los Angeles police department, in order to squelch rumors, was once forced to release a public statement to the effect that at no time has a psychic assisted it in solving a case. A Canadian psychic, whose name I won't help to publicize, claimed to have assisted various police departments. When I appeared with her on an episode of the "Shulman File" television program, host Morton Shulman revealed that his staff had investigated the claims and found them false.

One of the most publicized psychic detective capers was that of Dorothy Allison, the Nutley, New Jersey, clairvoyant. In 1980 she volunteered to solve the mystery of who was committing the many murders of black children in Atlanta. With great hoopla Allison arrived at Atlanta airport. The event was covered by every major television network. "I'll clear up this case in a few days," she announced. After those "few days" Allison quietly left the city, claiming she couldn't function with all the publicity. No doubt she was in a hurry to get back home to Nutley to write her autobiography. When it was finally published it was labeled "non-fiction."

Later, an Atlanta police official revealed that the woman gave the police forty-two possible names for the killer, all incorrect. "She rode around in a big limousine, ate real well for three days, then went home," he said.

Transcendental Meditation and the "unified field"

When it comes to being a magical entertainer, Doug Henning has established a reputation for being right up there in the top rank of current prestidigitators. But I have to disagree with his opinions on the paranormal.

During a long and interesting discussion I found Henning open and generous in discussing his pet theories on Transcendental Meditation and the theory of consciousness. There is no doubting his sincerity when he says, "I feel that I'm a pioneer in exploring inner space." Henning speaks of meetings he has had with world-class physicists who have shared with him their "edges of science" theories on how meditation can help an individual "contact 'the unified field' . . . an infinite field of energy where time and space collapse." As Henning expresses it, "If we can bring our awareness to the level of the unified field, we can control the laws of nature with our minds. The scientists have proven that all reality is just a force field, which they call supergravity." When I asked where the documentation is for this claim, Henning didn't answer directly, but acknowledged that the theory could be proved only theoretically.

This brings us to the bottom line in this controversy between paranormal and traditional science. The people who advocate these way-out theories support them in a way that Henning states quite clearly: "Real magic (like telepathy) is caused by laws of nature that are unknown." They say there's really no way the methods of science can clarify these unknown laws. So what we are looking at is largely speculation and blind faith.

Henning was initially influenced by the Maharishi Mahesh Yogi, the founder of the TM technique, who induced the young magician to study with him in Switzerland twelve years ago. Since then Henning has practiced TM devotedly. Without a doubt Henning has also been strongly influenced by a number of prominent physicists who are into Eastern religions and/or parapsychology. I say this because the jargon Henning uses is almost word for word that of these scientists, whose writings I have been plowing through for years. When Henning quoted the great physicist

John Wheeler to me as support for some of this nonsense, however, he was doing what others of these people have been guilty of—distorting Wheeler's position. Wheeler is no supporter of the paranormal. Wheeler's own words say it best: "Now is the time for everyone who believes in the rule of reason to speak up against pathological science and its purveyors."

Can handwriting reveal character?

You've just received a handwritten note from someone you don't know personally. The script is tiny and tight. Aha—here's a person who is very secretive. The lines are quite uneven. Definitely an unstable character. But look at the flourishes on some of the letters. An artistic temperament, without a doubt.

It's quite common to associate handwriting with personality. And the official use of graphology, or handwriting analysis, is so common that most people I have met accept it as a scientifically proven practice. It isn't. Media stories would lead you to think otherwise. After all, graphology has been used in business and industry to help in promotion and hiring decisions; by judges in juvenile work concerning educational direction; by police in crime investigations; by lawyers in selecting juries; even in compatability studies of couples planning marriage.

A recent *Los Angeles Times* story out of Jerusalem reveals some interesting facts. Some apartment owners in that city are requiring rental applicants to submit handwriting samples before they can be accepted. At least one young couple declined. "It kind of turned us off a little," they said. "It seemed like reading tea leaves." Graphology experts in Israel claim that up to 60 percent of all Israeli companies use handwriting analysis to help identify unsuitable or untrustworthy job applicants. Handwriting samples are routinely requested in resumes. Arie Naftali, one of Israel's best-known graphologists, claims that the Israeli air force is one of his clients, and that Israeli intelligence reportedly uses graphology to monitor Arab leaders.

In Europe the use of graphology in all these various capacities has been going on for years. It is taken quite seriously in many official quarters. A majority of French companies use handwriting analysis in recruiting executives, as do many companies in Italy, Belgium, Switzerland, West Germany, and Spain. The *Times* informs us that there are nineteenth-century French books on the subject. That doesn't startle me too much. How far back does the recorded information on astrology go? Am I equating graphology with astrology? Not quite. Astrology is definitely a pseudoscience. The scientific credibility of graphology has not yet been proven, or disproven.

For some time I've been trying to get research information on graphology, but without success. Now how's this for coincidence: at the 1986 conference of the Committee for the Scientific Investigation of Claims of the Paranormal, held in Boulder, Colorado, I asked a psychologist if he was aware of any research on the subject. "Sure," replied Professor Edward W. Karnes, chairman of the psychology department at Denver State College, "I've just completed a study on graphology myself." And what were the results? "I'll send you my analysis."

Said analysis sheds some light on a controversial subject. Several hundred people were involved as subjects in this well-controlled study. In brief, some of the experiments proved nothing as to the validity of graphology. Others did give it some support. Karnes concluded that the experiments "cast considerable doubt on the validity of graphoanalytic evaluations of personality." The jury is still out.

Lie detectors and beating them

President Ronald Reagan raised quite a storm when he allowed his administration to announce stringent new security measures in late 1985 subjecting thousands of government employees and contractors to polygraph (lie detector) tests. When even cabinet members were included in the possible list of "testees," Secretary of State George Schultz came down hard on the reliability of the polygraph, indicating he would not sit for the test. "From what I've seen it's hardly a scientific instrument," Schultz said. "It tends to identify people who are innocent as guilty and misses some fraction of people who are guilty of lying." The government of Ontario followed the same line a couple of years ago when it banned the use of the lie detector as a tool for screening prospective employees or measuring their trustworthiness.

Some research into the subject would indicate that Schultz knows what he is talking about. The lie detector does not actually detect lies. What it does detect is stress brought on by emotional reaction to specific questions. This stress can sometimes be caused by lying—but not always. That fact alone makes the polygraph unreliable as a scientific instrument.

The polygraph is a measuring device. A cuff around your upper arm checks blood pressure. Wires connected to the fingers indicate changes in electrical resistance caused by sweating. Rubber bands around the body check breathing rate. Telling a lie will normally cause an emotional reaction—a person will sweat slightly, breathe faster and experience a rise in blood pressure. But the same reaction can be induced by certain dictates of the brain brought about by other thought processes.

A person who wants to deliberately beat the lie detector can easily do so. There are many known methods and new ones are probably always being invented. The trick is to alter the readings taken during the pretesting given before the regular questioning begins. Biting the tongue, pressing on a thumbtack hidden in one's shoe, digging a fingernail under the nail of another finger—these methods of producing sudden physical discomfort will cause stress, which will be shown on the lines being traced on the lie detector graph paper. The polygraph operator will initiate a series of "control" questions, in which deliberate, known lies as well as truthful answers are called for. The readings from these answers are then used to make comparisons with responses during actual questioning. A knowledgeable subject will use the ruses to make the control responses inaccurate—thereby knocking the whole process out of kilter.

Another weakness in the use of the polygraph is that the results do not depend so much on the readings as they do on the operator's interpretation of the readings. This introduces the factor of human perception. This is not science.

Police departments in Ontario and all over the continent do make use of the polygraph, sometimes with positive results. It has been useful in obtaining confessions in some cases. This could be interpreted as a form of coercion, which was probably one of the reasons it was outlawed in the marketplace in Ontario. In that area, of course, it was also considered an abuse of the employee's right to privacy.

According to mythology, Diogenes strolled the streets in daylight holding a lighted lantern—looking in vain for an honest man. I wonder if the old Greek philosopher would have any more luck carrying around a heavy polygraph machine.

Psychics, Inc.

If you caught the Phil Donahue television program on June 22, 1984, you saw two parapsychologists who are on to a good thing. Russell Targ and Keith Harary are branching out. Targ, along with Harold Puthoff, is the scientist who made a name for himself and Uri Geller at California's Stanford Research Institute several years ago. The two scientists set up the experiments that ostensibly proved Geller's psychic abilities. They put Geller on the psychic map by endorsing his so-called paranormal powers. The fact that knowledgeable skeptics later demonstrated that the experiments were a mockery of scientific method and that Geller was in fact a fraud had no effect on the blind beliefs of Messrs. Targ and Puthoff.

Well, Targ teamed up with Harary, a parapsychologist with similar beliefs, and they went into business—definitely a more lucrative way of channeling psychic energies than doing laboratory research. They helped form a company named Delphi Associates to "conduct further research and explore new applications of psychic functioning." The idea was to give psychic advice to business people and corporations. Surprisingly, there's a tremendous market for this type of operation.

On the Donahue show Targ and Harary claimed to have predicted prices on the silver market, helping to make money for themselves and, by implication, for their clients. They also make this claim in their book, *Mind Race,* published by Random House. As with most psychic claims, there is little documentation to back them up. The pair also have diversified by going into the oil-discovery field.

All this without the benefit of crystal balls which they, of course, deride. Instead they use the "scientific" method of "remote viewing." This means that a person is sent to some distant location and the psychic, miles away, gets a mental picture of the surroundings at that location. When I first got into this game, this was known as clairvoyance, but the jargon has turned scientific today. The terminology is changing to keep up with the times and to remove the stigma of mysticism and fortune telling. What all this has to do with the price of silver is beyond me.

Targ and Harary also pursue a line that has now become quite popular with the purveyors of the paranormal: You Too Can Be a Psychic. No longer do these people claim supernatural powers only for superstars such as Geller. Now everyone, but everyone, has psychic abilities—just work at it and the whole smorgasbord of telepathy, clairvoyance, precognition, and more will be within your grasp. In other words—try it, you'll like it.

The superpowers and "psychic wars"

I learned long ago to take psychic stories from behind the Iron Curtain with a grain of salt. But Jack Anderson, an American syndicated columnist, has written columns on the subject—and seems to be taking the "facts" he is quoting quite seriously. What he is referring to is the alleged Soviet research into psychic warfare—the use of the mind to spy on other nations and to influence the outcome of future conflicts. The United States, he claims, has been engaged in combatting Soviet psychic research with a psychic warfare program of its own.

According to Anderson, the Pentagon once considered developing an "anti-missile time warp machine" to blast incoming missiles into a prehistoric era where they would theoretically harm only a few dinosaurs and Cro-Magnons. Right now, he says, the CIA estimates that psychic research is being conducted in at least two dozen laboratories in ten Soviet cities. The Soviets are supposed to have developed "remote psychological monitors" that measure the heartbeat and breathing rate of persons thousands of miles away. This research would eventually lead to controlling the heartbeat and respiration of distant victims—a modern form of voodoo.

If you would like to explore this esoteric subject in greater detail, get Ron McRae's *Mind Wars*. McRae is an investigative reporter who works for Jack Anderson. According to the dust jacket, McRae "reveals the suppressed results of long-term, top-secret research carried out by the U.S. Navy, the CIA, and the nation's most prestigious research institutes."

McRae claims that the Navy has used psychics and palm readers to keep track of the movements of Soviet missile-launching submarines. One of these, a mystical "Madame Zodiac," in Washington, D.C., was allegedly visited every third Tuesday by a Navy commander to get the locations of Soviet subs off the East Coast. He crossed her palm with $400 each time.

I wonder how the Navy kept track of these subs for the next few weeks. McRae names another psychic, Shawn Robbins, who not only pinpointed the sub locations, but predicted their future movements. Robbins came highly rated as one of the top ten psychics in the United States. The authority for that rating, according to McRae? The *National Enquirer,* no less.

McRae details one of the problems encountered by the CIA in carrying out this program. The source of funds paid out to psychics had to be
protected. Now, how do you do that with psychics? A problem, indeed. If
the psychics are genuine they might learn the truth telepathically. The
problem was brilliantly solved. The CIA used two middlemen for psychic
funding—one who knew the CIA connection and another who believed
the a cover story. A classic caper for confusing a clairvoyant.

It is significant that certain members of the U.S. Congress take much
of this nonsense quite seriously. Congressman Charlie Rose of North
Carolina, a member of the House Select Committee on Intelligence, is
concerned that Soviet research will open a "psychic arms gap." He also
has suggested that the Soviets might use dowsing rods deployed in satellites to pinpoint the location of American MX missiles.

U.S. Navy Captain Joseph Dick, who heads the Defense Intelligence
Agency team trying to track down Vietnam GIs missing in action, claims
that psychics have made contact with prisoners in Cambodian jungle
camps. Former Army intelligence analyst Lt. Col. Thomas Bearden says
the Soviets have "psychic hyperspatial nuclear howitzers that could de-
nude the strategic capabilities of the free world with a single shot" by
transmitting a nuclear explosion instantaneously anywhere in the universe.
All this, of course, according to McRae—I kid you not.

I'd like to borrow a phrase from an article by Phil Klass in the *Skeptical Inquirer*—the foregoing deserves to be called "Gullible's Travels."

Auras exist—in the eyes of the beholders

Have you ever noticed how well behaved the kids are during December,
the gift-giving season? You can almost see the halos around their little
heads. There is a certain aura about them. Well, if you visit a psychic who
stares at you for a few minutes with a glassy look, don't panic. Some
psychics like to contemplate your aura. They'd like to convince you your
aura has different colors that denote your state of health—that there is a
psychic energy field that emanates from all living things.

This is not a new development. In early Christian times it was fashionable to paint halos around the heads of saints, something we've all seen on
religious works of art. We can backtrack many more centuries to find
Greek holy people sketched with the same auras around them. But how

did it begin? Most likely the ancient clairvoyants claimed to see these auras, and so the artists reproduced them. There's another theory that seems to make some sense. The ancient sun worshippers would stare in the general direction of the sun, then back at their fellow humans. Due to the phenomenon known as persistence of vision, they would seem to see an aura around the figure of the person they were looking at. This is the same effect you get if you stare at a lighted electric bulb and then at a blank wall. The stimulus of the light remains on your retina for a few moments, maintaining the image of the bulb in your perception.

Updating all this in our technological age, the Soviets have developed Kirlian photography. This is a method of developing photographic film to produce an aura around almost any object—a person's hand, a leaf, a plant. The object is placed in a high-frequency electrical field and then projected onto photographic paper. The developed picture will show an interesting pattern, or aura, around the object. Spooky-looking and seem-ingly unexplainable, this phenomenon sent the psychic supporters into ecstasy. "Here's a perfect example of what we see. Modern science has proven our case." Soviet electronics technician Semyon Davidovich Kir-lian became an instant celebrity. He was now the discoverer of "bio-luminescence," another word to add to the vast collection of psychic jargon. Kirlian photography was exploited in books, newspapers, and magazines, not to mention radio and television.

In 1975, however, a damper was put on this latest psychic craze. The National Science Foundation in the United States issued a grant to a group of science undergraduates at Gonzaga University to do a study of Kirlian photography. The students investigated Kirlian's claim that the "physical, chemical and dynamic characteristics of the objects were trans-formed into electrical characteristics which were represented on film in dynamic, colored figures." The group did careful, scientific experiments with plants. The conclusion? The colored patterns on the film were pro-duced by the water content of the object being photographed. The glow around the photographed plants was affected by the amount of water it contained. Kirlian was all wet.

The question remains—why do some people still claim to see auras? Some answers: 1) some of them are commercial, psychic charlatans and are simply faking it; 2) some are partly self-deluded and partly fraudulent at the same time; and 3) some actually do perceive auras around people, which is quite possible when one is hallucinating. The aura exists in the mind of the viewer.

Soviet "eyeless vision" is as phony as ours

Many extrasensory-perception stories have emanated from the Soviet Union in the past few years. They are not easy to check out. Those that have been investigated have come up with the usual explanation—fraud. In 1963 one of those tales circulated in the world press. A psychic named Rosa Kuleshova had been tested at the Biophysics Institute of the Academy of Sciences in Moscow. She was able to see with her fingertips— describe colors and read newspapers by touch while blindfolded. This is the phenomenon known as "eyeless vision." The Kuleshova case was hailed as a scientific breakthrough. One of the scientists involved in the experiment was ecstatic. "The fingers have a retina," he was quoted as saying. "The fingers see light."

But there was nothing new about this supposedly special power. Back in 1816, in England, sixteen-year-old Margaret M'Avoy made a name for herself by performing the same feats. There was a slight problem. She couldn't do it in the dark. Her supporters dismissed this minor drawback. "Everything looks black in the dark." M'Avoy is considered to be the first to demonstrate eyeless vision, and to claim it as a psychic feat. Countless others have duplicated the act, including many stage magicians who just do it as an entertainment feature.

An amusing version of this act took place in New Orleans a few years ago. A well-known mentalist-magician was booked into a theater in that city for a one-week stand. When he arrived in town he arranged for the staging of a blindfold drive through city streets. This means getting behind the wheel of a car, heavily blindfolded, and driving through heavily trafficked streets—accompanied, of course, by press photographers and TV cameras. This procedure is often used by mentalists—I've used it to good effect myself. The publicity generated by this type of promotion usually hypes the box-office take for the balance of the week. In this particular case it was Mardi Gras week and the city was in a festive mood. Many people were carrying huge clusters of balloons. Just before the blindfolded magician slipped his car into gear, with dozens of cameras pointed at him —the unexpected happened. One of the revellers, in the spirit of good, clean fun, tied a huge cluster of opaque balloons to the hood of the car, effectively covering the windshield. The blindfold drive ended before it began. It would seem that the superman's psychic vision could penetrate layers of blindfold—but not a bundle of balloons.

The methods used for eyeless vision are numerous. The peek down the side of the nose is still the most effective. Even when plaster is first applied over the eye sockets, a movement of the skin caused by grimacing will dislodge it. There are many sophisticated magical methods which I cannot reveal, but I will tell you this—if anyone claims true psychic eyeless vision powers, simply tape the eyelids down very carefully. God-given powers will suddenly vanish.

The greatest of blindfold acts was that of Kuda Bux, the Man with the X-ray Eyes. He hailed from Kashmir and made Canada his home for a number of years. His method of operation was never revealed to other magicians. His eyes would be covered with baking dough. He would then permit anyone to wrap layer after layer of cloth around his head until he took on the appearance of a mummy. He would then go through a series of tests including an uncanny exhibition of marksmanship with a rifle. I always had great admiration for Kuda Bux. But he never claimed psychic powers.

An obsession with hypnotic regression

Roy Bonisteel's long-running CBC-TV program, "Man Alive," touched on a controversial subject one week in 1985. I was given air time. Producer Larry Gosnell covered reincarnation from its historical roots, as part of religious belief, to the modern North American practice of hypnotic regression to past lives—both the parlor game and the exploitation of gullible believers by the inevitable charlatans.

Hypnotic regression to past lives has absolutely no scientific validation, however. As pointed out on the program by Dr. James Alcock, psychology professor at York University, "A great deal of the information that people produce under hypnosis is often just pure fantasy. And if the person doing the hypnosis subtly leads the hypnotized person to believe that he or she is back in ancient Egypt . . . the person is set up to believe that whatever comes into their mind next is reality."

The same opinion has been voiced by British author Ian Wilson, who has done considerable research on reincarnation. He has theorized that the hypnotist triggers the phenomenon of "multiple personality" in the subject, who then takes on the new role that has been imposed on him or her. This in itself is controversial, because multiple personality has proved to be quite rare in psychological studies.

In his book on reincarnation Wilson has gone into great detail on the writings of parapsychologist Ian Stevenson of the University of Virginia. Stevenson has done a tremendous amount of field work in India and other Eastern countries, relating a great number of claims of reincarnation. Wilson has investigated a good deal of these anecdotal accounts—and debunked them.

Stevenson is one person who should have appeared on "Man Alive." It is no fault of producer Gosnell that he did not. Stevenson simply refused to take part, despite much effort by Gosnell. His reason? Stevenson was wary of the way he might be presented on the program. My own telephone call to Stevenson got no further than his secretary. "He does not give interviews on the telephone," I was told, "because of errors and things that could creep in. He would be glad to check over whatever you write if you want to send it to him." Ian Stevenson would seem to be particularly careful about any possible criticism.

My own contribution to the program was a point I've made repeatedly—there is harm caused to certain individuals when they are exploited by regressive hypnotists, or paranormal practitioners of any kind.

There is also another harm caused by belief in reincarnation, and that is the often related belief in karma, the contention that one's present condition is the consequence of one's actions in a former life. This belief often results in a lack of compassion for people suffering from poverty and disease. A good example of this can be seen in India, where higher castes hold the "untouchables" in such contempt.

Perhaps the most provocative question was asked at the close of "Man Alive." "Why do you think it is," asked Bonisteel, "that so many people believe in reincarnation today?" Alcock responded that the traditional religions had somehow failed a lot of people. He also offered the opinion, with which I thoroughly agree, that science has weakened religious belief but hasn't offered an alternative to anxieties about dying.

A Gallup poll once showed that over 20 percent of North Americans believe in reincarnation. It's strange—at a time when many educated people in the East are abandoning their belief in reincarnation, it has become a fad in the West.

Science also has its share of scams

Readers of this column know that I zero in on the fraud and deceit in the field of the paranormal. But it's not only the pseudosciences that are guilty —science itself has its share (a much smaller one, though) of deception. Oxford University Press has published a variety of scientific scams in Broad and Wade's *Betrayers of the Truth*.

Among these cases is one that was highlighted recently in a TV Ontario docudrama—the case of Sir Cyril Burt, the great British psychologist. Burt was a pioneer in research on IQ, the study of human intelligence, and was the first psychologist to receive a knighthood for his accomplishments.

The great controversy about IQ has always been: does a person's IQ stem from heredity or environment? Burt was a strong proponent of the heredity factor. He exerted such a strong influence on psychological thinking in Britain after World War II that he was instrumental in restructuring the English educational system. Children were given IQ tests at the age of eleven. The results of these tests influenced their assignments to higher or lower qualities of education. All this was largely based on Burt's theory that a child's IQ was determined by heredity and firmly established by the age of eleven—and unchangeable after that age.

When this system of testing came under attack in the 1950s, after he had retired from his professorship at University College, London, Burt published a series of articles revealing "evidential data" he had allegedly gathered. Burt claimed he had set up a detailed study of sets of identical twins who, for various reasons, had been separated and grown up in different environments. The idea, of course, was that if these twins exhibited similar IQs and yet had been raised in separate environments, then only the factor of heredity could be involved.

The results of this study were astoundingly clear—so astounding that they began to raise suspicions among certain psychologists. The trouble was that they were too good. Psychologist Leon Kamin of Princeton University, who appeared on the TV Ontario docudrama, read one of Burt's papers in 1972, a year after the eminent psychologist's death. Kamin's suspicions were aroused when he noticed that some vital details were missing in the published experimental reports—such as who had administered what tests to which children and when. After further research into Burt's work, in 1974 Kamin wrote a book that, for the first time, pointed a public, accusing finger at the great psychologist. Many psychologists found it difficult to accept the charges even then. It wasn't until 1979, when Leslie Hearnshaw, a professor of psychology at the University of Liverpool, published his biography of Burt, that Kamin's charges were confirmed. Working from Burt's personal diaries, Hearnshaw found many cases of falsified data. It seems that when the results of his findings were challenged, Burt would sit down and invent data to support the results.

Meanwhile, the IQ controversy continues to this day. And, human nature being what it is, the scam will never die, whether in science or pseudoscience—or in human affairs.

HIGHER LIFE
Chariots of the Imagination

Since the dawn of time man has looked at the heavens in awe and in fear—and with hope. To this day, even with the immense accumulation of knowledge gathered by the science of astronomy, the great mass of mankind seems to look skyward with the same emotions. Evidence for this emerges whenever public opinion polls on individual belief in the existence of flying saucers are taken. Invariably a majority indicate some belief in the existence of UFOs. Even though the media interest in UFOs has declined in the last few years, history tells us that some day there will be a resurgence. Whether flaming shields, flying chariots, angels with spreading wings, or flying, saucer-like aircraft, we always see what we want to see somewhere up there. The objects we perceive depend only on the current beliefs of the era we live in.

Let no one underestimate the strength of belief, almost religious in its persuasion, of the true UFO adherent. Whenever I have expressed my skepticism of the existence of aircraft from another civilization buzzing Mother Earth, I have encountered bitter opposition from the ufologists. My writings on UFOs have prompted some of the most outraged letters from readers, sometimes bordering on the vicious. When voiced from the lecture platform, my opinions are invariably strongly and determinedly attacked from the floor.

I have never, to my knowledge, written a column mentioning

Stanton Friedman, the "flying saucer physicist," without Friedman firing off a letter to the editor taking great exception to my statements and opinions. Well, that's what a free press is all about. I once appeared as a guest with Friedman on a Toronto-based television program called "The Shulman File," one of the most highly rated programs in the Toronto area at the time. The host, Dr. Morton Shulman, was an outspoken, acerbic, well-informed man who insisted on having controversial guests arguing controversial subjects on his program. Anyone appearing on the show usually understood that they would be an open target not only for the other guests, but for the host himself.

It was on this program that I first saw Friedman at a loss for words. He had been promoting *The Roswell Incident,* a book written by Charles Berlitz and William Moore that Friedman had "researched." The book describes a crashed flying saucer, a supposed cover-up by the U.S. government, and an alleged secret stashing-away of the bodies of the humanoid alien crew. Shulman suddenly interrupted Friedman's recitation of all the gory details with, "I've read this book from cover to cover, and I've never read such a pile of shit in my whole life." He leaned toward a momentarily stunned Friedman to ask, "Have you ever been committed to a mental institution—never had psychiatric care?" All this with a smile, to lighten the impact. Friedman quickly recovered and went on to describe the invasion of UFOs that has enveloped us poor earthlings for years.

The ufologists' arguments about secret government cover-ups that endure for years are hard to support when you consider some of the really important secrets that have surfaced after only a short period of time. The Watergate affair and the secret arms deals between the United States and Iran are only two.

The huge statues on Easter Island, the stones of Stonehenge in England, the mysterious figures on the Nazca Plains of Peru—these and other artifacts have at one time or another been credited to aliens from outer space. Most likely they were the cultural expressions of human beings—perhaps, in some cases, as observatories of the heavens or signals to the gods on high.

The controversy raging in science about the possibility of intelligent life somewhere out there in the cosmos continues to give some legitimacy to the claims of UFOs in our skies. After all, if science tells us life may be out there, why not the possibility that they are already getting neighborly? How such life gets from there to here, if indeed it does exist, is neither here nor there, of course.

I personally would settle for the confirmation of intelligent life on *this* planet.

$10,000 for alien craft or passengers

Philip J. Klass is a man who puts his money where his mouth is. The world's leading expert on the investigation of UFO claims has a standing offer: he will pay $10,000 to anyone who can prove the existence of flying saucers from outer space. The terms of the offer, in brief, are these: the U.S. National Academy of Sciences must clearly identify a crashed spacecraft, or major piece of a spacecraft, as extraterrestrial in origin. And if anyone can show evidence to the satisfaction of that same institution that the earth has been visited by spacecraft from other planets, or if a bona fide extraterrestrial visitor appears live before the United Nations General Assembly or on a national television program, the offer also applies.

The key word in the last sentence is "bona fide," the real thing—E.T. won't do. On the other side of the coin, anyone taking up this offer must agree to pay Klass $100 each year until the event takes place—up to a maximum of $1,000. The odds sound good, if you believe in the existence of UFOs. But the number of takers can be counted on the fingers of one hand. And the interesting part is that the leaders of the various UFO groups, the ones who hype ufology the most, will have no part of this contract.

Philip Klass, when he is not occupied tracking down some of the major UFO claims, is senior editor for *Aviation Week and Space Technology,* a leading journal in its field. In a recent interview at his Washington, D.C., home, Klass told me that the mere sighting of an unidentified flying object is no longer of much interest to the news media. It's been overdone. "If a flying saucer landed on the White House lawn tomorrow it probably wouldn't cause much of a stir," he said. I suspect Klass had his tongue in his cheek on that one, but it is a fact that UFO reports are no longer world-shaking events. Today you've got to be abducted by the little green men or it's no ball game. That's right, abducted—and by an honest-to-goodness, fourteen-karat creature from another world.

One of the first and most celebrated abduction stories was that of Betty and Barney Hill, of Portsmouth, New Hampshire. It sparked a two-part series in *Look,* and was the subject of a book and later a movie. The incident allegedly happened in 1961, but it wasn't until five years later that it hit the front pages—and international attention. One night, so the story goes, the Hills were driving through the White Mountains of New Hampshire on their way home from Montreal when they spotted a light in the sky that seemed to be following them. They were quite frightened by this and reported it after getting home. About ten days later, Betty Hill began experiencing nightmares in which she dreamed that she and her husband had been taken aboard this alleged spacecraft and examined by alien creatures.

This story was kept alive by the Hills for two years—while Barney was undergoing psychiatric treatment. Eventually they were both sent to a Boston psychiatrist, Dr. Ben Simon, who placed them under hypnosis, and they both "relived" their abduction adventure. It was from this experience with hypnotic regression that the big story broke in 1966. Klass reveals that after intensive investigation and interviews with Simon, he, Simon, turns out to have believed that the hypnotic recountings were fantasy, not fact. This fact was never disclosed in the sensational stories that followed. Betty Hill was a great believer in the existence of flying saucers. Couple this with a vivid imagination and you've got quite a combination.

"Today," says Klass, "even a story like this would no longer grab much public interest. There have been just too many 'abductions.' An Italian night watchman claimed a world record, having been abducted by aliens four times. A Des Moines nurse topped that—she claimed eight abductions. A woman in Tucson, Arizona, was not only abducted, she was taken to another planet." Plaintively Klass asks, "What are they going to do for an encore?"

Barney Hill has since died, but Betty "still pursues the UFO enigma with relentless compulsion," according to *Omni* magazine. Several times a week she visits an area near her Portsmouth home where the UFOs unfailingly appear—to her. She has had, she says, as many as eighty sightings on some nights, but no personal boardings since her celebrated adventure of more than twenty-five years ago. Hill also claims that when she calls out to the UFOs they respond with blinking lights. A couple of police officers showed up one night and explained that the lights were merely from airplanes. Hill counters that claim. UFOs, she says, can disguise themselves as airplanes. UFO skeptic James Oberg, a member of the Committee for the Scientific Investigation of Claims of the Paranormal, suggests that they might also disguise themselves as police officers.

Telufologists

When a publicly funded television network inadvertently helps spread a preposterous story that misleads the public, I find it difficult not to complain. And when this same network has a program with a principal guest who makes a career out of spreading this nonsense, and then has other guests who are not sufficiently informed to cope with his wild claims —either the program's producers haven't done their homework or they couldn't care less about the integrity of the production.

In a January 1985 broadcast of TVOntario's weekly "Speaking Out," the guests were UFO pitchman Stanton Friedman, Royal Ontario Museum curator Chris McGowan, and former journalist Cameron Smith.

Friedman went through his entire litany of UFO claims, which he can recite by rote. When asked for evidence by host Harry Brown, Friedman cited landing traces of spaceships, abductions of humans by extraterrestrial humanoids, and the U.S. government cover-up of a crashed spaceship in New Mexico, as described in *The Roswell Incident*. All of these pieces of "evidence," and others, have been investigated and explained by experts on the subject. These explanations have been published in books and periodicals. Unfortunately, the general public—and the other guests who were on this program—are not aware of these explanations, which put Friedman in the enviable position of expounding his theories with practically no opposition from the other panelists.

One of the incidents described on the show concerns a man by the name of Barney Barnett, who claimed to have seen a crashed saucer with dead bodies at Socorro, New Mexico. Bennett is dead now, but there is a character witness to his testimony—Holm Bursum, Jr., a former mayor of Socorro. There was another alleged UFO landing in Socorro in 1964. It occurred on property owned by the same Bursum—that's quite a coincidence. There were several other "witnesses" mentioned in this weird and wonderful tale, each of whom had a record of way-out UFO beliefs. All their claims are accepted without question by Stanton Friedman. The whole story is so convoluted, unconvincing, and ridiculous that it is an insult to one's intelligence to have to debunk it. When confronting the purveyors of all this piffle, however, one cannot put up a good argument without knowing some of the pertinent facts, including the non-facts.

This story was just one small portion of ninety minutes of nonsense on "Speaking Out." When Friedman spoke of "regressive hypnosis," the method by which people have been coaxed to "remember" their direct encounters with aliens, without being challenged by the other panelists, again my blood boiled. Cool it, Gordon, I told myself. This isn't the first time, and it won't be the last, you see this sort of thing on TV. On the other hand, someone once said you can come down with a case of CDS watching this stuff—Credulous Dementia Syndrome.

Maybe aliens will put Eric Gairy back into power

Headline in the *Toronto Star,* October 23, 1984: "One year after Grenada invasion colorful ex-PM wants old job back—Sir Eric Gairy promises prosperity, peace." The despotic former ruler of Grenada is back in the news. His latest public statements reveal that his thinking hasn't changed much since the days of his leadership. "God has not made all of us to be leaders," he says. "All of us can't have the same psychic and spiritual powers. He has appointed me. And I have come back to do a good job." Ronald Reagan isn't the only leader to have God on his side.

Gairy had divine guidance long before Reagan took office. He was, and probably still is, a great believer in magic, mysticism, and flying saucers. When it came to UFOs, Gairy was not only a believer, he was a great promoter. He was able, in November 1977, to have the United Nations carry on a debate about UFOs. Gairy was not the first to bring up the subject in that august body. In 1967, atmospheric physicist James E. McDonald addressed a U.N. committee on the matter and asked for a U.N. investigation of "UFO activity." He was turned down. McDonald was one of the first scientists to propagate the theory that UFOs are the vehicles of extraterrestrial intelligences visiting our planet. His wholesale acceptance of the authenticity of thousands of sightings was not unlike that of most ufologists today. In 1971, the Ugandan representative to the

United Nations, a Mr. Ibingira, told a U.N. committee that he was concerned about UFOs interfering with human exploration of outer space. The United Nations was soon to issue a statement about outer space exploration. Ibingira tried to get a warning included in that statement—a warning to space-involved nations not to provoke or antagonize any UFO that might be encountered out there. Ibingira didn't succeed.

Eric Gairy got a lot further in the United Nations than did the aforementioned gentlemen. He was able to get Secretary-General Kurt Waldheim to meet with him and several other ufologists to organize a steering committee to plan U.N. UFO research. This committee included such figures as J. Allen Hynek, Jacques Vallee, Stanton Friedman, and Gordon Cooper. Hynek, of course, was and is the high priest of ufology. Vallee has written several books on UFOs, including *The Edge of Reality,* co-authored with Hynek. Vallee is a computer scientist who started off writing science fiction. To me his UFO books are fictional science. My old friend and adversary, Stanton Friedman, continually dwells on the "Cosmic Watergate"—government cover-ups of UFO sightings and landings. Cooper is one of several astronauts who, after returning from space, adopted a new world view. He became intrigued by the UFO phenomenon. This steering committee, unfortunately, couldn't steer the United Nations into UFO research.

Gairy lost his job as Grenada's prime minister in 1979. During one of his numerous trips to New York, Maurice Bishop initiated a coup and took power. The new rulers claimed to have discovered evidence in Gairy's residence of paraphernalia used in voodoo and witchcraft. Gairy must have been disappointed that a formation of friendly UFOs did not swoop down on Grenada to reclaim his lost authority for him. But now he's back. It will be interesting to see if he can psychically will himself back into power.

UFOgate

It can't be done. Governments cannot keep a secret indefinitely. I state this categorically and emphatically. We read daily about Brian Mulroney's new government operating in a hush-hush manner, banning ministers from spilling the goods on threat of excommunication. Well, it won't work. Leaks have a way of developing and enlarging. The truth will out.

That's why I can't agree with my old friend Stanton T. Friedman, known in the ufology trade as the "flying saucer physicist." For some strange reason he has given up on physics and taken to lecturing all over the continent on The Coming—of UFOs.

Friedman shares a trait with other lecturers (even me)—he's not averse to publicity. So when a Toronto newspaper published an article on the fading interest in flying saucers, followed by a tongue-in-cheek editorial on the subject, Stanton wasn't laughing. He brought his case to the Ontario Press Council. It ain't true, he complained. The UFOs are still out there in terra firma's suburbia, but our governments are sitting on the saucer story. They won't tell. They've been covering up the facts all these years.

Of course most ufologists have been taking this line, but Friedman is in the forefront. It was he who coined the phrase "Cosmic Watergate." But Stanton, Watergate blew its cover years ago. Who's holding down the lid on the UFOs these many decades? If the U.S. government knows of the existence of UFOs, why are they wasting millions of dollars on the NASA program, using such primitive means as rockets for space exploration? Why not use the technology of the captured UFOs you claim the government is hiding? It is revealing that when the U.S. congressional panels were investigating the intelligence agencies, Friedman was challenged by UFO investigator Philip J. Klass to bring his cover-up evidence to the panels in Washington, at Klass's expense—and Friedman declined. His reason for throwing away the chance of his career? "The pressure has to come from somebody else other than me."

One of the most notorious government cover-ups was supposed to have taken place when "an extraterrestrial spaceship" crashed in Roswell, New Mexico, in July 1947. This resulted in a book, *The Roswell Incident,* by William Moore and Charles Berlitz. This is the same Berlitz who wrote that masterpiece of fictionalized fact, *The Bermuda Triangle.* Friedman was the "chief of research" for *The Roswell Incident.* He still claims that the U.S. government stowed away the spacecraft wreckage along with the remains of the little green men. It's been almost forty years since this event—and no leaks. I hope they kept the little men on ice.

A follow-up to this bizarre tale took place in mid-1984. A citizens' group filed a lawsuit against the U.S. Air Force to compel it to release the remains of extraterrestrial aliens being held secretly. A federal judge in Washington dismissed the suit. Perhaps they weren't kept on ice, after all.

I enjoyed the later comment by a Pentagon official. He said that they could not disclose the existence of the remains because of difficulties in locating the next of kin.

Friedman's complaint to the Ontario Press Council was dismissed. But all is not lost. After all, this column is all about Stanton T. Friedman.

Of Nessie and flying saucers

With another Hallowe'en approaching, goblins, spooks, and monsters will soon be roaming the streets again. But one monster hangs around all year —and has remained with us for many years. That's Nessie, the Loch Ness monster. It (she? he?) has been the subject of countless books, articles, broadcasts, and scientific expeditions. Loch Ness, near Inverness in the Scottish highlands, is one of the largest freshwater lakes in Europe in terms of volume. It is over six hundred feet deep in spots—definitely not recommended for wading. Add the murkiness of its water and the heavy vegetation surrounding the lake and you have an air of mystery attached to this body of water. This has helped develop the myth of the monster that haunts its depths. The myth is perpetuated by sightings every spring, when the tourist season begins. For some strange reason the local chamber of commerce raises no objections.

There's some similarity between the myth of the UFO and that of the Loch Ness monster. The Nessie sightings really proliferated in the 1930s and the myth has grown ever since. The modern flying saucer myth grew from 1946 on. But monster sightings in Loch Ness were first reported about fifteen hundred years ago by the Irish poet St. Columba. UFO sightings go back to antiquity.

We know that UFOs are usually described as cigar-shaped or saucer-shaped objects. But what does Nessie look like? It is said to be gray or brownish in color, with a long, giraffe-like neck and a small head. The body has several humps with large, projecting fins. The length of the creature is estimated at about twenty or thirty feet; some say three hundred feet. Reasonably close estimates, give or take a few hundred feet.

So there you have it—just an ordinary, everyday, run-of-the-mill monster. The first sighting, which really kicked off the modern legend, was in 1933. A Mr. and Mrs. John Mackay reported to the *Inverness Courier* that they had seen an "enormous animal" in the water. Just by chance, the Mackays happened to own a local inn that is still a major center for monster hunters.

Of all the people who have organized expeditions to verify the existence of Nessie, Tim Dinsdale has to be the most dedicated. He has written a book, *Loch Ness Monster,* which has gone into four editions over a period of twenty years. It has been regularly updated, and goes into great detail about Nessie sightings, statistics, and photographs. If you believe in monsters, *Loch Ness Monster* can be very convincing. Dinsdale is billed as an aeronautics engineer, author, photographer, and monster hunter.

Photographs of Nessie have much in common with the multiplicity of photographs taken of UFOs. A photo can easily be misinterpreted or even faked. To ask someone to accept a picture as strong evidence is to ask them to suspend their disbelief. Some cryptozoologists admit there may be some form of known creatures living in Loch Ness—perhaps some form of giant eel or sea otter. But none has ever been captured. That highlights another striking similarity between UFOs and the Loch Ness monster— never has a flying saucer, or part of a saucer, been captured or found on earth. Neither has the monster, in all these years, ever been caught and exhibited by man. Perhaps we simply haven't yet discovered the proper bait. We're still left with the basic question—is Nessie a monstrous fish or a fishy monster?

Desert markings still mystify

Anyone who has not read Erich von Däniken's *Chariots of the Gods?* has surely heard of it. It has sold in the millions. The theory that von Däniken puts forth captures the imagination. Between ten thousand and forty thousand years ago, he says, astronauts from a superintelligent civilization arrived on earth and impregnated the early humans, producing humans as we know them today. Later the space visitors returned and taught us the basics of technology.

In *Chariots of the Gods?* and other books that followed, von Däniken gives many examples of what he calls the "evidence" that proves his theory. One of the most interesting, and perhaps the best known, is the famous desert markings on the Nazca plain of Peru. On a 200-square-mile plateau about 250 miles southeast of Lima is a series of markings that, when viewed from the air, is spellbinding. It seems that sometime millennia ago the natives of the plain etched patterns on the desert floor. To do this they removed the dark, surface stones, exposing the light-colored soil beneath them. These lines, thirteen thousand of them, extend for miles. They form a number of geometric shapes and almost eight hundred large animal figures—birds, fish, lizards, a monkey, and a spider. Von Däniken claims that these lines represent airfields that the ancient astronauts built for future landings.

There are several reasons for rejecting this theory, even if we accept the premise that aliens have landed on our planet. First, many of the lines, or "landing strips," run right into the sides of hills and mountains. Second, aircraft would certainly get stuck in the soft, sandy soil. Third, and the most convincing reason, is that a spacecraft would not require a landing strip. Our present technology, surely inferior to that of a super-race that has mastered interplanetary travel, already can land spacecraft vertically.

If we reject von Däniken's wild theory, what then can we say about the origin of these strange drawings? A more conventional theory is that these were ancient Inca roads, but their nature, size, and position seem to rule that out. Professor Paul Kosok of Long Island University first photographed the Nazca lines from the air in 1939. In 1941 he noticed that one of the long lines pointed directly toward the setting sun on the day of the winter solstice. He later confirmed that other lines indicated the solstices and the equinoxes. Here was a theory suggesting a massive, two-dimensional astronomical calendar.

Marla Reiche, a German mathematician, devoted thirty-nine years of her life to studying the Nazca lines. With the help of the Peruvian air force she also took aerial photographs. She too was convinced the lines represented an astronomical observatory, probably built by a pre-Inca civilization around 1000 B.C.E. to calculate the coming of the rains needed for the crops. But why the figures of birds and other animals? An interesting hypothesis has emerged. It is known that the ancients worshipped the sun and moon—and, gazing up at the night sky, put their own interpretation on the star constellations. For instance, what we call the "Big Dipper" they might have seen as the figure of an animal they were familiar with.

If one superimposes the ancient constellations visible from the Southern Hemisphere over the figures on the ground, some of them match. Could the people of that era have been trying to catch the attention of their gods by reflecting the messages they thought were being flashed by the sky?

The power of the ancients

If you are not a reader of *Omni,* the science magazine for the masses, you are missing a highly educational section titled "Anti Matter." It deals with wild and woolly claims of paranormal and other far-out events.

The best item so far concerns one fellow's theories about the temples of antiquity, which were understood to be monuments to the gods. Not so, says inventor Paul Brown of Bliss, Idaho. "They housed huge electric dynamos that powered society much like the generators of today." The proof for this theory? Well, you may have seen the circular drawings called mandalas. The mandala is used as a motif to symbolize the universe and the power of the gods. Wrong, says Brown. The mandalas are actually electrical schematic drawings. The ancients left them behind to show how they built their generators. Strangely, archaeology has not yet come up with a discarded ancient electrical generator. Shocking.

Look closely at your next-door neighbor

If you're expecting to see the little green men alight when the flying saucers land in force, forget it. They're already here. But they're not little. They look much like you and me, and they are circulating among us right now. Your next-door neighbor could be one of them—or perhaps the young woman at the supermarket check-out counter. Please don't take my word for this—read General Publishing's *Aliens Among Us,* by Ruth Montgomery, and you'll get the full story.

Montgomery is the author of several books on psychic matters and a former Washington columnist on politics and world affairs. It was Montgomery who put prognosticator Jeane Dixon on the map by writing *The Gift of Prophecy* in 1965, in which Dixon was highly touted for her predictive abilities. For those who wonder where Montgomery gets all the strange information revealed in her current book, the foreword enlightens us. Montgomery has "guides," "souls like ourselves who have had many previous lifetimes but are currently in the spirit plane."

There's no doubt that the possibility of life on other planets somewhere out there does exist. Montgomery quotes some noted scientists on that score. For example, astronomer Richard Terrile, of the Jet Propulsion Laboratory in the United States, once said, "The time will come when we realize that we're not the center of the universe. The galaxy may be teeming with life. There may be millions of civilizations." Montgomery's book takes this concept a giant step forward. She says that representatives of some of these civilizations have already visited earth and have taken out local citizenship. They arrived on UFOs, of course. And what is interesting is that Montgomery claims that UFOs have now taken on different shapes than the conventional and accepted saucer-shaped discs. Some, she says, are now boomerang-shaped. This would seem quite logical to me. Would not the boomerang shape enable the craft to return more readily to its point of origin? Then again, maybe not all aliens have arrived on UFOs. As the author writes, "A high-minded soul in the spirit realm can exchange places with another soul who wishes to depart the physical plane, by entering as a walk-in." And these "walk-ins" are everywhere among us.

Montgomery relates another theory of alien transport as revealed by her guides. "Spaceships are nonessential for the conveyance of spacelings to earth. . . . [The aliens] are able to reassemble the atoms of their bodies within our atmosphere so that they become visible, physical beings, and can as easily disassemble the atoms when they wish to disappear." I'd like to point out to Montgomery's guides, wherever they are, that this is not an original concept. Sir Arthur Conan Doyle, creator of Sherlock Holmes and a dedicated believer in spiritualism, accused Harry Houdini of perpetrating his miraculous escapes by exactly the same method.

The travails of the ufologists

In an address before the 1985 symposium of the Mutual UFO Network in St. Louis, Missouri, Stanton T. Friedman raked this humble columnist over the coals. MUFON is a worldwide organization dedicated to "resolving the UFO mystery and all of its ramifications in a scientific manner," according to the *Encyclopedia of UFOs*. Many of its members are scientists, engineers, researchers, and authors who share a common interest, if not belief, in flying saucers. Friedman, whom I have written about and sparred with on television, is a nuclear physicist who has become a full-time lecturer on UFOs. He doesn't equivocate. The saucers have landed, he says—they've been buzzing around us for some time. His evidence for this is voluminous—very shaky, but voluminous.

When Friedman takes the time to launch a vituperative attack on me personally before this august symposium—sarcastically calling me Canada's gift to debunkdum, among other things—I can feel nothing but pride and satisfaction. I learned long ago that in the world of debate, when an opponent descends to a personal attack, his arguments have usually petered out. During the address, the flying saucer physicist blasted the "negativists" who have "vigorously, sometimes viciously, attacked the notions that some UFOs are extraterrestrial spacecraft and that governments have covered up the best data." We negativists are accused of replacing science with pseudoscience and using myths instead of facts. This is a clear case of the pot calling the kettle black. As a negativist I'm in good company—sharing the brunt of Friedman's attack with Philip Klass, senior editor of *Aviation Week and Space Technology* and an internationally recognized authority on the subject of UFOs. Klass has investigated and debunked some of the major UFO claims over the years.

I can understand Friedman's antagonism to Klass and myself, but I'm really surprised at his public spearing of J. Allen Hynek, the guru of ufologists, at the same symposium. Hynek was the technical adviser on the blockbuster film, *Close Encounters of the Third Kind*—as a matter of fact, he coined the phrase. Hynek too is included among "the noisy negativists," for making statements that don't agree with Friedman's theories. This is like Gromyko accusing Gorbachev of being a capitalist.

I have a feeling that some of the ufologists are getting too sensitive about the drop in public and media interest in their pet theories. Their movement is in big trouble. One of the largest UFO groups, the National Investigations Committee on Aerial Phenomena, has gone belly up. No more funds. The Aerial Phenomena Research Organization has discontinued its newsletter. Not a good sign (or should I say "omen"). Even Hynek's prestigious Center for UFO Studies is hinting that it would be useful to have a few extra bucks donated to the cause. The ufologists have always griped that governments are cold-hearted when it comes to granting dollars for UFO investigation. They simply can't understand why the taxpayers won't ante up a few million here or there to expand this worthwhile field of scientific research. If "Star Wars" merits billions, how about shelling out a few dollars to greet our other visitors from space?

Perhaps, if Friedman is right and the little green men are visiting us, this would be our only salvation. As Ronald Reagan recently remarked to Gorbachev at Geneva, "If suddenly there was a threat to this world from another species from another planet in the universe, we'd forget all the little local differences that we have between our countries and we would find out once and for all that we really are all human beings here on this earth together." But what if the ugly little humanoids were friendly?

The dean of ufology has passed away

The UFO movement lost its leader in May 1986, and his passing seems to have coincided with a decline in world interest in the flying saucer craze. The death of astronomer J. Allen Hynek in his seventy-sixth year was somehow symbolic. Hynek was born and he died in the only years out of the last hundred that Halley's comet was visible from our planet.

In the 1950s Hynek was associate director of the Smithsonian Astrophysical Observatory in Cambridge, Massachusetts, where he was responsible for tracking the earth's first artificial satellite. From that position he went to Northwestern University in Illinois, where he assumed a professorship in astronomy, remaining there for many years.

During the 1950s and 1960s, when the flying saucer flap was reaching its peak, the U.S. Air Force enlisted Allen Hynek to head Project Blue Book. The project had been initiated to investigate the many reported sightings of UFOs. The military was more than a little nervous about these reports. Perhaps more serious than the fear of extraterrestrial craft was the possibility of some new aircraft design by the Soviets. Hynek, an astronomer and scientist, was quite skeptical about the many claims, and his investigations shot down most of them. But it seems that the few sightings for which there were no apparent explanations weighed on his mind.

Hynek's views gradually began to change. In 1973 he established the Center for UFO Studies (CUFOS) in Evanston, Illinois, which immediately became a gathering house for UFO sightings worldwide. Computers were installed, claims were analyzed and given ratings for authenticity, or were discounted. For the first time the investigation of the flying saucer was given a more or less scientific patina, but it was becoming more and more apparent that Hynek's skepticism was gradually fading. Because of the scientific aura at CUFOS, Hynek's endorsement of many controversial sightings raised the hackles of true skeptics.

At some point Hynek began to take another tack. No, he didn't believe in the "nuts and bolts" theory—that actual spacecraft could traverse the immense distances from other worlds—but he did have another theory. UFOs were perhaps part of another reality, a parallel universe. They perhaps appeared spontaneously out of that other reality, then disappeared into it without a trace. But, of course, Hynek did concede that they sometimes left physical traces.

This was part of his "Close Encounters" terminology. It was Hynek who coined the phrase "Close Encounters of the First, Second, and Third Kinds." Encounters of the "First Kind" would be UFOs seen at close range. Those of the "Second Kind" would be actual physical traces left by UFOs, such as scorched grass or broken tree twigs. Encounters of the "Third Kind" would be reports of sightings of actual occupants of the spacecraft. Thus was born the film *Close Encounters of the Third Kind,* a movie for which Hynek served as technical consultant.

My first encounter with Hynek, although it wasn't a close one, was when he did the commentary on an award-winning, four-hour radio program on UFOs broadcast on Montreal's CJFM. In the four taped hours, Isaac Asimov and I were the only skeptics given a few minutes to air our views. The balance, all commentaries by ufologists, was distinctly out of balance. Hynek was given the opportunity to hear the taped comments of Asimov and myself and then proceeded to attempt to demolish our arguments, without, of course, our having a chance to answer.

I last saw Hynek at a presentation he and others gave at a scientific conference in New York. When the panel convened at the close for questions from the audience, Hynek had vanished. I never did get a chance to interview him directly. An interesting and controversial figure has departed the scene.

HEALING
Bring Back This Sinner's Sight

It is easily the most pernicious of claims of the paranormal. It can give people false hope. It can induce people to throw away their medicines. It lines the pockets of charlatans masquerading as men of religion. This is faith healing.

One must look at the practice of psychic or faith healing from two perspectives—the religious and the medical. The term originated in religious teachings and dates back to the beginnings of recorded history and probably beyond. *Faith* is the key word, and it does account for many so-called miracles from biblical times to the present day.

The mind-body effect so often referred to in medical journals and in the press today is considered the principal cause of the majority of faith healing "cures." More and more is being learned about the effect of the brain on the physiology of the body and vice versa. It seems that certain non-organic illnesses can be cured by suggestion and that the symptoms of more serious ones can be similarly (if temporarily) reduced. The experienced faith healer, or psychic, or shaman, or witch doctor, has learned to take advantage of this phenomenon.

This does not mean that recovery is a miracle or that it engages supernatural powers, as the faith healers would have us believe. Indeed, the trained medical therapist can produce the same results, and more consistently. More importantly, such a professional knows when to employ such techniques, and when other diagnoses and treatments are preferable.

I have met and interviewed many a faith healer, and it is important to realize that they often do have a self-deluded belief in their own powers. They incorrectly assume, and convince their patients to believe, that the recovery has been caused by supernatural powers. There is no doubt that their influence is also aided by the mental and emotional state of their patients. Fatigue and anxiety are powerful factors that can interfere with rational thought and increase gullibility.

Faith healing as practiced by such television evangelists as Peter Popoff, W. V. Grant, and others falls into a separate category. These people are out-and-out charlatans. They pre-select the patients they will "heal," and they install plants in their audiences. They perpetrate premeditated fraud.

When confronted by believers in the miracles of faith healing, I am often asked to explain the many miracles claimed to have taken place in Lourdes, France. Many labor under the misconception that miracles are a daily occurrence at that shrine. They may be surprised to learn that at last count there have been since 1858 a total of only eighteen miracles, so-called, at Lourdes. This with approximately three million visitors each year.

The controls at Lourdes are quite stringent. A medical board sits there. Certain regulations apply. First, it must be proved that an ailment really existed; second, it must be cured within a few hours, and it must be shown that no medical treatment was applied; finally, the cure must last for several years. I have found it impossible to confirm whether the eighteen miracles claimed at Lourdes were determined according to the established guidelines, but if you apply the above regulations to the claimed psychic healings of organic diseases across our own continent, you can probably discount each and every one.

Of all the columns and features I have written for the past number of years, none has received more determined and organized opposition than the two columns I wrote on the chiropractic profession. Shortly after the second column appeared I received a call from the *Toronto Star* asking if I could attend a meeting requested by members of that profession. Attending were the *Sunday*

Star editor, the *Star* ombudsman, the head of a Toronto chiropractic institution, and a lawyer who evidently was retained by the profession to represent it internationally.

The lawyer took the offensive from the start. My columns were inaccurate and derogatory to the profession, he claimed. I asked him to point out just one factual inaccuracy. No reply. My opinions were damaging, he claimed. The *Sunday Star* editor pointed out that I was hired to express my opinions. I asked the chiropractor some pointed questions regarding chiropractic. The lawyer jumped in each time, not allowing the chiropractor to respond. After almost two hours of such sparring, a fatigued ombudsman asked the protesters what they wanted. What was the bottom line? Simple. They just wanted the newspaper to publish a disclaimer of everything I had written, as well as an article of their own in defense. The ombudsman sat up straight in his chair. A disclaimer? No way. An article? No problem. Just write a letter to the editor—that's what the page was for.

So the whole matter was settled, but not to my satisfaction. Three different letters from the chiropractors were subsequently published. I had some pretty strong facts and arguments to counter some of the material in those letters, but my editor felt that there was no point in prolonging the argument. I suppose he was probably right. The power of the press is considerable, and it should not be abused. Press theory has it that the public can be trusted to read both sides of a controversy and come to a valid conclusion. Theoretically, yes, but the theory is skewed when one side presents distorted facts that go unchallenged.

The thrust of my thinking on chiropractic, as on all the alternative medical practices, has not changed. Let the buyer beware.

Peter Popoff and the secret hearing-aid acid test

The latest issue of *Free Inquiry* magazine covers the fascinating saga of Peter Popoff, whose televangelism ministry is based in Uplands, California. His TV programs are syndicated continent-wide. Popoff dramatically "heals" people on television and in mass gatherings during his crusades. His latest money-making gimmick is to solicit donations from the public to purchase and send Bibles to the Soviet Union. His goal: three million bucks—no less.

Magician and psychic investigator James Randi has headed an investigative team to pursue the Popoff pop-offs. The team attended a Popoff crusade in Houston, Texas. You may recall that the Rev. W. V. Grant was caught using the established methods of stage mentalists to secure information from members of the audience, and then feed it back to them—presumably as revealed to him from a divine source. Well, Popoff uses a far more advanced method in practicing his deceptions—shortwave radio, 39.17 megahertz, to be precise. The investigators observed that before the mass healings began, Popoff's wife circulated among the audience, gathering intimate facts from various individuals. When the faith healer went into action he rattled off people's names, illnesses and other details without any hesitation whatever. What the psychic detectives did was use an electronic scanner to monitor the airwaves. Presto, there was the solution. Popoff's wife was heard relaying the information to him offstage. He was equipped, of course, with a mini-receiver and an earphone.

This revelation, I must admit, came as no surprise to me. An old acquaintance of mine, Tommy Tucker, based in New England, has been supplying this specialized electronics equipment to the mentalists' trade for many years. It hurts my professional sensibilities that this delicious trade secret had to be revealed to the public. But there's no question—it did have to be revealed, in order to expose the deception practiced by this particular televangelist.

When the videotape of this particular Popoff crusade was shown on the Johnny Carson show, when he was shown repeating out loud his wife's "divine" communications—the cat was really out of the bag. Millions of people were eyewitnesses to the deception. You would think that these revelations would set Popoff back on his heels. His reaction to all this? When interviewed on television he appeared quite unflustered. "In the New Testament Peter was followed around by a magician—and I guess now in 1986 Peter Popoff is destined to be [too]. . . . I don't feel that the people in the audience or in our crusades are misled at all. Do you mean to tell me that thousands of people, week after week, support an organization like ours—and cram the biggest arenas in the country, when they're not being helped at all? He [Randi] is trying to discredit everything when, in fact, people are being touched—people are being blessed."

Popoff has told interviewers he considers the attacks on him a blessing in disguise. Not only is he being interviewed on TV, but two network magazine shows are preparing pieces on him. He's now getting publicity, he claims, that he never would have gotten on his own. Popoff's reaction might not be just bluster. Sure, the publicity is definitely on the negative side, but will it deter the great mass of gullible followers that keep him, and others like him, in business?

It was advertised as "Peter Popoff's Miracle and Blessing Crusade Through Prayer," to take place at the Toronto International Centre of Commerce. You had to see it to believe it. Just visualize four thousand people inside a huge hall, enthusiastically welcoming every exhortation shouted by the televangelist the Reverend Peter Popoff. The good reverend screaming, blessing, chastising, healing. And his stories! The long, drawn-out, childlike tales of his accomplishments and miracles in the service of the Almighty—with four thousand devotees hanging on to his every word. You wondered how adults could possibly swallow all that nonsense. But they obviously did. After all, didn't Popoff tell them, "You must have a childlike faith?" Faith in whom—Peter Popoff?

The afternoon started off with controversy even before the services began. A team of observers came up from the Buffalo office of *Free Inquiry* magazine. They joined a team from the Toronto area, including myself. Here was our chance to see Popoff in the flesh, and to watch his miracles before our very eyes—how he was using a radio earphone to get messages from his wife backstage, then calling out people's names, addresses, and supposed illnesses. This information was supposed to be coming from a direct pipeline from God. The American group brought a quantity of "consumer alert" leaflets with them. These same leaflets were distributed at other Popoff crusades across the continent, to advise attendees that his methods had been exposed.

As people entered the center they were handed the leaflets. It was interesting to watch their reactions. The first woman to get one glanced at it, tore it up, and harangued the man who had handed it to her for ten minutes. I later spoke to her and found that she had been a Popoff follower for years. Others read the leaflet, carefully folded it and held on to it. Still others threw it away in disgust.

Eventually Popoff's front man, Reeford Shirrell, accompanied by a few of his stalwarts, came bursting through the door, threatening the leaflet distributors with expulsion from the area if they didn't cease and desist. After a confrontation with Shirrell and a representative from the center, the leaflet distributors were advised that Popoff had rented the whole area in addition to the hall. We had no option but to withdraw. All this time, unknown to me, my good wife, Zita, was innocently handing out leaflets inside the hall. Obviously she had not been noticed.

When the program began, Shirrell took the stage. His job is to stride up and down, exhorting the crowd to get them into a frenzy when Popoff takes the stage. The first thing Shirrell did was to wave one of the leaflets at the audience, vehemently shrieking, "The devil is here with us today, and we'd better pray for their souls. Throw these away—it's the devil speaking." I noticed a few people responding, but not too many. Curiosity is a powerful force. One woman later told me, "I'd like to take it home and look it over."

When Popoff took the stage, he too referred to the leaflets, and to Satan. It seems that this attempt to publicize Popoff's deceptions touched a raw nerve. When first exposed, he had taken it with some humor— claiming that, yes, he sometimes used radio—but other times he was getting divine guidance.

Faith healing sometimes works—for a reason

Few subjects that I write about or speak on stir up so much controversy as that of faith healing, also known as psychic healing or spiritual healing. When you cast doubts on a practice that has endured for thousands of years, you're asking for brickbats along with the rare bouquet. I'm getting ready to duck.

I should first make it clear: I agree that faith healing is a reality. It does work—in some cases. But there is nothing magical about it. We all know about the placebo, or sugar pill, effect. If patients are given what they believe to be a drug, the non-medication will sometimes have a beneficial effect—providing the illness is of a psychosomatic or neurotic nature. One of the reasons for this, according to medical science, is that the brain is triggered to release endorphins, pain killers, which act in the same way as morphine to reduce pain and promote a feeling of well-being. Some instances of faith healing can be quite dramatic, particularly when an illness is neurotic in origin. An hysterical person, confronted with a situation he or she finds difficult to cope with, will sometimes go temporarily blind, or suffer some form of paralysis or loss of speech or hearing. These are the cases that, when cured by the laying on of hands, spark cries of "miracle."

A miracle is a violation of the laws of nature. There is nothing unnatural about the autosuggestion that helps cure one of a neurotic illness. It's a perfectly natural function of the human body. Of course, you might say that the workings of the body are miraculous in themselves. But that's a miracle of a different kind.

In many cases the taking of certain drugs and the action of so-called psychic healers has the same effect. Hypertension, or high blood pressure, can be controlled by drugs. It can also be controlled, to some extent, by the influence of a yogi who teaches transcendental meditation. The ability to learn to relax, which is what TM is all about, is certainly conducive to controlling hypertension.

There are many illnesses seemingly cured by faith healers that would cure themselves in any case. These are the self-limiting illnesses such as colds, flu, laryngitis, backache, and infections of various kinds. Have you heard the old story about the cold that was magically cured in seven days? If left on its own, it would have taken a week. Then we have the cyclical diseases such as multiple sclerosis. A patient will have regressions in which there is a marked but only temporary improvement. This happens, too, in many cancer cases. The many claims of cancer cures by phony psychic healers arise from these regressions. Faith healers visited just prior to such regressions will usually be given credit for a miraculous cure. Here again, nature has taken a hand—but doesn't get the credit.

The medical profession is being criticized today for becoming too technical, too specialized, too remote. I wouldn't join in the first two gripes. I would in the third. I would cast a strong vote for the return of the family practitioner, the doctor who takes a more personal interest in the patient and inspires more trust. That is what the successful faith healer does—perhaps the disappearance of this personal touch is what provides the opening for so many charlatans to get in on the act, and what causes more naive believers to get hooked.

Nothing against religion

Richard Gray of London, Ontario, has fired off a letter to the editor in which he takes me to task on several points. I think he is setting up straw men when he criticizes me for attacking people's faiths and religious viewpoints. In all my years of writing, lecturing, and broadcasting I have never once alluded to religious faith in a derogatory manner. I *have* attacked those charlatans who have capitalized on the faith of clients in order to exploit them. Spiritual mediums are a good case in point. Some faith healers are another example. Some of the prominent television evangelists are still another. I have no argument with those who express a faith in the supernatural. I do take pains to point out the natural explanations for certain phenomena when these explanations are available. When they are not available, I simply note that science is still searching for them. My argument is only with the frauds, the cranks, the pseudoscientists, and the peddlers of psychic gobbledygook.

The Reverend W. V. Grant

When *Free Inquiry* magazine sent investigators to check on the authenticity of faith-healing "miracles" wrought by some of this continent's leading televangelists, Rev. W. V. Grant was a prime target. Apart from his television and stage appearances, Grant runs a mail-order business from a post-office box in Cincinnati. He sells booklets such as *I Was a Cannibal, Men in Flying Saucers Identified,* and *Freedom from Evil Spirits.* He also sells, according to *Free Inquiry,* a Bible course that offers the subscriber a diploma as a real "Reverend" with an "honorary Doctor's Degree" and a "license to preach." At Grant's revival meetings, or "miracle services," according to *Free Inquiry,* people are commanded to get up out of their wheelchairs and run, not walk, up and down the aisles. Canes and crutches are "dramatically broken and thrown onto the stage, while those who used them moments before trot about in ecstasy."

The investigators at one of these services, held in St. Louis, Missouri, in November 1985, uncovered some very interesting phenomena. First of all, Grant used the psychic's well-established method of making a big impression on his audience—he circulated among them and revealed to some of them various personal facts that it would seem he couldn't possibly have known. He could address them by name, specify their illnesses, identify their physicians, and provide other intimate details of their lives. This display in itself was enough to get the audience hooked. Standard, but effective, procedure. There are many methods known to the mentalist-magician for acquiring this information. One of the methods used by Grant is childishly simple. Believe it or not, he simply asks these people for the information—and gets it—beforehand. A couple of hours before the meeting began, he spoke to some of the early arrivals and got the information. During the meeting, when he called out the details before a packed auditorium, the people he referred to thought he was merely checking the accuracy of what he remembered. But the great bulk of the audience got the impression that Grant was receiving his messages from some divine source. Devilishly clever, isn't it? But that's what the craft of magic is all about.

But how about the wheelchair occupants and their miraculous cures? Again, very simple—when you know the method. Let me quote from the article by investigator James Randi in the Spring 1986 issue of *Free Inquiry:* "Those people who did rise from wheelchairs and run in the aisles did so because they were quite capable of doing so, and always had been. One of them . . . told [us] that 'a pastor told him to sit' in the wheelchair they provided even though he could move about without it. We visited this man at his home and discovered that he lived in a room on the third floor of a walk-up. He managed the trip up and down those stairs several times a day! The fact is this: Grant supplies the wheelchairs to appropriate subjects. It is no miracle at all that they get up and at his command wheel *him* about in those very chairs. Witnesses assume that the subjects arrived in the wheelchairs and will leave in them—unless treated to a miracle healing. That is just not so. Deliberate, cruel hoaxes are perpetrated to make miracles where there are none."

Reverend Angley and his cooperative audience

Faith healing has been with us for thousands of years, but only recently has it been able to make an impression on a truly mass audience. Some of the televangelists, using the medium of the electronic church, have used their dubious methods to take advantage of the afflicted. There has been very little detailed investigation of faith healing since Minnesota surgeon

Dr. William Nolen, a few years ago, revealed the fraud perpetrated by the late Kathryn Kuhlman, one of the best-known "spiritual healers" in America. Nolen took the trouble to follow up on some of the so-called cures that Kuhlman was supposed to have effected—and revealed that some persons were not only *not* cured, but that their conditions had seriously worsened.

Now, at last, there has been a well-organized, responsible effort to expose the methods of such well-known personalities as W. V. Grant, Ernest Angley, Peter Popoff, Pat Robertson, and others. *Free Inquiry* magazine devotes a good part of its Spring 1986 issue to a field investigation it organized to "analyze and evaluate faith-healing televangelists and their methods."

Editor and philosophy professor Paul Kurtz, psychic investigator James Randi, professor Joseph Barnhart of North Texas State University, along with several others formed a team that concentrated largely on Grant and Angley. Kurtz, with a seven-member team, attended one of Angley's services at Grace Cathedral in Akron, Ohio. The "Ernest Angley Hour" and the "Ninety and Nine Club" are aired over television stations all over the United States, Canada, the Philippines, and Africa. On his shows Angley "heals" cancer, diabetes, deafness, and blindness among other afflictions.

At Grace Cathedral Randi posed as a cripple and was led by the hand by Kurtz. Other members of the team were scattered among the large crowd in the auditorium. A nattily attired Angley appeared after a half-hour musical program. He opened with an appeal for funds. Ushers passed through the audience, making two separate collections—one for a "tithe offering," the other for a "love offering." With about eight hundred people present, and most giving twice, the collection, according to the investigators, seemed fairly ample.

Then Angley got down to business. He droned on with a long, "incomprehensible sermon." He then moved among certain spectators who had been placed at the front by the attendants, touching each one on the forehead and shouting "Heal, Jesus!" Each immediately fell back into the arms of the waiting attendants, and was laid out on the floor, poor Randi among them. He had to play along—couldn't remain standing. One of these people, a young man named Steve Bruch, attested he could now straighten his knee, and the pain had disappeared—after Angley had claimed a miracle. When questioned later by Kurtz, Bruch revealed he had a cartilage problem. "The knee often goes out," he said. "But if you stretch it, does it go back in?" asked Kurtz. "Yes." "Was that a genuine miracle?" Bruch just smiled. Another man was asked what miracle had been wrought for him. He showed Kurtz a finger that was crooked. It had been broken a few months before. "It's still bent," said Kurtz. "Yes, but it is a bit straighter than it was before."

Edgar Cayce and his bedbug juice

"What about Edgar Cayce?" That's the question usually tossed at me whenever I come down hard on the swindling psychics or the fake faith healers. Somehow, those who are uncertain as to the genuineness of psychic advisers have a vague feeling that the "Sleeping Prophet" was for real, and for good reason. The Edgar Cayce myth has grown over the years, with a multitude of books about the great man feeding the multiplicity of anecdotes about his miraculous healings and prophecies.

The establishment of the Association for Research and Enlightenment at Virginia Beach, Virginia, has added to and perpetuated the myth. This institution stores and distributes printed material on the Cayce "miracles" and is the nerve center of a huge number of Edgar Cayce study groups in cities all across the continent. These study groups can have a profound effect on people who, for various personal reasons, have found it necessary to join some sort of social group to ease their psychological pain. I personally know of individuals, originally quite rational-thinking and sensible, who have joined these groups and now have become full-fledged occultists, ready to believe almost anything. What of it, you might say, if it has made life more bearable for them. Nothing wrong with it at all—if you don't mind relinquishing control of your own fortunes.

Edgar Cayce was a mild-mannered, introverted, deeply religious man who became a world-famous psychic diagnostician. He would lie on his back, his head facing south (later north), and go into a deep trance. These trances can be quite real—they are really a state of self-hypnosis. While in the trance someone (usually an osteopath) would ask Cayce questions about the health problems either of a person present or someone who had written in. Cayce received thousands of letters asking for help. Cayce's followers cite the fact that he was not a physician and had no medical training: How could he be so knowledgeable without possessing some occult powers? Overlooked is the fact that for years Cayce did a tremendous amount of reading on the subjects of osteopathy and homeopathy. In those days "home remedies" were in fashion, and he consistently recommended many of them. How would you like your friendly physician to prescribe some of the following for you: peanut-oil massage; oil of smoke; ash from the wood of a bamboo tree (for tuberculosis); bedbug juice; or fumes of apple brandy from a charred keg.

Cayce prescribed these and many other goodies, and got away with it. Why? Why did so many write letters of thanks and appreciation—letters on file at Virginia Beach? There are several answers to these questions. One of them is the same reason for any faith healer's success in impressing a responsive subject. The key word is *faith*. The believer will accept almost anything the miracle worker asserts. Just attend any faith-healing session. Hear the great man intone, "Rotate your head—your neck pain is now gone." And the believing subject responds, "Yes, it's gone, it's gone." Such are the wonders of psychosomatic cures.

It is well known that those who subject themselves to the "cures" of faith healers will seldom complain when not cured. Their faith in the miracle worker is not diminished. Conversely, they often do blame themselves for not having sufficient faith in the Almighty—and will often suffer psychologically from this. Another reason that patients uncured by Cayce and others fail to complain is that they can't. Many of them are dead. There was one interesting case of this sort in which the patient was dead before Cayce gave his remote-control diagnosis. He had prescribed a cure for a young girl named Theodoria Alosio, who died of leukemia on a Sunday. The diagnosis and the prescribed cure (a special diet) were rendered on the following day.

This and other booboos were rationalized at a later date by Cayce supporters. When I interviewed Hugh Lynn Cayce, Edgar's son, several years ago, I asked him if his father had ever been in error. "Of course," he replied. "We've even written a book listing these errors—*The Outer Limits of Edgar Cayce's Power*." What Cayce didn't say was that the book contains all kinds of outlandish and unreasonable excuses and rationalizations for the errors—a standard ploy of the occultists. I have a thick file in my records for this type of maneuver. It's headed, "Psychic Copouts."

Edgar Cayce was much more than just a long-distance faith healer. He branched out into many phases of the occult. Take dowsing, for instance. At one point Cayce combined his resources with those of Henry

Gross, the famous dowser. They put their heads, or dowsing sticks, together, and pinpointed a location along the seashore where they claimed was buried a king's ransom in treasure. After much digging and messing around, all they came up with were piles of sand and strained backs. But this error, too, was explained. Maybe the treasure was once there, but had been removed. The psychic impressions were picked up through the spirits of the departed pirates. Perhaps the playful spirits were playing a joke on the living. The occult information Cayce received might have been supposed to be applied at that time, or in the past—or in the future. As I said: psychic copouts. They are endless.

The Sleeping Prophet didn't get his title without reason. Cayce made many predictions that were recorded and taken quite seriously. Some of them are still slated for the future, so we'll have to wait and see—if we live that long. One of the things Cayce talked about most frequently was the lost continent of Atlantis. He claimed that some day Atlantis would rise again. Those who interpret his vague predictions figure that he foresaw Atlantis emerging from the depths in 1968 or 1969, and that worldwide catastrophes would then follow. Great earthquakes would cause New York and Japan to vanish. The asteroid Icarus was to come close to the earth in June 1968, and might even strike our planet, causing great devastation. Well, it did come close to the earth—within four million miles. Before the end of this century, Cayce predicted, much of North America's east and west coasts would be destroyed. The waters of the Great Lakes would empty into the Gulf of Mexico. We can now add these items to our list of present world problems—and look forward to more sleepless nights.

The mind-body relationship

When Norman Cousins speaks, the believers in faith healing listen. At a recent conference on "Hypnosis and Psychosomatic Medicine" in Toronto, Cousins was a featured speaker and a prime public attraction. He certainly does pull in the public, as the attendance at his lecture attested. Cousins, you may recall, is the well-known writer who caught the public imagination by narrating how he licked a debilitating disease his doctors had pronounced incurable. He did it, he claimed, with laughter. Cousins's premise is that the emotions can affect a bodily disease. He checked out of the hospital, repaired to a hotel room, rented some Marx brothers films, and laughed his way back to good health. Of course, as Cousins says, there was some exaggeration to that story—but he does claim that his positive emotions hastened his recovery.

It could be true—but there are some questions. Is it possible that the doctors' prognoses could have been off base? It has been known to happen. And is it also possible that the illness was such that he would have improved even without the film fun? We'll never know. But these questions certainly remove Cousins's claims from the realm of scientific certainty. That is the crux of the whole matter. How does anecdotal evidence stack up against valid, controlled scientific studies?

In his address to the conference Cousins cited case after case of people whose illnesses improved with faith in themselves and in their doctors. I have no argument with that philosophy. Faith healing does work—in certain cases. Particularly in illnesses of an hysterical or neurotic nature. There is no doubt that a mind-body effect can take place. When Cousins refers to the possible helpful effects of faith in the cure of cancer, however, I believe he's treading on shaky ground.

There is a tendency today to lay great stress on the possible effects of brain function on bodily diseases. But science is still a long way from making positive claims. The supporters of faith healing and psychosomatic cures have been quick to leap on the bandwagon—which is also a characteristic of those who support claims of the paranormal. They seek instant answers without waiting for science to corroborate their claims—if it ever does. It is significant that when I questioned Cousins directly, he admitted there is no scientific evidence to back up his claims. There was a major, controlled study being organized in California, he said, to take a look at the mind-body relationship—a study that would probably take years. Until all the data are in and the study is concluded, the jury is out on this one.

Dr. Wallace I. Sampson is a highly respected oncologist on the faculty of the medical school of Stanford University in California. He addressed the 1985 conference of the Committee for the Scientific Investigation of Claims of the Paranormal on the subject, "Meditating Away Your Cancer." Sampson concluded a well-reasoned and informative lecture with the following: "Putting together the lack of theoretical basis and hard evidence for the proposal of mind over cancer with the often-seen drawbacks of depression and unrealistic expectations, one can only conclude that commercializing and franchising this method is not often in the public interest.

It is in all likelihood a soft-core type of quackery, and suffers from the usual type of pseudoscientific thinking."

"I never had cancer—and lived!"

The television station is WBZ-TV, Boston. The program is "People Are Talking," broadcast daily, live, before a studio audience. The host, Nancy Merrill, usually has two or three guests who discuss and argue controversial issues. Participants have included former president Jimmy Carter, Rev. Jesse Jackson, Gloria Steinem, Erica Jong, John Erlichman, and Milton Berle. The program is one of the most popular in the New England area. My first appearance on the show, in 1983, propelled me into a hot and heavy debate with two Boston-area psychics. On a recent broadcast I found myself sharing the camera eye with two of America's leading faith healers, Etel DeLoach, a woman from New Jersey, and Bryce Bond of New York.

Bond, who prefers to be termed a "spiritual" healer, seems to be eminently successful in his field. He has been a psychic teacher at Drew University and has his own cable-TV program in New York, "Dimensions in Parapsychology," soon to be syndicated. He claims to have travelled the globe teaching his technique of laying-on of hands. Arguing with Bond about the merits of faith healing is like trying to nail Jell-O to the wall. His arguments consist of a series of cliches—"As you sow, so you will reap"; "Everyone is made in the image of God"; "You have to get in touch with yourself"; "The powers that we possess are immense and often untapped."

When Bond claimed that "all sickness is 100-percent psychosomatic," I was quick to take issue. But Merrill's constant interruptions made it difficult for me to make my points. It was an exercise in frustration. The program, slanted for maximum viewer response, regularly showcases psychics. Infrequently, a skeptic like myself is brought on to give some appearance of balance. The studio audience is loaded with psychic supporters bused in for the program. Merrill gives the paranormalists on the panel maximum time to express their views. I found myself fighting for every chance to present my arguments.

I would have loved to question Bond on the subject of Yul Brynner, but didn't get a chance. He claims that the actor was cured of throat cancer through faith healing, but is evasive about whether he, Bond, did the healing. That was in August 1983. A wire-service story carried in the *Toronto Sunday Star* of March 18, 1984, stated that Brynner had been diagnosed as having lung cancer six months previously. Somebody was stretching the truth.

The most interesting part of the program for me was when a third guest, Lynn Hambro, was brought on. She claimed to have had several forms of cancer for many years. She claimed that several doctors, in a number of hospitals, had failed to cure her—until she finally was healed by Etel DeLoach. DeLoach sat beaming during this tribute to her psychic powers. Merrill asked my opinion on this. I answered: "I cannot accept anecdotes. I would have to see documented evidence of the cancer diagnoses. It's well known that many cases of so-called psychic cures are nonsense because the claimed illnesses never existed in the first place."

Later in the program, to my surprise and satisfaction, my opinion was vindicated. A telephone interview with Dr. William Nolen, a noted surgeon in the U.S. Midwest, introduced a dramatic note. Nolen has spent much time investigating faith healing and writing books on the subject. He was well informed on the case of Lynn Hambro. He actually had copies of her medical records. His words say it all: "There isn't any documented evidence that I could find in her records . . . of cancer."

Nancy Merrill laughed self-consciously. Hambro slumped lower in her chair. DeLoach kept a fixed smile on her face. The studio audience looked uncomfortable. My reaction? Just another psychic balloon deflated. There are thousands more floating up there. Incidentally, Lynn Hambro has now herself become a faith healer.

Psychic surgery is just sleight of hand

The patient is lying on the surgical table. The surgeon approaches and quickly makes an incision in the abdomen—with his bare hands. Blood spurts out. The surgeon removes some internal tissue, disposes of it in a bucket and closes the wound—again with his bare hands. He cleans up the area—there is no scar. The patient gets up and walks away. At no time was the patient sedated or anesthetized.

You have just witnessed a demonstration of psychic surgery. The August 1984 issue of *Discover,* the science news magazine, has a piece on this subject by Martin Gardner. He recounts the sad story of Andy Kaufman, the mechanic on the TV show "Taxi." Kaufman had cancer. In March Kaufman had flew to the Philippines, where fraudulent psychic surgeons can practice openly, to be "operated on." You would not believe how many people from this continent make this expensive trip.

You may recall the group of Canadians from British Columbia who were killed in a fiery bus crash in the Philippines a couple of years ago. These people were on one of these futile, hopeless journeys, looking for a miracle cure. There are several travel agencies that specialize in arranging these trips. In the United States, the Federal Trade Commission has ordered some of these agencies to discontinue this practice. I'm not aware of any similar restrictions in Canada.

Kaufman underwent several "operations" performed by psychic surgeon Ramon Labo. He died two months later in Los Angeles at the age of thirty-five. Kaufman's girl friend, who accompanied him to the Philippines, witnessed the "surgery" and endorsed it as authentic. She claimed to have been only a few feet away and said there was no possibility of deception.

The practice of sleight of hand does not require the viewer to be at a distance. As an experienced magician I can back up that statement. Last year I appeared on a CBC "Take 30" television program, on which I demonstrated the phenomenon of psychic surgery. I "operated" on host Harry Brown, removing a huge piece of "diseased tissue" from his upper arm. The closeup camera was two feet away from the area, and no hanky-panky was revealed. It really looked authentic—until I explained the method. The psychic surgeon conceals the tissue in a small container carefully palmed. In my case it was a chicken liver obtained from a cooperative butcher shop. A tiny, thin, plastic vial containing animal blood is also concealed. The fingertips are pressed into the soft flesh so that they disappear from view, seeming to penetrate the skin. The vial is broken, blood flows, the tissue is produced, and the "wound" is cleaned up. The illusion is truly realistic.

When the patient has faith in the psychic surgeon's abilities there often is a temporary sense of well-being. This is the same effect that most faith healers induce—autosuggestion. When this euphoria wears off, the old problems, the old pains, return. Most of the psychic surgeons do not set a fee—they accept a donation. With more than a hundred patients a day, the donations can add up to quite a bundle.

Why do so many otherwise sensible people make this useless pilgrimage? Most are desperate. With illnesses that have been pronounced terminal or merely remain uncured by standard medical means, patients are often ready to try anything.

They have also been misled by the broadcast media. For example, in 1977 NBC aired a prime-time TV special on the paranormal. It was hosted by Burt Lancaster and featured a sequence on psychic surgery in the Philippines. The manner in which it was presented almost endorsed the authenticity of the phenomenon. Andy Kaufman was one of those who viewed the show.

Medicinal sandals and other devices

To add to the international aspect of the 1984 Psychics, Mystics and Seers Fair held in Toronto, one of the booths was selling sandals manufactured in Australia. These were not ordinary sandals. They were designed to help stimulate and treat the wearer's lungs, brains, sinuses, stomach, bladder, liver, gall bladder, pancreas, adrenal glands, intestines, kidneys, thyroid, sciatic nerve, knees, shoulders, neck, eyes, and ears. Did I omit anything?

According to the accompanying sheet, the insole consists of rubber nodules that massage the nerve endings in the soles of the feet as one walks. A detailed sketch illustrates each section of the sole and its connection to its respective part of the body. This is supposed to be an ancient science with its roots in China. "After all," the pamphlet states, "man and woman in their natural state didn't pamper their feet with footwear with a protective sole. They received their stimulus by walking or running on rough ground." Are we to assume that people were healthier and lived longer thousands of years ago?

Moving along through the crowded aisles at the fair I spotted another pseudoscientific display. This one featured something called a "Bodydisc"— "a new scientific device to help you improve the functions of your body in minutes. It is easy to use and profoundly effective." The crowd around the booth was attracted by the sight of a woman lying supine on a couch. A man seated beside her was verbally instructing her in various therapeutic movements.

Under the small of the woman's back was the aforementioned disc. It consisted of a flat plastic disc about six inches in diameter and coated with foam rubber on one side. As one balances on the disc and moves according to instructions, tensions will be relieved in various parts of the body, it was claimed. In interviewing the marketer of this amazing, magical apparatus, I was relieved to hear that it was scientifically respectable, because "in all the Eastern disciplines, the pelvis seems to be where the intelligence is" with respect to movement.

Another display offered quartz crystals guaranteed to radiate energy. They came in various lengths and thicknesses. The pleasant woman who was vending these crystals pointed out that they would help to make a person more alert, give stronger memory retention, and help the eyesight so that one would never have to wear glasses. One could buy a crystal for various prices ranging from $15 to $125—depending, I suppose, on how wide-awake one would wish to be, how clearly one would want to see, and how much one would wish to remember. Strangely, I couldn't find even one booth selling snake oil.

One thing remained—to find someone to give me a psychic reading. I found just the person I was looking for—imposing-looking, intelligent, busy. He was a lawyer from Rochester, New York. He used his psychic powers, he told me, to listen to what his clients were thinking rather than what they told him. These powers were of tremendous help in cross-examination, he said. He extracted three cards from a tarot deck, glanced at them, and told me all about myself. In addition to the usual generalities, the psychic was quite specific about one thing—"Your guidance comes from your emotions, not your logic," he said. "You are not a skeptic."

Voodoo

Mention the word *voodoo* and you conjure up visions of someone shoving pins into a rag doll while someone else, miles away, is writhing in pain. Well, there's a lot more to voodoo worship than remote-control hexing, though it is true that the practice persists, and that it sometimes works.

Voodoo operates on the same principle as faith healing. Accordingly, it does sometimes work. If a person suffers from a psychosomatic illness and if he or she has faith in the healer who is laying on hands, in many cases a problem will be cleared up, if only temporarily. The voodoo hexing will, of course, have a negative effect—but only if the recipient is aware that the practice is taking place. The principle is no different from that which makes hypnotism work—autosuggestion. The unfortunate individuals on the receiving end of the voodoo ritual are simply convincing themselves that they will be affected—and they often are. People have been known to die from this phenomenon. There's no magic involved. It's the good old scientific principle of cause and effect.

Voodoo is derived from an ancient West African religion. The word comes from the African *vudu*, which means spirit or deity. When the slave trade moved into the West Indies, particularly Haiti, voodoo moved in with it. From there it was just a short hop to New Orleans, where it also thrived. The Louisiana government eventually outlawed voodoo as a religion, forcing it to convert into a cult—and it survives.

In New Orleans the name of Marie Laveau is still a force. She was the nineteenth-century voodoo queen of the area. Laveau would lead ritualistic musical ceremonies in Congo Square, now known as Louis Armstrong Park on the edge of the French Quarter. These ceremonies are supposed to have been the precursors of jazz. The really orgiastic rituals for the faithful were always held in secret near Bayou St. John, on the shores of Lake Pontchartrain, the huge lake that crowds New Orleans onto the banks of the Mississippi. Pilgrimages are still being made to Laveau's tomb in St. Louis Cemetery Number 1, although there is still controversy over Laveau's true burial place. The tomb is covered with hex signs—if you make an X on the tomb, rub one foot three times on the ground, and knock three times, the legend says, you will be granted a favor.

In this century voodoo has taken off in different directions. It has become a spiritualist-drugstore cult involving the sale of magical potions and various fetish artifacts. It has joined the modern occult movement, integrating astrology, superstition, witchcraft, and various symbolic rites under a single umbrella. And it still has a faithful, if confused, following from an older generation that retains it as part of its religious beliefs.

When the invitation arrived from the Physics and Maths Department at Tulane University, I was quite pleased. Not only would I lecture on "Science and Pseudoscience" for honors students, but I would have a chance to visit New Orleans and explore a hotbed of superstitious beliefs and voodoo practices. New Orleans is an amalgam of the old and the new. The World's Fair there triggered a construction boom in the downtown core. Modern high-rise hotels are springing up like mushrooms. Elsewhere, the old architecture and the old ways prevail. The fabled French Quarter has been preserved as it was hundreds of years ago. At Tulane, the buildings are old, musty, and tradition-laden—at least the buildings I was in were.

The audiences at my two lectures were the same as my university audiences everywhere—interested, reasonably enthusiastic, and loaded with questions about the paranormal. I always find it amazing how poorly informed the average student is about the pseudosciences. For that matter, it's no secret how little is known by the majority of students, as well as the public, about science in general.

A good part of my few days was spent hunting down the famed New Orleans Voodoo Museum, which had departed the French Quarter. I finally located it in a decrepit part of town a friendly hotel clerk had advised me to avoid. Visualize an old, alabaster-white, two-story stucco building, pockmarked with age, circa 1850. Appropriately, it has a reputation as a haunted house. You enter the narrow doorway from street level, mount a flight of dimly lit, rickety stairs. The walls are covered with all sorts of symbolic artifacts—shields, drums, skulls, voodoo dolls.

On the second floor you are cordially greeted by the high priestess, Lygia Maciel deCastro, a pleasant-looking, dark-eyed, dark-haired, 33-year-old woman who is enthusiastically prepared to initiate you into the history of voodoo. DeCastro hails from Brazil, where African voodoo practices combined with spiritual beliefs from France to produce a hybrid sort of voodoo religion. She tells you that the religion is practiced principally in the black Baptist churches in New Orleans. A large number of immigrant Haitians and Cubans have also swollen the ranks of voodoo followers in the past few years.

A glance around the museum reveals a number of small altars. Two things catch your eye: a long pole at the center of each altar, and a number of Catholic statues surrounding them. The poles, you are told, are there for the spirits to descend; the statues are a reminder that the early French inhabitants of New Orleans taught the African slaves about Catholicism, and so the voodoo beliefs were tempered much as they had been in Brazil.

At this point deCastro introduces Charles Gandolfo, founder and curator of the museum. Gandolfo is a serious-looking young man of medium height with piercing black eyes. He is Creole, a mixture of Spanish and French blood. Gandolfo said he inherited voodoo beliefs from his grandfather. It seems the old man was dying of lockjaw. The medical profession couldn't help him, so he went to a voodoo priestess. She treated Gandolfo's grandfather with a potion brewed from certain grasses mixed with ground white cockroaches. The treatment saved his life. Today we would get an anti-tetanus injection—but, then again, do we know what that syringe really contains?

Chiropractic

Like many of you, I wonder about chiropractors. Are they charlatans, or do they honestly provide a much-needed health service? Or does the field consist of a mixture of both elements? Come to think of it, a parallel question keeps surfacing about so-called psychics. Are they fakes, or do they really believe they have supernatural powers? Or are there some of both kinds of psychics?

A book published by Fitzhenry and Whiteside entitled *Chiropractors: Do They Help?* takes a look at the chiropractic profession. It is written by three sociologists who have done considerable research in health and health care. Professors Ian Coulter, Merrijoy Kelner, and Oswald Hall dig deeply into the chiropractic field but, like the title of the book, they leave us with a question mark. I still wonder about chiropractors.

We're told that chiropractic students take a four-year course in a specialized college. These colleges, however, do not have government support, so they lack "some of the elaborate training facilities available to other kinds of professional education." This sets up question mark number one in my mind. An important point often brought up in criticism of chiropractic is "How scientific is it?" The authors say, "It seems to the objective observer that chiropractic education is not as dependent on science and scientific research as medical education is. . . . Chiropractic students can learn the art of the practitioner's therapies without scientific proof that they work." So chiropractic medicine is an art, not a science. For me that's question mark number two.

The authors follow the chiropractor's career after he or she leaves school. During the first year of practice it seems that chiropractors expect to continue the learning process. "There is no suggestion that they consider their training completed just because they have graduated from chiropractic college; they recognize that much of their education still lies ahead of them." I feel a little uncomfortable about the thought of donating my spinal column to enhancing the education of a budding chiropractor. Question mark number three.

We then face the controversial problem of the use of X-rays by chiropractors. This is a practice long condemned by the medical profession. At one chiropractic college the teachers urge caution in employing X-rays. Most practitioners use them, however, according to the authors. One chiropractor reported that, "Patients who have invested money in

X-rays come more regularly for treatment and are more reliable. Paying for X-rays gives a patient a vested interest in health care." Is this another way of saying the patient is hooked? Also, is this just one chiropractor's philosophy, or is it pervasive in the profession? The question marks are adding up.

Some chiropractors go a lot further than hand manipulation of the spinal area, which is supposed to be their basic skill. Some have added sidelines: giving advice on nutrition and diet, suggesting vitamin therapies, prescribing "natural remedies" such as herbs and seeds—sometimes they even practice a little acupuncture. If I seem a little critical of chiropractic, I should make it clear that the authors of *Chiropractors: Do They Help?* seem to lean over backward to endorse the practice, even though they claim an objective outlook.

The practice of chiropractic is supposed to have begun in 1895. Daniel David Palmer claimed to have restored a man's hearing by adjusting a bump on his spine. Palmer accomplished this miracle, he said, by releasing pressure on the nerve to his "patient's" ear. Palmer was a grocer who also claimed to be a "magnetic healer." Obviously he was ignorant of the fact that the nerve from the brain to the ear is not situated in the spinal column. Before the year was out Palmer had established the Palmer College of Chiropractic. In 1906 he was jailed for practicing medicine without a license. Palmer's son, B. J. Palmer, took over the college and expanded its activities. Graduates established their own schools, and soon the profession was booming.

But as pressure was applied by the authorities, the multitude of chiropractic schools ran into a problem. It seems their graduates were unable to pass the strict medical licensing tests because of their ignorance of the basic sciences. So the colleges tossed in courses on anatomy, bacteriology, pathology, obstetrics, and other subjects. A study conducted by the American Medical Association in the late 1960s revealed that less than half the teachers in chiropractic schools had graduated from college —many more didn't have degrees in the subjects they were teaching. And remember, a basic science course will only prepare a student for the study of a disease. It does not prepare a student to make a diagnosis or to prescribe the proper treatment. It would seem that your average chiropractor gets on-the-job training—on the patient. A key question is this: What types of medical problems are chiropractors competent to deal with—and do they stay within their limitations, or do they venture into fields beyond their scope?

Several U.S. government inquiries have elicited this kind of response from chiropractic officials: "Our chiropractors specialize in treating musculoskeletal problems—mostly backaches and stiff necks." Sounds fair enough. But several studies over the years have revealed a different scenario. A huge percentage of these practitioners have attempted to treat asthma, pneumonia, appendicitis, tonsillitis, ulcers, heart problems, cancer, hepatitis, diabetes, kidney and liver disease—the list goes on and on. One of these studies was conducted by the American Chiropractic Association itself. In 1973, Ottawa pediatrician Murray Katz visited many of the chiropractic offices in the area to conduct a survey of his own. Over 70 percent had pamphlets on display exaggerating the treatments that could be performed, according to Katz.

One of the great dangers involved with chiropractic treatment is the indiscriminate use of X-rays—and most chiropractors use them. The full-spine X-ray subjects the sexual organs to up to a thousand times as much radiation as the usual chest X-ray. The effects on future generations could be far-reaching. The medical profession takes a very dim view of this practice by chiropractors, and with good reason.

In Canada the various medical associations differ in the degree of their opposition to chiropractic medicine. The Canadian Medical Association takes a hard line. Chiropractic is a false doctrine, it has said, and it hasn't hesitated to call it outright quackery. Of course, the chiropractors charge that the medical profession has a vested interest in protecting its own territory.

So how do you feel about chiropractors? Do you have back pain? Forget all the other illnesses. Let's face it—many, many of us walk around in a semi-crouching position. What does your doctor say? "Learn to live with it." Well, you've had enough. You're not going to take it any more. Want to gamble? Visit a chiropractor. You pays your money and you takes your chances.

TRUTH
Forces of Darkness and Light

I could not have written three years of weekly newspaper columns plus many feature articles on the paranormal without dipping into the world of magic, what we in the profession prefer to call conjuring.

One should write from personal experience, and if there is one thing that has influenced my life more than any other, it has been my experience of the conjuring art and all that it encompasses. The people I have met, the exposure to the underground world of deception (whether practiced for entertainment or for fraudulent purposes) have given me a valuable perspective on the functioning of the human psyche.

Conjuring as practiced today is a far cry from the magic of the ancients. The old magic still exists in all its paranormal forms. But from the occult magic of the ancient priesthood has developed today's art form of conjuring, the magic we see on stage and television.

The hobby of magic offers perhaps more satisfaction than any other one can think of. For the collector, it is possible to collect magic paraphernalia or books on the subject. For the person interested in self-help, the ability to prestidigitate offers a source of confidence. For those who seek contact with others, there are worldwide magical fraternities. For those who merely seek an intellectual challenge, conjuring is no slouch.

The list of prominent personalities in every field of endeavor who have practiced magic as an avocation would amaze you. Medical authorities such as the late and great Dr. Jacob Daley of New York, actors such as Tony Curtis and Mickey Rooney, authors such as Charles Dickens, sports personalities such as Mohammed Ali, executives, academics, journalists, lawyers, businessmen, scientists—the magic bug has bitten all of them. And, of course, the great professional magicians of the past and present, from France's Jean Eugene Robert Houdin to America's David Copperfield, have carved out a niche for this great art in the history of the theater.

When the Committee for the Scientific Investigation of Claims of the Paranormal was formed in 1976, the founders, in all their wisdom, decided it would be advantageous to have a few knowledgeable magicians in their ranks. After all, who could better disclose the methods used by so many psychics, methods quite familiar to the experienced magician? This decision has paid off over and over again.

CSICOP has probably accomplished more than it ever dreamed it could in its brief existence to date. It has shed much light on the forces of darkness. And much credit has to be directed to its chief organizer, Paul Kurtz, not only for his guidance of CSICOP, but equally for his policy of publishing skeptical material through his publishing company, Prometheus Books.

Prior to the promotion of skeptical tomes under the stamp of Prometheus, you would have been hard put to find many books of this kind on library or bookstore shelves. When I first took an interest in the paranormal I could find only two books that would give me some sort of guidance: Martin Gardner's *Fads and Fallacies in the Name of Science,* and D. H. Rawcliffe's *The Psychology of the Occult,* now published as *Occult and Supernatural Phenomena.* Now, thanks to Prometheus, there is a tremendous range of skeptical literature on the paranormal. Inquiring readers can now find some rational explanations to balance the bombardment of occult nonsense they've been exposed to for so many years.

Whenever I debate, broadcast, write, lecture, or simply have a one-on-one discussion about the paranormal I invariably encounter the same bottom-line question. "So what harm is there to all this stuff?" After all, I'm told, astrology is a fun thing. So is visiting a psychic. UFOs, Bigfoot, and extraterrestrial visits are interesting and exciting. The television programs featuring the occult are entertaining. So why all the fuss? Who needs CSICOP? You're just practicing overkill.

Any harm? Plenty.

Just look at our youth today. The New Age, the occult epidemic that has swept the West—is it just chance that the drug culture has accompanied this explosion of irrationality? Speak to some of the kids in schools, as I have. You'll find them confused, not knowing what to believe. They are fed all the paranormal gobbledygook through the print and electronic media. They have lots of questions, but the answers aren't forthcoming in their regular curriculum. No harm?

You just have to receive the mail that I do, as a writer on the paranormal, to be aware of the fears experienced by so many impressionable people: "My Ouija board has given me this message—what shall I do?"; "Our family has been haunted by this ghost for years. Is there any way we can get rid of it?"; "This psychic on the radio has advised my husband to leave his job. What do you think?" No harm?

The television evangelists make a strong impression on their followers with their fake faith healing. Old people, ill, confined to their homes, watch these TV charlatans faithfully, cling to them for sustenance, and send them money that would be better spent on groceries. No harm?

It seems clear: Once a person comes under the influence of these supernatural beliefs, his or her mind ceases to function at a normal level of reasoning. The only solution, if there is one, is widespread dissemination of the natural explanations for so-called psychic phenomena.

The great Houdini

Fifty-six years ago this weekend, Harry Houdini, the world-famous escape artist, died on Hallowe'en in a Detroit hospital from abdominal injuries.

Nine days earlier, McGill University student Sam Smiley was witness to the fateful incident in Montreal that resulted in Houdini's tragic death.

On the afternoon of October 22, 1926, Smiley was sitting in Houdini's cramped dressing room sketching a portrait of the great magician. Houdini was reclining on a couch, thumbing through his mail. Smiley, a budding artist, sat near the foot of the sofa while his friend Jack Price sat beside him. The magician chatted with the two young men, recounting some of his theatrical experiences.

The door opened and in walked a tall, sandy-haired man in his early thirties. He identified himself as Gordon Whitehead, a McGill divinity student. He was returning a book Houdini had lent him. Whitehead was offered a chair. After a few minutes of conversation he asked Houdini, who took great pride in his physical condition, if he could take blows to the abdomen without discomfort. Still perusing his mail, the magician nodded absent-mindedly. Without warning, Whitehead stood up, leaned over the recumbent Houdini, and delivered several heavy punches to the stomach area.

"Jack Price and I were shocked," Smiley recalls. "He must have punched him three or four times. I remember Houdini gasping, 'That's enough, that's enough.' Jack asked Whitehead to leave, which he did." Houdini, a proud man, pretended to be unruffled and asked Smiley to continue drawing. The students finally left, saying goodby to Houdini, who seemed to show no effects from his recent experience. This was not surprising to them, considering that here was a man who was renowned for his superb physique and his superhuman feats of skill and endurance.

Houdini was born Erich Weiss in Hungary, in 1874—the son of a struggling Budapest rabbi. As a baby he was brought to the United States, where he spent his boyhood years plying his trade as a magician. Houdini borrowed his new name from Jean Eugene Robert Houdin, the famous French conjuror who was the father of modern magic. Houdini's new bride, Bess, became his stage partner, and together they worked the circuses, the small theaters—wherever they could perform and eke out a living. Houdini began the handcuff act that was to make him famous. There were escape performers before Houdini, but he was the first to challenge people, particularly the police, to bring their own handcuffs and fetter him.

Houdini's challenges became more and more daring. He escaped from ropes, from chains, from boxes and trunks, from jail cells, from combinations of all these confinements. His reputation spread. In 1900, Houdini made the move that was to make him world famous. With Bess he sailed for England to perform in what was then the hub of show business. Success followed success. Booking agents on the continent fought to engage him. He triumphantly toured Germany and was a sensation with his daring challenges and escapes. In the Soviet Union Houdini escaped from the infamous Siberian Transport Cell, an all-metal prison van used to move prisoners to exile. All this under the eyes of the secret police. He was the talk of Moscow.

Houdini had a sense of theater second to none. He was the first escape artist to realize that making it look easy was the wrong approach. He learned how to build up suspense on stage, to create the illusion of danger to himself. When he was bound and manacled he was able to free himself in a few moments in many cases. Instead he would sweat and struggle for up to twenty minutes or more to release himself from the restraints. He would often be placed behind a curtain or in a cabinet. The audience would not see him struggling but would hear the sound of his efforts, while the orchestra played some rousing music. Houdini would then emerge, dripping with perspiration, triumphantly holding chains and handcuffs aloft, to thunderous applause. Things moved at a slower pace in those days. Today the audience would probably walk out of the theater before such a performer reappeared. In those simpler times they were content to enjoy the music and wait patiently for the miracle. Always the superb showman, Houdini would simply have adapted to today's standards. He knew exactly how to capture the public imagination. He took advantage of every situation, whether while performing on stage or feuding with a rival performer in the newspaper.

As a youngster, Houdini excelled in track and field and concentrated on building a powerful physique. He became an expert diver and swimmer, learning to swim underwater for long periods. He later went to work for a locksmith, becoming a master of the craft. This early training became invaluable in later years, when he was tossed off bridges into deep rivers, chained, locked up, and jammed into sealed packing cases. Houdini never left anything to chance. He was always fully prepared for any contingency. He had a handful of well-trained, reliable assistants who looked after every detail. To the public, Houdini was the miracle man no locks could contain—but the miracles resulted from hard work, preparation, ingenuity, and skill.

In 1910 Houdini toured Australia and made headlines in still another medium. Airplane flight was then in its infancy. It had been only six years since the Wright brothers had made their historic first flight. Houdini, the innovator and headline-hunter, plunged into aviation. He learned to fly, and had his own plane built. In Australia he flew it for the official measured mile, becoming the first man to successfully fly on that continent. Many people are not aware that Houdini had a short career in the early movies. He always played the daredevil hero who got out of tight situations and rescued the heroine in distress. He performed many of his famous escapes in these movies, many of which are now collector's items in private hands.

In the late nineteenth century and early 1900s spiritualism was at its peak. After World War I the fake spirit mediums were out in full force, pretending to receive messages from servicemen killed in the conflict. Houdini launched an all-out campaign against these charlatans. He exposed them by duplicating their effects and revealing their methods to the public.

One of Houdini's most publicized feats was his challenge and exposure of Mina Crandon, known as Marjorie, the Blonde Witch of Boston. Marjorie was the Canadian-born wife of a Boston surgeon. Her first spirit manifestations were reported in 1923, after which she became world famous. Marjorie's surgeon husband, an intelligent man, was among the first to corroborate her contact with the spirits. Evidently the good doctor was unable to diagnose the true source of her powers, and believed that she was a genuine medium.

As Marjorie's fame grew, she attracted Houdini's attention. After much negotiation, he was finally allowed to attend one of her seances. At these sessions everyone would sit around a table, in the darkness, holding hands. Marjorie's husband would always be at her right side, holding her right hand. He swore she never got loose. At this seance Houdini sat to her left. Marjorie had placed a closed box containing a bell on the floor between Houdini's feet. The bell would ring without outside physical contact when the spirit entered the room, she promised.

What Marjorie didn't know was that Houdini, as was his custom, had prepared for this little encounter. Before the seance he had wrapped his right leg tightly with surgical tape. This caused the leg to be highly sensitized after he removed the bandage, just before the seance. When he pressed his leg against the calf of the Blonde Witch, he could feel the slightest twitch of her leg muscles. When the mumbo jumbo of the seance began, Houdini felt Marjorie's left leg moving ever so slowly. Her foot curled from the right side of his sensitized leg to the inside. She wasn't playing footsy—she was pressing the top of the box and causing the bell to ring.

Houdini's classic tilts with Marjorie finally resulted in her exposure and gained Houdini further fame and prestige. This opened up a whole new career for the great showman. He always found a way to keep a few steps ahead of the competition. Now he was receiving more publicity and reaping richer dividends than ever before.

But Houdini still had one unfulfilled ambition—to present a large-scale, full-evening magic show. He finally produced this extravaganza and toured the continent, bringing the show to Montreal's Princess Theatre on October 18, 1926. In his role as a spook-buster Houdini was usually called on for speaking engagements wherever he appeared. In Montreal he was invited to speak at McGill University one afternoon. The students jammed McGill Union to hear him lambast the charlatans and reveal their methods. Smiley busily sketched Houdini during the talk. When the magician saw the drawing at the close of the lecture he said, "Come to the theater tomorrow morning . . . I'll autograph this if you'll make another sketch for me to keep." So it was that Smiley found himself in the great man's dressing room the next day, a witness to the events that would lead to tragedy.

After the punching episode, Houdini began to develop acute pain, but continued with his performances. He travelled to Detroit with his production, but finally collapsed backstage in a Detroit theater. He was rushed to a hospital, but it was too late. A ruptured appendix brought on peritonitis. After battling valiantly for several days, the great Houdini lost his final struggle. He died on October 31—Hallowe'en 1926.

An old-time magician who knew Houdini once told me a strange theory regarding the date of Houdini's death. The doctors, I was told, had expected him to succumb two days earlier. But the great magician had fought on until the thirty-first—so that he would pass away on Hallowe'en, an anniversary that would never be forgotten.

Normally, this would be another anecdote added to the folklore of Houdiniana. But knowing the man's penchant for publicity, I wouldn't put it past him. Perhaps there is just a grain of truth to the story.

Houdini left a secret code word with his wife, Bess, so that he could possibly contact her from the other side. This perpetuated his memory in the public consciousness for years to come. Every year since 1926 seances have been held to bring Houdini back. He hasn't returned yet—but I have a hunch he's just waiting for the right time and the right place.

It is not widely known that Houdini actually posed as a psychic in his younger days. At an early stage in his career as a magician, Houdini and his wife were literally going to bed hungry each night. They were performing with a travelling medicine show, the California Concert Company. Doc Hill was the owner, director, manager, and star of the show. He pitched the magic elixir. Bess sang on stage. Harry moved around among the spectators, passing out the bottles. He would then present his magic act as a bonus.

When the whole operation began going downhill, Houdini and Hill came up with a brainstorm. Harry would become a psychic, conduct a seance, tell people "secret" facts about themselves, give advice, and contact the departed. The new formula was an instant success. Spiritualism was in its heyday at the time. The crowds flocked to hear the intense young man with the piercing eyes, probing the unknown.

Hill would rent a theater and Bess would double as a hat-check girl in the lobby cloakroom. She checked more than hats and coats. Now and then she would check the contents of a customer's coat pockets, note where he or she was seated, and pass on the information to Houdini backstage. The mind reader would feed the facts back to the stunned spectator during his performance. An amazed audience would shake its collective head in disbelief. Of such methods are miracles made.

Houdini was so successful in his venture that he branched out on his own as a psychic. His reputation spread quickly. Now and then, like all psychics, he would make a chance prediction that would come true. When this happened his followers multiplied like weeds. Houdini had learned what several magicians have discovered in this day and age. Tell the public you're a magician or a mentalist and you'll get a fair, good, or great turnout, depending on your abilities. Tell them you're a psychic and that you *in fact* can see their future or read their past—they'll stand in line to pay for your services.

But with all his faults, and he had many, the legendary Houdini was a man of conscience. When he saw how many bereaved and anxious people came to him for spiritualist advice and consolation, he packed in the psychic act. Once again it was Houdini, the magician and escape artist. Of course, he went on from there to develop his challenging escape act, which was to make him world famous and his name immortal.

When his mother died, Houdini was propelled into another phase of his career. In the forlorn hope that he might make contact with her on the other side, Houdini visited one medium after another. This despite the fact that from his past experience he should have known better. When he saw the consistent deception practiced by the spiritualist charlatans, he was sufficiently enraged to mount a campaign against them. From then until the end of his life, Houdini conducted a one-man crusade against spirit mediums. He wrote and lectured extensively on the subject. His knowledge of the methods used by them made him a formidable adversary. He went after the big names in the business, challenging them directly and generating tremendous publicity.

The magic of Orson Welles

When Orson Welles died in 1985, it was somehow fitting that the announcement was made at a magic convention. An enthusiastic magician, Welles had been planning to attend that same annual convention the following year. Methuen Publications' *Orson Welles: The Rise and Fall of an American Genius,* by Charles Higham, covers the boy genius's life in great detail, but refers only briefly to his interest in the conjuring art. It was a consuming interest, however. In his later years, when most of his public appearances were on television interview programs, Welles would invariably whip out a deck of cards or some other magical prop and proceed to amuse and amaze the host and the viewing audience. His prodigious acting ability helped dramatize each effect into a small miracle. During World War II Welles staged many illusion shows for the armed forces—levitating and sawing in half such luminaries as Rita Hayworth and Marlene Dietrich.

There are a couple of anecdotes on Welles's magical abilities that sound highly exaggerated, but I wouldn't have put them past him. One was his presentation of the "rising card trick" at a lawn party in England. This is the effect of a previously selected card visibly rising out of a shuffled deck. Welles went a little further. On this particular occasion the card not only rose out of the deck, but continued rising straight up until it practically left the country. The story is that Welles made use of a war-surplus barrage balloon concealed by low-lying clouds, and moored to a tree in the garden by a thin, almost invisible wire. He somehow attached the wire to the back of the card, released it, and the card took off.

Another story has it that a sky-writing airplane spelled out the name of a card selected by a Welles audience member. That one sounds a little more plausible.

There's no question that Orson Welles was catapulted onto the world scene by his radio broadcast of H. G. Welles's novel, *The War Of The Worlds.* His Mercury Theater on the Air, on Hallowe'en 1938, created panic across America when it faked a news broadcast of an invasion of Martians. Higham does cover this episode in his book. The "news announcer" first broke into a musical program with a bulletin describing several explosions on Mars, as reported by an observatory in Illinois. This set the listeners up for a later report of a flaming object falling on a farm at Grovers Mill, New Jersey. A Professor Pierson at nearby Princeton University was interviewed to lend authenticity to the event. Later, a reporter "on the scene" described the horrible creatures emerging from a "spacecraft" and the killing of at least forty bystanders.

By this time actual, full-scale panic was setting in among the thousands of radio listeners. People rushed into the streets, made hysterical phone calls to the authorities, filled churches and prayed, and fought for bus and train transportation. Many believed it was the end of the world. The streets of almost every city in New England were filled with cars trying to flee. The panic was concentrated in the northern United States, but some spread as far as Alabama and Texas.

CBS, which carried the broadcast, was later involved in a furor of condemnation, but gradually the fuss died down. Welles himself was shocked by the gullibility of the radio audience. The program had featured several announcements that the broadcast was fictional, but thousands either did not hear, or failed to mentally register these announcements. Later, many media commentators and scientists deplored the lack of education in rational thinking that would have enabled listeners to discern the hoax. That was almost half a century ago. Are things any different today?

My hobby, the world's greatest

The magic of the Christmas season has often led my daydreams back to another kind of magic—the wonders of the world of conjuring, a world in which I have spent a lifetime—first as a transfixed and unbelieving spectator, then as a dedicated amateur performer, and finally as a polished (?) professional and student of magical lore.

The scenes flash by as in a kaleidoscope. My earliest memory of a magic show is seeing Hardeen, brother of the late Harry Houdini, performing on the Steel Pier in Atlantic City. As a ten-year-old I had only one explanation for the wonders I witnessed that afternoon—Hardeen had hypnotized the entire audience, myself included. Then there was the immortal Howard Thurston, mesmerizing a packed house in Montreal's Loew's Theatre sometime during the 1930s. Later that season came his greatest competitor, Harry Blackstone, with his shock of white hair and his great stage presence. Could I have guessed that, years later, the Great Blackstone would visit my home and pose for movies that would become a collector's item?

The years flash past to my shaky start as a prestidigitator in front of a captive audience during World War II. My fellow airmen in the Royal Canadian Air Force were tolerant and demonstrative—a definite assist to my self-confidence. Later, like many budding magicians, I went through the crucible of performing at children's parties. If you can successfully surmount that obstacle, you've got it made.

Then came the big milestone—my first magic convention. The 1951 combined convention of the International Brotherhood of Magicians and the Society of American Magicians in New York City was an eye-opener. All the greats of magic were there. My camera never stopped clicking. More collector's items. The worldwide fraternity of conjurers was suddenly revealed to a wide-eyed enthusiast.

My television debut was a little out of the ordinary. With a group of Montreal magicians on one of CBC's earliest programs—at a time when just a few hours of TV were scheduled each day—my trembling fingers attempted to outwit the camera (only one) with a bit of hanky-panky. Mercifully, that memory is very vague.

Another flashback—a memorable evening in 1970 at NATO headquarters in Naples, Italy. The scene: a Canadian magician and his wife as guests of noted American magician Mike Rogers at the NATO officers' club. Mike, an old friend stationed at Naples, is an officer in the U.S. Air Force and doubles as night manager of the club. "C'mon Henry, they're tired of my magic here. How about showing some of your stuff for a change?" So here I am in far-off Naples, seated at a table with a Turkish colonel, a Greek general, and various and assorted brass, selling some Canadian sorcery. Very satisfying—I've made my contribution to the defense of the West.

Another scene is etched on my memory—a wild night on the luxury cruise liner, SS *Roterdam*. There's a near-hurricane raging on the Atlantic. In the night club salon the evening show is in full swing. I try to keep my balance on the rocking stage as I perform for a sparser-than-usual audience. Those who haven't retreated to their staterooms are watching with dulled enthusiasm, greenish faces expressing their inner feelings. It isn't the act, I tell myself, it's the storm. I finish just in time to make it backstage myself.

So the memories advance and retreat. A lifetime in magic, the world's greatest hobby—and second-oldest profession.

Some tricks of the trade

Walter B. Gibson's *The Bunco Book* kindles a lot of memories for me. An expose of games of chance and of the questionable methods used by unscrupulous gamblers and con men, the book was first published in 1946. The graphics may be a little dated in their design, but the material is just as relevant today as it was forty years ago.

If you have ever spent a few hours and a few bucks at a carnival sideshow, you have certainly made a small investment on the "Wheel of Chance," on "Ring a Watch," on throwing darts, on three-ball bowling, and on hoop-tossing, among many other games. You might think most of these games are merely a test of your skills. Well, I hate to be a spoilsport, but most of these games of chance give you no chance. If they are honestly run, they are designed so that the odds are all against your winning. And if they are gaffed, as many are, your chances are almost nil.

Gibson covers the construction of these devices in detail in this fascinating book. He also lets you in on many of the questionable methods of crooked gamblers: how dice are loaded, the intricacies of marked cards, some of the ways roulette wheels can be controlled. One chapter is really educational—you too can learn how to guard against being shortchanged by your friendly storekeeper. If you get to New York City and stroll down Broadway you'll still see the three-shell game and three-card monte being pitched by the sidewalk entrepreneurs. If you study *The Bunco Book* and read the chapter on these ripoffs, you'll find it quite enlightening to watch how the gullible and uninformed are relieved of their ten- and twenty-dollar bills. Gibson's knowledge of the methods used by the con man and the criminal was the foundation of his later career as a prolific novelist.

My mind goes back to the many interesting hours I spent talking with him in New York City, years ago. Gibson was a phenomenon. To the public he was perhaps best known under the pen name of Maxwell Grant, the creator of The Shadow, the nemesis of criminals, always lurking in the dark to expose the forces of evil. This series alone consisted of 283 novels. Anyone who has ever attempted writing will appreciate the fantastic output of Walter Gibson's typewriter. When producing these novels he would average eight thousand words per day, usually completing a story in six to eight days. Three days to outline the plot and the characters, six or seven days to write it up. When each novel was completed he would turn it in to his publishers and begin another.

When "The Shadow" began its successful run as a radio series in 1937, the first person to assume the star role was Orson Welles. I can still hear his sonorous, "Who knows what evil lurks in the hearts of men? The Shadow knows . . ." A film was produced on the subject, and later it was even turned into a comic strip.

But The Shadow was just part of Gibson's prolific output. All his life he was associated with magic and with magicians. Gibson wrote a great number of books on the art of conjuring and on the many colorful characters in the magic field. He was a friend and confidant of Houdini, of Howard Thurston, of Harry Blackstone, and of Joseph Dunninger. He cooperated with these master magicians professionally, writing about and glamorizing them, ghost-writing many of the books they turned out, traveling with them and soaking up the backstage life of the great magicians. After Houdini's death, Gibson wrote two volumes on the great escape artist's methods. These are probably the most authentic in existence, since Gibson worked from Houdini's personal notes.

Walter B. Gibson died in December of 1985, at the age of eighty-seven. He was active into his eighties, appearing as a guest on all the major television talk shows and recounting the endless anecdotes of an amazing career.

David Copperfield

Let's face it. We all encounter deception in our daily lives. Open your daily newspaper and there's another front page story of hanky-panky on the political scene. Turn the pages and scan the headlines. Items about rip-offs in everything from advertising to zodiac readings. For a writer in the debunking business—and most likely for his readers—the subject can some-times become downright depressing. That makes it particularly refreshing to refer to a type of deception that brings a little sunshine into our lives— the deception practiced by the magician, the conjurer, the individual who temporarily takes us back into the wonderland of our childhood.

Give David Copperfield credit. The twenty-nine-year-old wonder-worker improves every time I see him. I first witnessed his performance at a magicians' convention several years ago. He drew a standing ovation from his peers. He has gone on from there to become, in my estimation, the leading stage and television magician of the present day. But I can't share the opinion of a reviewer from another newspaper that David "has been popularly accepted as a worthy successor to the great Harry Hou-dini." I strongly doubt that any magician will ever again capture the public imagination as did Houdini. Neither, I would guess, will another magician have a name that will become immortal, as did the great Houdini.

Comparing magicians from one era to those in another is like compar-ing the hockey players of different decades. The rules of the game keep changing. And in showbiz, so do the audiences. Can you imagine a con-temporary audience sitting while a magician in manacles, behind a screen, takes twenty minutes to escape—while the orchestra plays on? That was the way Houdini operated. When he emerged, dripping with sweat and unfettered, the audience would bring the house down. If a magician tried that today, he would come out to find the best trick of all performed by the audience. They would have vanished. In any case, Houdini wasn't even recognized as a great conjurer. He was undoubtedly the world's greatest escape artist—and a master of acquiring publicity unequaled by anybody to this day.

This doesn't take anything away from David Copperfield. He con-tinues in the tradition of the greats—Kellar, Dante, Thurston, Blackstone. His presentation has been updated, and fits the contemporary scene. In magic, as in many other things, it's not what you do, it's the way that you do it. The youthful Copperfield has an appealing personality, great stage presence, and is slick and smooth with his sleight of hand. The large stage illusions almost work themselves; it takes a showman to sell them. Copperfield sells them.

Show-business audiences are pretty jaded today. Television has saturated us with every type of entertainment. We've seen the greatest in every branch of the business—not once, but many times. Magic, in particular, has had a rough time in recent years. How can you compete with the miracles of modern science and technology?

Imagery is the basis of most memory devices

You can't trust your memory. Time and again, descriptions of UFO sightings and accounts of so-called psychic experiences have been shown to be erroneous due to additions, omissions, and distortions in the subject's memory. You don't have to look further than some of the scientific studies of eyewitness testimony to find the potential weakness of this type of evidence in many court cases. Poor memory is often the culprit.

Can we do something about this human failing? Can the student who wishes to improve his or her studies find a solution to this ongoing problem? Can we improve our ability to recall names, faces, telephone numbers and all the other information required in our complex society? We certainly can, if we want to make the effort to learn a memory system. Believe me, anyone can do it.

Memory devices, known as mnemonics, are not new. They date back to the ancient Greek philosophers. Later, Roman orators used them to help remember their lengthy speeches. The foremost exponent of the artificial memory system today is Harry Lorayne, the New York dynamo—who incidentally is one of America's leading experts on card magic, and who has written numerous books on the subject.

Holt, Rinehart and Winston has just put out Lorayne's latest tome on memory, *Harry Lorayne's Page-a-Minute Memory Book*. It's his eleventh book on that subject—and I am sure the system works.

If you've read any of Lorayne's previous books on the subject, it's basically the same system, but presented in a more concise manner, with a lot more punch.

Artificial memory depends on a few basics: association, interest, and observation. As Lorayne points out, "In order to remember any one thing it must be associated with something we already know or already remember." As for interest, "It is always easier to remember things you're interested in than to remember things you're not interested in."

The importance of observation is easy to prove. We often see things but don't observe them. Which traffic light is on top, red or green? Are the numbers on your wristwatch in arabic or roman figures? Are there any numbers at all? Which two letters are not on the telephone dial? These are things you see every day but don't observe.

Imagery is the foundation of most memory methods. It's much easier to remember a picture than a name or a number. When you have a system in which you can link mental pictures to a series of numbers, and then merely remember the pictures, you've got a workable memory system that you can use for a lifetime. Learning the nuts and bolts of the system takes some application, but it's well worth the effort.

Harry Lorayne's standard stage presentation is dramatic. If he's appearing at a convention Lorayne will mix with the delegates at one of the gatherings prior to the show, asking their names and the towns they hail from. He will not write down anything.

On stage, Lorayne will ask the entire audience to stand, saying, "When I call your name please sit down." He will then point to each person and rapidly reel off his or her name and hometown. Occasionally he will quote some amusing additional information about the person that he has picked up. That's Lorayne's whole act. It's an amazing demonstration, and an applause-getter. Nothing magical about it—it's the memory system applied in an entertaining manner.

As I said earlier, Lorayne's memory system works. But there's one thing I still find difficult to understand. I've met Harry Lorayne and spoken with him many times over the years—in magic shops, at magic conventions, and at various other magical gatherings. He still can't remember my name.

Paul Kurtz's humanist commitment

If there is one man who has the courage of his convictions, it is Paul Kurtz. A professor of philosophy at the State University of New York at Buffalo, he is also founder and editor-in-chief of Prometheus Books, a publishing house, editor of *Free Inquiry* magazine, on the editorial board of the *Skeptical Inquirer,* former editor of *The Humanist* magazine, and founder and chair of the Committee for the Scientific Investigation of Claims of the Paranormal. Kurtz has also been a member of more international boards and councils than I would care to list. When I asked him what he does in his spare time, Kurtz replied, "I jog three and a half miles and work out in the gym daily." Hobbies? "I specialize in French food and travel." Happily married, he has three children.

Kurtz has been an outspoken champion of the cause of secular humanism, which isn't an easy cause to espouse in the United States these days. The fundamentalists, led by Jerry Falwell, have declared outright war on the humanists. And it's no secret that the evangelical fundamentalists pack a powerful political wallop and have strong support in very high places. Kurtz has had the dubious distinction of having been singled out by President Reagan in a debate involving an exchange of letters between the president and humanist Norman Lear, the well-known television producer. Reagan was critical of writings by Kurtz in defense of humanist philosophy. A high-profile scientist like astronomer Carl Sagan, although a humanist and winner of a Humanist of the Year award, still does not often declare himself publicly on the subject of humanism. Kurtz, on the other hand, takes a strong stance in espousing the humanist cause.

In 1980 Kurtz founded *Free Inquiry* magazine, in order to respond to attacks by right-wing fundamentalists on secular humanism, and because of the effect ultraconservatives were having on the system of education in the United States. The attempts to insinuate "scientific" creationism into the public school curricula is just one of the actions of this powerful lobby. *Free Inquiry* features the writing talents of such scholars and thinkers as B. F. Skinner, Isaac Asimov, Mario Bunge, Karl Popper, Sidney Hook and others of similar caliber. Kurtz has taken the initiative in book publishing as well. He established Prometheus Books in Buffalo in 1970, and immediately began publishing the types of books other publishers shied away from—those that were skeptical of paranormal claims and that exposed and debunked charlatans in the psychic field. In addition, Prometheus has become one of the largest publishers of books on philosophy in the United States.

Kurtz organized the Committee for the Scientific Investigation of Claims of the Paranormal (CSICOP) in 1976. It began as a loose organization of scientists, scholars, science writers, magicians, and informed skeptics. Since that time Kurtz has been the driving force behind CSICOP, which disseminates critical information to a previously uninformed public.

I first met Kurtz during the early days of CSICOP. Since joining the organization and founding (with Dr. James Alcock) the Canadian section, I've seen CSICOP grow into a worldwide movement that is expanding so rapidly even Kurtz is surprised at its growth.

It's an old story. Someone has to come up with an idea—then sell it—then promote it. *Who's Who in the World,* in its section on Kurtz, has a brief statement of his philosophy: "Two passions have dominated my intellectual and professional life: one, a commitment to critical intelligence ... two, a belief in the importance of human courage, particularly of defending reason in society and in attempting to reconstruct ethical values so that they are more democratic and humane."

Our case in thirty essays

Prometheus Books has published *A Skeptic's Handbook of Parapsychology,* which covers more phases of the subject than a number of individual books. Edited by Paul Kurtz, this massive, 727-page volume consists of thirty essays by experts in the field. Refreshingly, even though it is entitled *A Skeptic's Handbook,* there are several chapters by parapsychologists, who certainly have a viewpoint quite contrary to that of your average skeptic. This is quite a switch from most books on parapsychology, which are written by the believers, for the believers—with a very one-sided view of the paranormal.

Kurtz, in his introduction, has an interesting definition of skepticism. It is derived from the Greek *skepticos,* meaning thoughtful, reflective inquiry. Kurtz points out that there are several forms of skepticism. One is the idea that the reality perceived by the senses can't always be trusted—which is a point I have always stressed and which is easily proved in the deceptions practiced by the conjuring magician—and the so-called psychic.

One can go too far in one's skepticism, creating a "universal" skepticism that is negative and self-defeating. No matter how skeptical one is, it's important to keep an open and inquiring mind. This is the essence of the scientific method.

The handbook contains a fascinating overview of the history of parapsychology from its early days, when it was called "psychic research," to the present, when the tools of modern technology have been brought into play. For anyone interested in the growth of spiritualism, the book contains a rare gem. The modern spiritualist movement began with the toe-cracking shenanigans of the Fox sisters in Hydesville, New York, in 1848. The sisters hit the road and conned the public for years with their demonstrations of "paranormal phenomena." When Margaret Fox finally confessed, publicly, that it was all a hoax, spiritualism had already been firmly established. The confession was overlooked by the great majority of the public—and to this day the believers and the practitioners of spiritualism conveniently ignore it. The handbook contains the complete confession of Margaret Fox as it was originally published in the *New York World* on October 21, 1888.

Those who have an unfounded belief in extrasensory perception would do well to read the chapters on fraud and deception in ESP research. Some of the most well-established, prestigious experiments, some of which stood up for years as proof of the existence of ESP, were shown to have been fudged or subject to loose controls.

For anyone partial to a good detective story, these essays make intriguing reading. The chapters by the parapsychologists are understandably critical of the skeptics. Susan Blackmore, of the University of Brisbane, England, presents a well-reasoned essay—but she is a parapsychologist who has the honesty and courage to make the following kind of statement: "I get negative results. Indeed, I have been doing so for ten years. The dilemma I now confront is how to weigh the results of my own failures against the published successes of others. This is just the last and most difficult in a long series of dilemmas forced on me by my failure to observe psi [psychic effects]." It would be "universally skeptical" to say that ESP does not exist. But to say that it has already been proven to exist is certainly untrue.

The origins of CSICOP

The Committee for the Scientific Investigation of Claims of the Paranormal had its beginnings in 1976. A group of authors, scientists, scholars, and a few magicians decided it was time to combat the spread of occult and irrational belief among the general public. This group was centered in the United States, with a few members in other countries, but there are now sections of the committee in Canada, West Germany, Belgium,

France, the Netherlands, Great Britain, Mexico, Australia, New Zealand, and Ecuador. James Alcock, of York University, and I helped to establish the Canadian section in 1978.

The Committee for the Scientific Investigation of Claims of the Paranormal (CSICOP) really owes its beginnings to astrology. In a 1975 issue of *The Humanist,* 186 leading scientists, including 19 Nobel Prize winners, issued a statement disavowing astrology. This precedent-shattering pronouncement was picked up by the media and published in major newspapers across the continent. The *New York Times* headlined its article "186 Top Scientists Dismiss Astrologers as Charlatans." Other papers carried similar headlines. The controversy stirred up by the statement triggered the formation of CSICOP, which has now developed into a worldwide organization.

CSICOP can boast a large roster of very capable members—a number of them of international reputation. Among them are the prolific author and chemist, Isaac Asimov; the eminent astronomer, broadcaster, and public figure, Carl Sagan; the long-time writer for *Scientific American* and mathematical writer, Martin Gardner—also a magical authority; the leading behavioral psychologist, B. F. Skinner; Harvard zoologist Stephen Jay Gould, *Discover* magazine's Scientist of the Year (1982); noted philosopher Sidney Hook, of New York University; Evry Schatzman, president of the Psychics Association of France—and many other prominent people.

CSICOP maintains a network of people interested in critically examining claims of the paranormal. It publishes books and articles regarding these claims. The basic reason for its existence is to encourage critical investigation of paranormal claims, to look at them from an objective viewpoint, and to disseminate the results of these investigations to the scientific community and to the general public. CSICOP's quarterly journal, the *Skeptical Inquirer,* evaluates fringe-science claims from a scientific point of view. It is packed with news and articles covering the entire field of things that go bump in the night, from astrology to UFOs, from poltergeists to faith healing. It is the first debunking magazine ever, and it is available to the general public.

Members of CSICOP have taken an active part in testing psychics who have come forward to be evaluated. One of the organization's earliest actions was to invite celebrated psychic Uri Geller to be tested. Understandably, Geller, who has been exposed as a fraud, ignored the invitation. One highly publicized participant was Suzie Cottrell, a young woman from Kansas. Suzie had aroused a good deal of interest when she appeared as a psychic on Johnny Carson's "Tonight Show" and amazed Carson and millions of viewers by performing an astonishing "psychic" feat with a borrowed deck of cards. Carson is a former professional magician, and not easily taken in. Cottrell's father contacted CSICOP and asked that she be tested for her psychic abilities. Evidently he, too, was impressed. After mutually agreeable arrangements were made, Cottrell finally sat for the tests. She was assisted, and observed, by two CSICOP members—Martin Gardner and magician James Randi. Her every move was monitored by a video camera.

Cottrell didn't do too well. It seems that she used some very adept sleight of hand—not sleight of mind—and she was caught red-handed, not to mention red-faced. Carson, probably a little rusty in the magic department, had been had, along with a few million others. That's why the committee has a few knowledgeable magicians on its roster—it takes one to know one.

CSICOP—a public service

In the past hundred years, to my knowledge, there has never been an organized movement to rationally discuss and debunk the worldwide spread of pseudoscience . . . until 1976. At that time the Committee for the Scientific Investigation of Claims of the Paranormal was formed. Let's look back at developments in the world of the paranormal since the group was established.

The organization was founded in order to help combat the forces of irrationalism sweeping the globe. Its accomplishments are well documented in the Winter 1985 edition of its journal, the *Skeptical Inquirer*. In this issue, the editor, Kendrick Frazier, a noted author and science writer, traces the development of a movement that began modestly in Buffalo, New York, and has spread worldwide. The circulation of the *Skeptical Inquirer* has increased tremendously in the past couple of years. Scientists, scholars, teachers and libraries draw on its contents for information as applied to critical thinking. It is far from being just a medium for debunking. As Frazier points out, "We seem to have helped create, or at least to bring together, a community of concerned people dedicated to furthering good science and opposing bogus science—and to exploring the distinctions between the two."

Frazier also outlines how, in the past few years, there have been significant changes in popularity of the various pseudosciences and paranormal beliefs. Erich von Däniken's *Chariots of the Gods?*, with its theory of ancient astronauts, has declined in public interest. Also, one seldom reads these days of mysterious ship and plane disappearances in the Bermuda Triangle. The UFO flap is in eclipse, if only temporarily. A good indication of that is the news of the Soviet missile that went astray over Norway and Finland in 1984. A few years before, the event would have generated UFO headlines all over the world.

I would certainly agree with Frazier that, "The psychology-based fringe sciences are having a heyday." The so-called psychics are more active and more publicized than ever. More and more we read of police departments calling in psychics to find missing persons or sought-after criminals. The lack of results is usually overlooked. The stories of U.S. and Soviet government agencies competing on a "psychic" basis keep popping up, and are being accepted without much critical inquiry.

The unsubstantiated claims for remote viewing, which is updated jargon for clairvoyance, have become quite fashionable and are also accepted by many as proven fact. Creationism is a powerful force that won't go away, even though it has been defeated in a couple of court battles. Medical quackery, too, has increased recently. This includes spiritual healing and other practices.

But what progress has been made in the resistance to all this nonsense since CSICOP was formed? There has been one unforeseen development. Local groups inspired by CSICOP have sprung up all over the continent. They've been monitoring their own areas, checking on irrational claims, putting out their own publications and newsletters—providing a public service. In a comparatively short time a good-sized network has developed.

They were right all along

It all started with a phone call in early April. Professor Paul Kurtz, chair of the international Committee for the Scientific Investigation of Claims of the Paranormal, was calling from Buffalo—"Henry, there's a lot of excitement in the scientific community down here. They're testing a psychic at Stanford Research Institute, and he seems to be authentic. Two of our investigators are flying down to observe the tests. We'd like representation from Canada; can you join them?" Within twenty-four hours I'm Air Canada-bound to California. This could be the event of the century—or any other century. A clear-cut proof that human beings have the supernatural power of projecting thoughts over great distances, or of receiving communications without using normal senses—this has been sought for a hundred years, and never conclusively established. There have been countless experiments in parapsychology—and many claims of success. But no solid evidence to support the claims. The field has been riddled with hanky-panky, with loosely controlled experiments. Will this be the key test that will turn it all around? If three confirmed skeptics from CSICOP put their unqualified stamp of approval on a psychic's abilities it could lead to further tests, and a possible gigantic breakthrough in science.

Arriving at SRI, I find my colleagues already there. We're ushered into a small lab. There, we meet Russell Targ and Harold Puthoff, the two scientists who had tested Uri Geller in that same lab in 1972. We were introduced to the psychic who was to be tested—a dark-haired, pleasant-looking man of medium height, probably in his early fifties.

Without wasting any time we go right into the first experiment. A number of sealed envelopes are placed on a table in front of the psychic. We have each previously inserted a small, personal article in an opaque envelope and then placed this envelope into a larger one, also opaque, and sealed it. There is no way the psychic can be aware of the contents of these envelopes—by normal means. He passes his hands slowly over them and, without hesitating, identifies the contents of each envelope. The experiment is repeated with different objects, with the same results.

We all proceed to the engineering building, where the psychic is locked into a small compartment about double the size of a telephone booth. It is enclosed by a double wall of copper mesh. This is called a "Faraday Cage." It is completely isolated from radio waves or magnetic fields. Communication with the compartment's occupant is impossible. The psychic is supplied with pencil and paper. We then attempt our key experiment in telepathic communication. A number of randomly selected targets consisting of photographs of various American urban areas are scanned by the experimenters and concentrated on.

If the psychic can produce accurate drawings of these scenes while in the Faraday Cage, there is only one way it could possibly have been achieved—through thought transmission. The controls have been rigid. After about an hour of this concentration the psychic is released and we carefully examine his drawings. Their similarity to the photographs is not exact, but close enough for us to admit that the seemingly impossible has finally happened. Extrasensory perception is confirmed a reality.

I was shocked by these events. I never expected to witness this in my lifetime. Who was this man? What was his name? Elchonen, I was told. Elchonen? But that was the name of the Montreal magician who staged a hoax that got newspaper headlines in 1977, by posing as a psychic and hoodwinking both an astounded theater audience and the media. And that magician was myself. At that moment I woke up, trembling and perspiring, from this incredible dream. That's what can happen on April 1.

James Randi's reward

The year is 1975; the scene is the Howard Johnson restaurant on Broadway, in New York City. Two magicians are seated in a booth with their breakfast, uneaten, sitting on the table. A waitress is looking on in astonishment as the bearded prestidigitator is demonstrating a small miracle to his colleague. Is it some subtle sleight of hand with a deck of cards, or a carefully crafted coin caper? No—he's bending a key!

That's when James Randi initiated me into some of the flummery behind the so-called psychic feats of Uri Geller. The Amazing Randi had just written his book *The Magic of Uri Geller,* in which, after considerable investigation, he exposed many of the secrets of that renowned trickster. Since then he has put out a revised version, *The Truth About Uri Geller—* followed by *Flim-Flam!,* an expose of many other deceptions in the psychic field.

It would be hard to ignore Randi's writings about the paranormal. As a co-founder of the Committee for the Scientific Investigation of Claims of the Paranormal (CSICOP), he has been the most active of that organization in the field of investigation. I first met Randi, a native of Toronto, many years ago at a CBC-TV studio in Montreal, during a magic program we were both engaged in. After that he migrated to the United States and made quite a name for himself as an escape artist. His first book, and his involvement with CSICOP, put him in the public eye, and he hasn't looked back since.

Randi stirred up quite a tempest in the parapsychological community a few years ago, when he set up a sting operation dubbed Project Alpha. He trained two young magicians in the intricacies of "psychic magic," bending keys and spoons, reading messages in sealed envelopes, and all the other nonsense involved in that dubious trade. He then had them apply to the McDonnell Laboratory for Psychical Research, in St. Louis, Missouri, in the guise of psychics requesting that they be tested. They were selected from among several other applicants, and for three years underwent a series of tests. Incredibly, they were endorsed by the institute as being true psychics.

Randi had proved a point. For years he and others of us in the skeptical community had argued that parapsychologists and many scientists were being taken in by opportunists posing as psychics. We argued that conjurers should take part in controlling the experiments used to test these people. Randi held a press conference uncovering the operation. It got wide media coverage and had the parapsychologists reeling—and some of them incensed. But many do now agree—there is a place in their labs for magicians.

Randi is now almost totally immersed in exposing the shenanigans of the television evangelists who practice faith healing. Probably due to that, he has once again hit the headlines. Just a few days ago he was informed that he had won the 1986 MacArthur Foundation Award (known as the "genius award" and usually given to poets, scholars, and scientists). The award means $272,000, tax free.

On the phone to his home in Florida, I reminded Randi that we skeptics don't believe in miracles. So what was his opinion on this fantastic prize? "If it were really a miracle," he chuckled, "I guess I'd have to go out of business. So I'd better not accept it as an absolute miracle." Randi thinks he was chosen as a recipient in acknowledgment of the work of CSICOP.

For a number of years Randi has carried around a personal check for $10,000, offered to anyone who can prove, by means of a demonstration under properly controlled conditions, that the paranormal exists. Many have taken up this challenge but none has succeeded. The check is getting pretty dog-eared by now, so I have a proposition for Randi: Why not stash away the $10,000 and offer a new challenge—a check for a quarter million? Why worry—it will be just as safe.

We must inform the young

One of my main concerns in the years I've been in the debunking game has been the attitude of our youth toward the paranormal. Our students, from the elementary school up to high school and university, have been exposed to a heavy diet of bunkum—both in the electronic and print media. They are provided very little in the way of enlightenment when it comes to rational explanations for all sorts of strange phenomena.

A mailing I once received from a local high school teacher is a good example of some of the thinking that goes on in our institutes of learning. The enclosure consisted of an essay by a student entitled, "A Step into the Unknown." This essay was a project of an English class at the senior level. "Would you care to respond?" the teacher asked. A call to the school revealed that the idea of the project was for students to get some feedback from outside sources on their efforts—as compared to simply receiving a grade from their teachers.

The writer of this piece opens by referring to the phenomenon of anticipating that the phone will ring just before it actually does. "You probably just set it aside as being a coincidence," she writes, but "you have probably been experiencing psychic phenomena." I wonder if the writer ever took note of the times she thought it would ring and it did not. A statistical study of this sort of happening would be very revealing.

"Everyone has some psychic potential," she goes on, "some people more than others, and it may be developed through meditation and awareness of the power itself." It's easy to guess how this argument was picked up. This is a line that has been pushed by the purveyors of the paranormal for many years. "Everybody has the powers. Buy my book or take my course, and you too can be a psychic. Think of the unrealized potential you possess. Now you can use that 75 percent of your brain that has been lying dormant." I've often wondered how these experts on the brain have found a method of measuring the brain's potential, and why they don't publish it so that all of science can benefit.

Another quote from the essayist: "Psychic phenomena are most interesting because they are unexplainable to humans. There is no explanation for the strange feelings and predictions made by psychics." There is some truth to this statement. Yes, so-called psychic phenomena are interesting. That's one of the reasons why belief in UFOs, ESP, spiritualism, and the whole mess in general is so widespread. But when the young lady states that there is no explanation for these things, I take it very personally. My ego is shattered. Obviously she hasn't read my column. She goes on to relate several psychic anecdotes she has heard, which merely adds a few more to the millions now in circulation. She quotes a psychic—"Before you can accept the psychic, a psychic prediction must happen to you." There's more than a little truth to that. Because, very often, credulous people will have a strange experience for which they cannot immediately find an explanation. This will often lead them down the slippery path to believing almost anything.

I cannot be critical of the student who wrote this essay. I am critical of an educational system that does not effectively teach the rules for critical thinking, for rational and logical analysis. Call it the scientific method if you like, but it should be taught beginning in the early grades. What's more, it can be more interesting and exciting than all the psychic slop in existence.

"... but your money had not come."

A *Toronto Star* headline from 1984 read "Better Business Bureau Says Rex Humbard 'Robbing Canadians.' " The accompanying story said the American TV evangelist was mailing local viewers a pair of cheap Mexican coins, asking them to wrap the smaller coin "with your largest bill and rush it back to do the Lord's work." A few weeks before people had received letters enclosing "holy oil," and asking them to bless their money with it and forward the currency to him. A glance back through the *Star* files unearthed an article of January 1982 revealing the same scam by the same Humbard. It's an old and continuing story.

The big difference between some TV evangelists and the practitioners of the traditional religions is that these TV performers invade our homes through the boob tube, instill fear in the hearts of people who are least able to handle it and then proceed to extract money from them in a highly organized manner. They prey on the elderly and the lonely. Many of these people are sick and have lost their mobility. Having lost contact with their local congregation they've joined the electronic church, which comes right into their home. They've fallen under its influence. Many viewers have established an intimate relationship with the TV preacher who visits with them regularly—a real bond exists. They have become emotional, and, eventually, financial partners in the electronic church. These viewers feel that they belong to a family, and feel a responsibility to contribute.

The televangelists use two powerful tools—television and the computer. TV gets them into the home and the computer builds the mailing list. Once the individual's name is known it goes into a computerized list for direct mailing. The receipt of a letter with one's personal name on it has a very strong effect. Many people don't realize it is automatically printed by the computer; they think it is a personal mailing.

The televangelists usually open their campaign with ads offering free gifts—magazines, books, pamphlets, cheap jewelry. This elicits a mail response. After a few more mailings the request for money begins. The donations are monitored carefully by computers. When a correspondent's contributions drop off, his or her name is automatically removed from the mailing list. You can imagine the effect this has on impressionable people who have been hanging on to this lifeline.

Rex Humbard has kept a "Prayer Key Family Book," a directory of sinners for whom he would pray. People's names would go into that directory when they sent money. If they stopped contributing Humbard would send a letter stating, "Last week I knelt at the prayer altar for every member of the Prayer Key Family Book, and I wanted to pray for you . . . but your name was not there."

A common plea on television is, "We must have your dollars or this program will be taken off the air." You could argue that public television makes the same plea, but many televangelism viewers are those who can least afford to pay—widows, pensioners, the deprived, and others in straitened circumstances. Our consciousness is shaped by the messages we receive through the mass electronic media. Many polls have shown that television is a stronger influence than the printed word.

TV evangelism is not only a North American phenomenon. Humbard tapes his syndicated programs, has them translated into seven languages, and sends them to eighteen foreign countries. They are broadcast on more than four hundred TV and radio stations. He has offices in Canada, Japan, the Philippines, Australia, Brazil, and Chile. This is a very big business.

Abetted by evil spirits

"What's all this debunking about, Gordon? What's wrong with people visiting psychics, getting readings, having a little fun? Most don't take it seriously, so why take off on the psychics?"

In 1984 the *Toronto Star* carried an item about ten fortune tellers drawn up on fraud charges before the courts. They had allegedly bilked their victims of anywhere from $200 to $5,000. Most of the victims, it was reported, were from the Caribbean. Many cases, it was pointed out, are not reported because the victims are too embarrassed to go to the police. What is the scam that helps separate these people from their money? In most cases they are promised that the "psychic" will help rid them of evil spirits.

The next week the *Star* carried another item about a North York woman who, having read the previous piece, decided she'd better report a ripoff perpetrated on her. It seems that a palm reader had advised her to stow her family's life savings into a cloth bag and to hide it in a safety deposit box to "take the curse off the money." When the victim finally checked the bag she found only shredded newspaper. The old switcheroo, of course.

When I look through my files I find almost identical stories dating back for decades. The methods haven't changed much. The success of these operations hinges on one factor: superstitious fear. The unscrupulous fortune teller often finds an easy mark in the person who comes from a country where superstition still flourishes. Some of the Caribbean islands fall into that category, which doesn't mean, of course, that *all* people from that area are easily taken in. Some of the methods, like the switching of a bag of paper clippings for a bag of currency, seem quite crude. Or the old gimmick of secretly introducing a small frog into a freshly broken egg, which convinces the victim that something occult is taking place. You might ask: "How can anyone in this sophisticated age be deceived by these ridiculous shenanigans?" I'll answer that with another question: How can educated, rational people I have known personally—scientists, businessmen, journalists—have been impressed and taken in by trickster Uri Geller, actually believing he bent spoons and keys through the power of his mind?

Sometimes the desire to believe in fantasy outweighs the need for logical and rational thinking. Accomplished psychics, if they are charlatans, know how to take advantage of situations. They will tell subjects what they want to hear. The fact that victims will not testify against psychic charlatans is also an old story. The *Star* notes that many are simply too embarrassed. There is another reason. Many of the victims, believe it or not, retain a great faith in the frauds who take advantage of them.

I've seen court cases, particularly involving psychic healers, where the "patients" testified in their defense. Just last week I came across another example of how superstitious belief can influence the thinking process. I had just finished participating in another "People Are Talking" TV program for the Westinghouse Group, this time on WJZ-TV in Baltimore. It was my usual confrontation with a couple of "psychics." As we left the set a young lady from the studio audience approached me with the words: "I really enjoyed your presentation—I agree with you 100 percent . . ." A rational thinker, I thought. There aren't enough of those around today. But her parting words, as she walked away, gave me even more food for thought—". . . because I think these psychics are aided and abetted by evil spirits."

Both sides deserve airing

Some readers may recall a controversy some time ago at York University between the administration and a professor dismissed from the institution. A long letter from this gentleman to the *Toronto Star* has taken issue with observations in this column about spiritual science, among other things. The dismissal, as he puts it, was for his "explorations of spiritual and mystical teachings." He says, "I am well familiar with the intolerance prevalent within our educational system towards such ideas," and claims that his dismissal raises "essential questions of academic freedom and the rights of individual professors to explore the areas of mystical, spiritual, and occult teachings, as well as the psychic sciences within our university system."

The question of academic freedom is one that surfaces regularly at universities and colleges, and I suppose each institution deals with it in its own way. It seems to me that imparting a belief in the occult to students whose minds are in a formative stage, as they are in a university, is to encourage irrational thinking—a dangerous manipulation of maturing intelligences.

The teaching of the paranormal and the pseudosciences in universities and colleges has become quite common in recent years. Unfortunately, the courses I have sat in on, and those I have investigated, have had one failing—the professors or instructors have neglected to present both sides of the psychic controversy. For example, when Uri Geller was in his heyday, students were often informed of the various "psychic" effects he accomplished—but never did I hear the rational explanation for these effects. Whether it was ignorance on the part of the teachers or was deliberate, I could not always be sure.

I can still recall a symposium at McGill University at which the professor, a psychologist who should have known better, spoke of Geller altering the molecular structure of a bent key through the power of his mind. Coming from an academic who was a strong proponent of the existence of flying saucers, I wasn't too surprised. But I wondered what effect this statement had on the minds of the more gullible members of the audience. I've always felt that teaching critical thinking to young students is far more important than the mere accumulation of facts traditionally emphasized.

Academic freedom should not give professors the right to teach *any-thing*. They should be answerable to a broader context of professional standards. The responsibility borne by teachers in our school systems is tremendous—whether in the university or in grade school.

We probably see more purveyors of the paranormal in extension courses than anywhere else. There could be a good reason for that. Universities find it useful to add to their coffers by running these courses. Courses on UFOs, human auras, extrasensory perception, faith healing, astrology, and other pseudosciences appear very attractive in an advertisement. The enrollment is usually quite satisfactory. These particular courses raise revenues that help underwrite other, more respectable courses that perhaps do not attract too heavy a registration.

It is a sad commentary on the education system across North America, but it is a state of affairs that will most likely continue.